What readers are saying about *Off the Leash*:

Brilliant! I laughed. I cried. This is real life in America, Jean. You're becoming my 21st century Steinbeck. — *Michael, Houston, Texas*

Your evocative writing draws the reader in. Your words and experiences resonate with many. You are a gifted writer. — *Linda, St. Louis, Missouri*

The reality of your landscape is so compelling and painful, yet your words cut through with such originality, meaning, and humor. — *Gerry, St. Louis, Missouri*

Your writing is addictive, I just hope it's not fattening! — *Sue*, Graford, Texas

My kids are wondering why I'm crying into my smartphone. Thank you for sharing your story with the world. — *Jessica, St. Louis, Missouri*

I am transfixed by your honesty and willingness to share such beautifully written tales. — *Craig, St. Louis, Missouri*

This is a book about discovery, humanity, humility, brokenness and the realization that our most futile struggle is the pursuit of non brokenness ... because it does not exist. The book is about finally seeing one's life in perspective and recognizing that the frailty is life. The screw ups are life. And ultimately, the ability to accept and embrace that brokenness, is life. — *Drew, Des Moines, Iowa*

Beautiful and moving. I admire you so much for having done it and can't thank you enough for sharing it with us! — *Alysa, Paris, France*

Your authenticity and transparency warms my heart. Thank you for your courage. — *Cheryl, Salida, Colorado*

Soft and beautiful ... sheer poetry. — *David*

The only thing I can say is thank you. — *T.*

D1115430

OFF THE LEASH

How my dog inspired me to quit my job, pack my car,
and take a road trip across America to reclaim my life.

a memoir

Jean Ellen Whatley

Blank Slate Press
Saint Louis, Missouri

A Blank Slate Press Book

Published in the United States by Blank Slate Press. Visit our website at www. blankslatepress to learn more. To view companion photos and videos of *Off the Leash*, visit www.jeanellenwhatley.com.

Cover by Kristina Blank Makansi

Library of Congress Control Number: 2012948093
ISBN: 978-0-9850071-3-3

www.blankslatepress.com

PRINTED IN THE UNITED STATES OF AMERICA

For Nathan, Patrick, Lauren and Sean,
I love you so.

In memory of
Beverly G. Garcia
Donald Wayne Whatley
Garrett Daniel Whatley

OFF THE LEASH

How my dog inspired me to quit my job, pack my car,
and take a road trip across America to reclaim my life.

Contents

An Invitation   5

1 - One Woman, One Man, No Witnesses   9

2 - The Midwest Winter of My Discontent   17

3 - Somebody Broke In Here In the Middle of the Night
     and Stole My Sanity   29

4 - Merge   45

5 - Blue Ridge Transfusion   58

6 - Where the Kudzu Wraps Around You in a Loving Embrace   80

7 - When You're Feeling Low, Buy a Cowboy Hat   100

8 - My Cousin Benny   124

9 - The Zen of Washing Your Panties in the Sink   138

10 - Land of Enchantment, Trail of Tears   153

11 - The Privilege of Breathing   168

12 - I Know About You   181

13 - Duty to the Dead   199

14 - I Will Never Leave You   210

Epilogue   219

Acknowledgments

About the Author

Libby, off the leash, on U.S. Highway 50 near Delta, Utah.

An Invitation

Have you ever felt like running away? I mean truly running away—quitting your job, checking out, going off the grid, saying goodbye to your family and friends, leaving town, the grocery store, the gas station, the lady who cuts your hair, the boy who cuts your grass, the stack of unpaid bills. Has your life ever gotten to the point where you felt like your robotic obedience to the norm is steering you off a cliff? Can you look at yourself in the mirror and say, "I am doing what I am meant to do?" Or has it come down to, "Is this it? Is this what my life is about?"

What happens if you do step off? What happens when so many bad things have been thrown your way, you just can't clear the hurdles anymore? What happens when you awaken to a longing in your heart so deep and so powerful that to ignore it would be like leaving a baby in the road? What would it take to change your life? What are you willing to risk to walk away from it all, to simply say, *"I can't do this anymore"*?

I did it. Last summer I risked everything: my reputation, my family's shoestring existence, my safety, even my sanity. I risked it all to do something radical. I wigged out. I split. I took off. The spark of an idea became an obsession calling me out, daring me to do something I had never done before. I broke all the rules. I blew off my soul-killing, sixty-hour-a-week job, took every last dime I had to my name (which wasn't much), loaded up my dog and a lot more baggage than I realized, and hit the road. I needed to attend to the things I longed for. Do you ever feel that way? Like there's some empty space inside you waiting desperately for you to fill it up? Sometimes we know what that empty space needs. Sometimes we don't. I just knew I had to go.

I'm not the irresponsible type. Look up the word "reliable" on Wikipedia, you'll find my picture there. For the past fourteen years, I've been a single mom with four kids. Half of that time, my former husband was behind bars. It's not like we were trailer trash either, not to cast aspersions on people who live in trailers—and at the rate I'm going, I just might end up there, too. Nope, when this unraveling began, we were what you could consider the ideal family: two-career household, enviable jobs as broadcast journalists, great kids, a dog, a cat, a guinea pig, a two-story house in the suburbs on a cul-de-sac with a minivan in the garage. Life was as normal as normal could be, except for the part about my husband liking boys. And so began the Decade of Disaster: his downward spiral into Internet addiction, a failed marriage, divorce, bankruptcy, and the crowning blow, the sex crimes which sent him to federal prison. He went down in flames and left me and our four kids buried in the wreckage.

But we climbed out.

We climbed out of the acrid heap of black rubble by our bloody fingernails, each one rescuing the next, clawing our way back into the light, where we sat atop the buckled wings, flicking off shards of metal. We made it. We survived.

I just didn't realize how tired I was. It's hard to process trauma while you're in the midst of battle. After the smoke cleared, with the kids raised, the old man out of prison, they began to figure out the rest of their lives and I began to consider mine. I held no grudge; there was far too much life to get on with, until death dealt me a bitter blow.

My brother died, the second of two brothers to die inside a few years. I hit the mat. I couldn't rally. I felt a staggering grief and hopelessness beyond anything I had ever felt before. "What's the point?" I kept asking myself over and over again. "What exactly is the point in all this?" And then, *snap!*

Nobody wants to be a test dummy for heartache and misfortune.

Nobody wants to be a lifetime member of the bitterness club.

Nobody wants to be the poster child for unrealized dreams.

I began to listen to my inner voice. It was nagging me like a fever in the night, challenging me to change my life. How many times had I ignored it? I'm here to tell you, I paid a hefty price for silencing mine.

But if you'll indulge me for just a second, I'd like to share something with you.

Lean into the madness.

When something calls you out, daring you to do something drastic to make you feel alive again, *follow that voice.* I know it's not easy, but an unattended inner voice is like an unruly child sent to her room, silenced but resentful. It's hard to take her by the hand and encourage her to speak the truth, and trust me, there will be consequences.

But your inner voice will help you; it will heal you and it will make you happy. You simply need to be still enough to hear it. It's like a clock in the hall, counting off every moment of our lives, always there, that reminder. It's the ever-present cadence of our days and nights, seldom heard, drowned out by the noise of our daily lives, until those lucid moments when the house is still and we hear its rhythm, strong and steady.

Quiet your house. If I could sit down in front of you, right now, take both of your hands in mine and look you straight in the eye, this is what I would say to you: "Quiet your house."

And come with me.

Come with me on this journey. I'll shove the junk to the floorboard and let you ride shotgun on the most enlightening, life-affirming trip I have ever been on. Come on, the dog won't bite and there's plenty of room. I suspect we'll make good traveling companions. We're a lot alike, you and I. That's what this journey has taught me—we are so much more alike than we are different.

So, come on, let's go. Boy, do I have some stories for you: some tragic, some shocking, many hilarious. You won't believe the things you'll see, the people you'll meet, the emotions you will feel. I promise. Come with me. Allow me to share this trip with you. I'll tell you about numbing fear, staggering losses, the grace of forgiveness, and the astounding bliss of living in the moment. We'll kick up some transcendental gravel, I guarantee. But maybe, just maybe, somewhere along the road, whether it's the pizza boy in Toledo, the musicians on a California highway or the thundering silence of the Utah desert with my dog by my side, maybe, just maybe, some of these sounds and images will echo inside your heart, making my journey all the more purposeful and rich beyond measure.

I invite you. Come with me.

1

One Woman, One Man, No Witnesses

The windows are down. I've gotten used to the sound and sway, the relentless battering of cross-wind, like a blow-dryer across my face, whipping the seat belt strap in the back.

Flap, flap, flap, flap.

Seems easier than fighting the wind with the windows up, the way a gust will suddenly lurch a car sideways, prompting a *"holy shit!"* tug on the wheel. Wakes you up in a hurry, especially when you're daydreaming or texting.

Damn, I need to be more careful.

Flap, flap, flap.

I'm leathery. Well, parts of me. My left arm is more brown than my right. I meant to put on sunscreen. I think it was back in Ohio somewhere. Too late now. I push my cowboy hat down farther on my forehead. Damn wind. There's some kind of passivity going on here, allowing myself to be blown around in my own car in the middle of the Utah desert, trying to make good time to Colorado. Already I am feeling the pressure. It's eating at me. I've started tapping my fingers on the steering wheel; I've checked my iPhone six times since I left Nevada and all it says is "E," as in "error" or "no service." Really it stands for edgy. I'm feeling so fucking edgy again and I know damn well it's not because I'm out on a two-lane highway in the middle of nowhere and it's 96-degrees and I have no cellphone service, with nary a sign of a human being or QuikTrip as far as the eye can see. Hell, there aren't even any telephone poles out here!

This has become routine, S.O.P., standard operating procedure, being out on the open road, just me and the dog. We've put 7,600 miles behind us and we've got a thousand more to go.

I sing sometimes. Not today. I'm feeling edgy because with each eastward mile I am that much closer to home. What a loaded word, "home." I am getting closer to the responsibilities I abandoned to take this journey, and soon it will be time to pay the piper. And everybody else on the fucking planet.

Cross that bridge when you come to it, Jean.

There has never been so literal and meaningful a phrase. I've been taking it one bridge at a time for eight weeks. Ever since I crossed the miserable Mississippi and got the hell out of St. Louis, heading east; the jubilation when we crossed the Verrazano Bridge into Brooklyn; the primordial peace when I parked overlooking the Golden Gate; the appreciation when a moment later I looked into the rear-view mirror at my wise companion, who sat patiently observing, never rushing me. She looked puzzled when I hopped out of the front and climbed in the back seat with her, putting my arm around her neck, sharing the view with her: my silent partner, my muse, my canine confidant.

I check my mirror now. Libby's sleeping in her prayer pose—the one where she tucks her hind legs, her front legs straight out in front and buries her nose into the corner of the car seat. Traveling with a dog is a lot like traveling with a baby. I try not to stop when she's sleeping: something about letting sleeping dogs lie.

I love her so much, it is indescribable. This is what happens when you travel across the country with your dog.

My eyes come back to the road. Up ahead I spot what appears to be a person at one o'clock. Out here? A man. He's walking. He's pushing something. He's headed my direction on my side of the highway, rolling something in front of him. At first, I think it's a mirage; I mean, who would be out here, out in the middle of nowhere? They don't call this "The Loneliest Road in America" for nothing—U.S. 50, the sun-baked, two-lane highway I've been traveling since I left Reno. I bought a burger at the truck stop at the Nevada line and played video poker with zero luck while I waited for my lunch. Filled up and fueled up, I was planning to blow straight through Utah and make it all the way to my friend's house in Colorado by nightfall. Ever since El Dorado Hills, since learning about my real father from someone who actually knew him, it's been mission accomplished. Now it's time to get back home. Every mile east of California has simply been a geographic necessity. Fuck Utah. I was going to blast through it, eighty-five miles per hour. The whole damn state had left a bad taste in my mouth since the former in-laws flat-out abandoned the kids and me after their fair-haired son got sent to the slammer. Seven years, they did nothing to help. Seven years, he did his time. I guess I've done mine. Just look where it got me. I'm a fifty-six-year-old woman, the epitome of responsibility for, hell, I don't know, thirty years? I'm on the final leg of a wild hare road trip that smacks of insanity because I walked away.

I walked away. At a time when people are desperate for jobs, I walked away from mine. I had to. And now my eyes are bathed in watercolor brushstrokes of terra-cotta, golds, browns, blues and whites, dazzling bright, piled skyscraper-high atop the desert floor. Thank you, Utah. I'd written off the entire state, but it's beautiful. It is so beautiful. I wasn't expecting to love it this much.

And truth is, now that I'm here, I'm trying to make it last just a little bit longer. Practicing what I profess, don't you know? That "be here now" stuff. There's plenty waiting when I get home. I'll be glad to see my kids, glad to see my other dog, but man, there's a lot of stuff I don't really want to face. Cable's been cut off. I barely have this month's mortgage. Car payment's due, the shower's still stopped up and I don't have a job. And, right now, at this moment, I've got some folks in Salida expecting me for dinner. That's another 300 miles from here. Shit. I told them I'd make it tonight. I don't have time to dilly-dally.

It's all starting to get under my skin.

And now there's this guy up ahead! *What in the world is he doing out here?* I'm less than a quarter of a mile away now. Is that a grocery cart? There's a flag, a small American flag waving from a pole. He's got it attached to his cart like a car antenna.

Poor dude. Rough place to be homeless. Lord knows I've seen my share of down and outers this summer, in every city from New York to San Francisco, sleeping in bus shelters, on sidewalks, park benches, curled up inside doorways, all their worldly possessions stuffed into trash bags or piled inside a grocery cart. He's wearing a bandana; the wind is whipping it around, just like the scrubby tufts of golden grass bent sideways in this sandy soil, desperately clinging to their miserable beds. I felt like that not long ago: dried up, beaten down. Everything gets beaten down by this wind, everything and everybody, today and every day.

He looks young! He looks like a kid, *like one of my kids,* I say to myself as I zoom by. What the hell is a kid doing out here on the highway, all alone, pushing a—wait a minute, it's a baby jogger. Looked like it was all zipped up. Wonder why?

"Surely he doesn't have a baby in there, Lib," I say out loud, but Libby pays me no mind as I continue blazing down the highway, eighty miles an hour and then some. "Where in the hell is he going? There's nothing out here, and it's gotta be fifty miles to the next town!"

Damn. I almost wish I hadn't seen him. If my lousy iPhone was working, I might have been checking emails or texting and I could have missed him all together. Then I wouldn't have this ping-pong match going on in my head. It's like that fucking Clash song, except this time it's should I drive or should I stop? Damn it! The curiosity is killing me. What if he needs help? Oh, but I've got people waiting.

"Waiting for what, exactly?" The voice of the enlightened Jean rises above the conditioned Jean. What if I'd been texting in Texas? I wouldn't have seen the road sign with my name on it, "Jean," followed by "Kindley Park". What if I'd taken the Interstate instead of the back roads in Virginia? What if I had not gotten out of my car at that wreck on I-10? What if I had actually listened to my gut, all those years ago? Would I have passed on Rick? Well, I wouldn't have had three more babies. That guy back there, he looked to be the same age as Patrick.

This is going to bug the crap out of me. I am still thinking about him, even though I've lost him, can't see him anymore. "It's too late," I say aloud. "I've gone too far to turn back now."

Gone too far to turn back now. Are you kidding me? Have you not learned anything? You've come too far to not turn back now!

I check my mirror—nobody in back of me, nobody in front. I slow down, downshift to fourth gear, then third. Libby's head pops up. Third gear, every time. She is like a human: the way she wakes up, stretches, and then sits up near the window, surveying the countryside. "Where are we now?" her doggie gaze asks, casting her bottomless brown eyes out over the golden high desert.

She was supposed to be a cat, truthfully.

"Mom, you've got mice or squirrels or rats or something running around up in the floorboards," said Nate. My son and daughter-in-law had come from Los Angeles for Christmas. They'd braved the elements of the basement bedroom. "We could hear them running around all night."

Aside from being embarrassed, frankly, I was worried about the house burning down from chewed electrical wires. So a few weeks later, Sean and I—he's the youngest of the four—were at the Humane Society looking for a mouser.

"Do not even look at the puppies," I told him as we crossed the snowy parking lot to go cat shopping. We had a dog already, Pete, who was thirteen, and I was thinking within a year or so, I might be dog-free, meaning that once Sean left for college I might be able to sleep over at my boyfriend's house. If I had a boyfriend. "Do not even go into the dog building."

An hour later we walked back out with an eight-month-old reddish-gold dog, Libby. She doesn't even look like a cat. With her widow's peak, heart-shaped face and Cleopatra eyes, we were done for the minute Sean sneaked off and spotted her at the end of puppy aisle four. She's always been a sweet dog, if not a little timid. Neurotic too. She won't walk through half-open doors. She jumps and barks at my toes under the sheets and she has weather anxiety. She hides behind the TV or under the dining room table every time the wind picks up. I think she's forgotten all that now; the battering of the desert wind against the car doesn't seem to faze her. She loves the car. Of course I hoodwinked her, not bothering to tell her it would be eight weeks and nearly 9,000 miles when I asked, "Hey Lib, wanna go for a ride?"

Twenty states later, we're thick as thieves, my girl and me. We've seen mountains and deserts and prairies and cornfields, terrible traffic, three fatal car accidents, and, oh, the ocean too. She went to Huntington Beach a couple of weeks ago. She had never seen the ocean, much less romped in the surf, shaking the water off so hard, her whole body lifted off the sand. Have you ever experienced a joy so divine? I laughed and cried at the same time to witness her bravery and excitement. Like a mom with her kid on the first day of kindergarten, I was proud and scared. But Ol' Lib and I, we ain't scared o' nothin' now.

My daughter's brave like this. I have mixed emotions about how she came to be this way. In fact, all four of my kids, good, bad or indifferent—are largely fearless now, having grown up before their time. But none of my boys ever articulated their genuine bravado quite as pointedly as Lauren did one night in the parking lot of the grocery store. Lauren, who was fourteen when Rick was arrested, had just celebrated her fifteenth birthday when she got caught shoplifting. I was in the dairy section.

"Will Jean Whatley come to the customer service counter, please?"

There she sat in the store office looking unnervingly calm, mascara and a lip gloss lying on the metal desk. They let her off with a slap on the hand and told her never, ever to come back.

"What in the world were you thinking?" I screamed at her once we got out to the car, asking the stupid question for which every parent knows there is no real answer. "Why did you do that?" Another pointless question. I followed up with "Weren't you afraid you'd get caught?"

"What do I have to be afraid about?" she yelled back at me, one of the rare moments she'd actually let her feelings show. "My father's in jail! He's going to prison for God knows how long! What the hell do I have to be scared of now? I'm not afraid of anything!" And then she began sobbing.

I felt the same way, truthfully. *What the hell did I have to be afraid of now?* Not that you want to go around borrowing trouble, but even then, after what I'd been through, it took quite a bit to move that fear needle up to the red zone.

It all started with a phone call informing me that my older brother Garrett had died suddenly in his San Francisco apartment. He'd had his problems, but still, it was a shocker. Half numb, I'd flown home to New Mexico where we held his memorial. The day after I got back from the funeral, *the very next day,* I was back at work, barely functioning, when my assistant called while I was at lunch.

"The St. Louis police department just called," Amber said apologetically. "They said you need to arrange for somebody else to pick up Sean from school because your ex-husband has been brought in for questioning."

"Questioning for what?" asked Patrick, a few hours later at our house. He was the oldest child at home at the time, a senior in high school. My eldest, Nate, was in college in North Carolina. I'd gathered the three kids still at home, in the family room—how apropos—to break the news that their dad was in custody.

"What'd he do?" Lauren pushed.

"I'm not sure, honey," I said, even though I already knew at a gut level so deep you could plumb the depths of my fear with a submarine, that it couldn't be good. "Maybe he witnessed a crime or something," my ridiculous wishful thinking trying to convince me that maybe he had not actually *committed* one.

After I had arranged for Pat to pick up his little brother at school I'd called my good friend Mick in the cop shop, the chief investigator for the Circuit Attorney. Being in the news business comes in handy sometimes.

"I won't be able to tell you anything until they actually file the charges," Mick told me. "My buddy in booking will call me the minute there's any paperwork."

Suppertime came, but still no word from Mick. I took the kids out to eat.

I wanted them out of the house before there was the chance of hearing any breaking news. With him being a big shot at the number-one TV station in town, it would be all over the news. We hid at a neighborhood restaurant: wings, burgers, nachos and nothing but hockey on TV. Somehow it seemed easier to be near other people. We sat and picked at our food. My cellphone rang in my purse. I hopped up and told the kids I'd be right back and walked out to the parking lot. I felt like throwing up what little I had swallowed when my friend Mick read off the list of charges.

So, let me tell you about *fear*. Fear is knowing you've got to take your kids home, sit them down and tell them something horrible about their father in the thirty-seven minutes remaining before his face shows up in a mug shot on the ten o'clock news. After this, everything else seems easy—even a runaway trip across the country, all alone with your dog.

"We're turning around, Lib," I tell her as I swing the car all the way around, heading westbound. I tell Libby everything. I fully believe she understands it, too. I'm traveling the same direction he's walking now. I spot him once again, no mirage. He's walking at a fast clip. Yep, it's a baby jogger. And he's got a backpack, and yep, he's young, tanned, athletic, and strong. *Stronger than I am.* I drive beyond him and hook another U-turn, pulling up about fifty yards in front of him. *I'm probably scaring him!* He's walking toward me now, the wheels on the baby jogger kicking up the fine pebbles along the shoulder of the road.

I roll to a stop, the right tires in the straw-like tufts of grass. A tractor-trailer rig thunders by, rattling my car. It's the first truck I've seen out here in half an hour. *Wow, what would it be like to have cars and trucks almost blow you off the road all day long? That must be scary. What if a driver gets too close, gets distracted?*

And then, snap. *What the hell am I thinking? How many trucks have gone by in the last half hour? How long would it be before somebody found me?* Here I am, a woman, out here all alone, with a sympathetic dog who'd gladly hop in the car with a band of gypsies or ax murderers in exchange for one simple pat on the head. She's that friendly and that needy.

I pull off my cowboy hat and set it on the floorboard, don't want it to blow all the way to New Mexico. "Stay here, Libby, I'll be right back." I reach into the back seat and scratch her head. I get out of my car, my safety zone, my escape vehicle. I raise my hand in a friendly wave. The sun is intense and the wind blows my hair sideways, as I push away the glinting strands, of cola-colored lattice over my eyes. I shove my keys far down in my left pocket; and in my right, my business card "Jean Ellen Whatley, Writer."

I start walking his direction, now twenty yards away. I'm out here all alone, a divorced mother of four, former soccer-baseball-football-tennis-basketball mom, former TV news "celebrity," exclusive provider of all things financial and familial for my kids, who are grown now, on their own. So am I. There's not another human being for miles around, save for this man, clearly bigger than me, who could, in a heartbeat, beat me over the head, steal my new hat, my car and my dog and leave me to the coyotes, snakes and vultures.

I'm out here all alone, and yet everything I have experienced up to this point on this journey across America and my time on this planet so far is telling me that walking out to meet this man is precisely what I'm supposed to do.

"Hey there," I holler and smile, big, so he can see it. He waves back. I approach him, my hand extended.

2

The Midwest Winter of My Discontent

I'd grown reclusive in the months leading up to my little coast-to-coast jaunt. That's not like me. Hell, I am a textbook extrovert. You know, like on those lame personality profiles one has to take for a team-building exercise or dating profile? They do come in handy, I suppose, for pigeonholing human beings into some kind of generalized types. The good ones are amazingly accurate, or so we'd like to flatter ourselves—provided the assessment is indeed flattering. According to the gold standard of personality tests, I was characterized thusly: *"Warmly enthusiastic and imaginative. Sees life as full of possibilities. Spontaneous and flexible, often rely on their ability to improvise and their verbal fluency."* Spontaneous? Warmly enthusiastic? Who wouldn't want to be with somebody like me?

Nobody. At my last job, especially in the last few months, I had turned creepy, more like the worst traits of the classic introvert, described in this way: *"Skeptical, sometimes critical, always analytical."* Also known as *pretty fucking miserable to be around.* That was me: not conducive to winning clients and influencing co-workers. At my last day job, I was a video producer for a creative agency which produced multi-media events for huge organizations, like 5,000 tax preparers, doughnut-makers, chicken-fryers, or, say, professional football players. And with all these large-scale events came lots o' videos: videos to be played at their big-ass gatherings and videos to be played on their big-ass websites. Producing corporate propaganda was like falling off a log backwards after being in TV news and politics. The similarities are frightening.

So we were busy all the time, unlike other shops that were hurting for business after the downturn. To the credit of the guys who ran the joint, they weathered the bad economy. Course they cut everybody's pay and worked us sixty hours a week sometimes, but, hey, I'm not bitter. I just felt like a hamster. Or more like some gullible fool who'd signed up for a treadmill at the gym, except nobody told me I was expected to keep the pace of the guy who used the machine just ahead of me. At first, you know, you're all smiles, like, "Hey, no prob, I've got this," but after a while you find yourself breathing harder and harder. And you're slipping, slipping, grabbing at the handles. You're running so fast you can't even lift your feet off the rubber to the side rails to slow the fucking thing down! You miss a step; you fall and bust your lip. You look up, bloody, sore, tired, just in time to greet your new boss, who's twenty-five. She's all chipper, oh, and she's willing to work for half of the half your salary's been reduced to. OMG. Good luck on that, dude; just let me crawl back into my office so I can hide. I hope they won't ask me to think outside the box for a while.

Really, they were actual glass boxes in a tall, red-brick warehouse that used to be a showroom for luxury cars back in the 1920s. Partial floors had been built, like balconies all around, on three floors, with the glass-fronted offices overlooking the open area in the middle. Reminded me of a cellblock. My Plexiglas cell was on the bottom floor, kind of tucked under the stairs but near the front door. That was great, because at least I could see the path to my freedom. I could see the sun-shiny sidewalk, which lay beyond my reach, not twenty feet away from the mini-blinded cage with my name stenciled on the door. I could see it, but I couldn't touch it. I couldn't breathe it in. I monitored the seasons by the gingko trees: bare, green, yellow, bare. I marked the hours by a lime-green plastic K-Mart clock on the wall, the nagging tick of its second hand like a finger wagging at me: *You cannot make this train go backwards, sister,* and the annoying rattle of the air vent above my head—on-off, on-off, reminding me of a death rattle, which sadly I knew too well the sound of. On-off, on-off, warm air in the winter, cold air in the summer. On-off, on-off; I was beginning to think I'd lost my sense of humor, I'm sure the folks I was working with did too.

There was secured parking on the side of the building. I would take the parking spot closest to the gate, near the street, park, hop out and run back through the automatic gate before it closed, back out on the sidewalk. I did this so I could walk in the front door instead of the employee entrance around back. This helped me avoid co-workers in the parking lot with whom I might have to be pleasant. I'd ring the front bell, get buzzed in by the secretary who was in her cell on the third floor, and with any luck avoid contact with all other human beings. I would make a beeline for my office, quietly closing the door behind me, hang my coat on the cheap, tippy coat rack and then I'd be right back in the saddle, or in my harness, behind the laptop I never turned off overnight. Energy conservation be damned! I had zero time to wait for it to spring to life every morning; I had too many deadlines, too many unreturned emails, too many mind-numbing, nattering details. Nobody even noticed one minor detail in my office, which I found funny. On my bulletin board, right behind my desk, directly over my shoulder, was a page ripped from a motivational calendar. In bold letters it read,

"THE TOP FIVE THINGS I NEED TO DO TODAY"

under which I wrote, "Figure out a way out of this" five times.

I minimized the need for conference calls although I would frequently pretend I was on one when anybody came hunting me down. I cannot even begin to tell you the number of fake calls I jumped on when I spotted my boss heading toward my door. It works every time.

"Sure, we can accommodate their needs with a one camera shoot, an SVX500." I'd make some shit up, with nobody on the other end of the line, as I'd smile and wave to him, holding my index finger in that "Just give me one minute" gesture people use when they're on the phone. But he could never wait for more than two seconds. He's hyper that way.

I avoided brainstorming sessions like the plague. I scheduled off-site edit sessions on staff meeting mornings and on my happiest days I could have worn my fucking pajamas to work and nobody would have noticed because I conducted all my work via email, never stepping outside my office. I honestly don't know why we needed to be in the same building. What a waste of fossil fuels.

There was a lunch clique that you could set your watch by. About 12:07 the clump, clump, clump on the stairs would begin and anywhere from three to seven co-workers would emerge from their glass cages and tromp down the stairs and walk to lunch. Together. I'd been invited a time or two in the beginning, you know, the obligatory "ask the new girl to lunch" overture. But after a year of me saying no thanks, they quit asking. I didn't want to eat lunch with people who were going to talk about work, for Christ's sake! I would have poked my eyes out with my fork! Even as anti-social as I'd become, the fact that they never asked me anymore did kind of hurt my feelings. See how screwed up I was? And a hypocrite to boot! There's a great scene in an episode of

M*A*S*H where Margaret Houlihan breaks down in heaving sobs in front of all her nurses when she accidentally crashes a little tent party. They're laughing and drinking in their hair curlers, throwing their bras around and shit when she stumbles upon their little pajama party. On the one hand she doesn't care, but on the other, she feels like she's grown a second head or something. She beseeches them, "Did ya ever think about including me? Did ya ever think about asking me if I'd like to have a lousy cup of coffee?"

It had gotten to that point at the office—a Mexican standoff. I wasn't going to waltz out there and ask the lunch bunch, "Hey, can I go too?" And nobody was going to invite the troll under the bridge who, unbeknownst to them, was flipping them off under her desk every day. Okay. I know this is terrible. I realize it's aberrant behavior. I mean, who does this? I'm confessing this to you to establish my state of mind. I submit to you, ladies and gentlemen of the jury, that I was a crazy woman. A hateful, driven, fucking crazy woman who spent her lunch hours hunched over her laptop in the car at the park or the Internet café down the street, trying to pound out a few more lines, a few more chapters, one more scene of whatever book or screenplay held me in its grip at the time. Because, you see, that's what I really wanted to be doing and increasingly resented not having the time to do it.

It was the dream, dawg, the *dream!* Ever since about 1977, the dream was to be a writer, not a journalist, not a political speechwriter, nor corporate propagandist. I wanted to be a real writer. I yearned to publish something that did not include "Police say they have no motive in the killing" or "Operators standing by!" No, I longed to tell my own stories. Oh, there had been near misses with success: a finalist in a national memoir contest, a look-see by CAA on a screenplay, but you know that old adage about horseshoes and hand grenades. Close just wasn't cutting it. The dream was barely breathing. It was dying and I felt like I was dying a little bit more every day.

Then one day in January, hunched over my desk in my troll cave, I got an email from a real live New York literary agent. She said:

"I think that your voice on the page is just incredible. It's rare that I see writing that is so honest. I think that you could write a beautiful book—and I think that yours is a story that publishers would be very interested in."

This was in response to a story I'd published on Open Salon. It is a great forum for writers. Well, let me tell you what, boys and girls, I was crazy with excitement. *Crazy!* I read the email, and then reread it and reread it. Then I stood up, strode out of my glass cubicle, walked out the front door of the building and ran down my beloved sidewalk. And then I turned around and ran back, past the front door to the office, back down to the corner and back again. I had not the foggiest notion where I was running; I just ran down to one end of the block and back again. In hindsight, this is the exact same thing Libby does when I pull up in the driveway at home. With our electric fence, she has the run of the entire yard, front and back. When I come home at night, she's frequently asleep in a hollowed-out place in the grass, which she's worn down to the dirt. I pull up, she springs to her feet, looks me square in the eye as if to make sure I see her, then bolts like lightning straight to the backyard, galloping around in a huge loop. She then comes racing back through the open gate and sprints out to the front yard, making a big loop all around the perimeter of the front yard too. This is weird. It's as if pulling up in the driveway and catching her asleep in the yard is tantamount to catching the guard asleep in the guard shack. Hell, she *was* asleep! But this is what I must have looked like: a crazy woman, bolting out the door, running around the block, checking the perimeter.

"I heard from an agent! I heard from an agent! I heard from an agent!" I phoned both my older boys, one on each coast. Both Nate in Los Angeles and Patrick in New York City are filmmakers. They know what a tough nut an agent is to crack. "She wants me to call her. She wants to talk to me about my book!" The boys were elated. I thought carefully about my reply to the agent: not too needy, but not too aloof. I suggested a time for a call and hit "send". How liberating a simple command can be:

"SEND!"

"SEND!"

"SEND!"

My dreams flew through cyberspace with the chance they just might land on a receptive heart that would see and hear mine.

"SEND!"

That night, I took Lauren and Sean out for Mexican food and a margarita. It was one of the happiest days of my life. After decades of rejection letters, I printed her email and pasted it to my desk and covered the whole thing with tape so my coffee drips wouldn't mar the precious affirmation which could change my life:

"Your voice on the page is just incredible."

She used the word incredible again a month later, when she let me down easy.

"I think that this would be incredibly hard to sell to a commercial publisher. The memoir market is harder than ever … and this isn't an easy subject to publish."

I had been holding on by my fingernails up until then. She didn't realize that. She didn't know it had been a rough year. Hell, it had been a rough decade. I'm just saying. But the few months preceding her gushing and then bailing had been particularly arduous. My oldest brother Don died in August. Two brothers gone just a few years apart, with my mother's death about halfway in between. Three family members gone. Pretty damn tough. Don had pancreatic cancer, the Steve Jobs kind, but Don lasted only eleven months after he was diagnosed.

I had flown home to New Mexico to see him four times after he got sick. Each visit got progressively harder, but Don tried to make it easy. He was a bigger person than most people I know. I should try harder to be like he was. I don't know what was more difficult: the last time I saw him alive in hospice care or flying home for his funeral. I spoke at Don's funeral just as I had at my brother Garrett's and my mother's, but this time Don had requested it in advance. Garrett didn't have any time to think about it; death got the jump on him. My mother knew she didn't have to ask.

You have to man up in circumstances like this. You don't really get to be alone with your grief. As with any family—and I know many of you have been through this—when someone dies there are details, details, details. You're grateful for the distraction. But when you've been asked to eulogize someone, you also have to perform. You're given a solemn duty of getting a life right, remembering all the extraordinary and ordinary things which separate that person from all others on the planet. Don was only sixty-four. He was very handsome. Tall, blue eyes, golden brown hair when he was younger, mostly grey by the time he passed. He looked a lot like Jeff Bridges. Think of *Crazy Heart*, only not quite so puffy. By the time he left us, it was painful to see how cancer had eaten him alive. That cancer, it's the fucking devil.

There were more than 300 people at his funeral. He left behind a wife of forty-six years (yes, they were high-school sweethearts), two grown kids, five grandsons, and hundreds, if not, thousands of lives he touched as an educator. For twenty years, he was the president of the teacher's union. He was powerful. By the time he was set to retire, he was running a program to keep homeless kids in school. In his younger days, when we lived in Fort Worth, Don had gone to seminary to become a preacher. He earned a Bachelor of Divinity degree, which has nothing to do with confectionery. He grew disillusioned with the racism and hypocrisy of the church he was about to pastor and figured there was a larger flock he could tend to, kids in need of a decent education. He was right. He did a lot of good.

And I did a good job at the funeral, wasn't a dry eye in the house. With twenty years as a writer and a reporter under my belt; what would you expect? Write and talk; it was my job. Write and talk; it's what I do. The funeral was on Labor Day. Albuquerque was hotter than hell the first weekend of September as all of us mourners sat out in the front yard in our funeral black like so many crows on the lawn, eating plates piled high with all manner of macaroni salad, drinking cold beer and telling stories about Don. Would have been great if he'd been there.

Just three weeks later we gathered again, a blessed reprieve from sorrow when my oldest child got married. We needed the joy. Nate and Melissa's wedding in the San Fernando Valley was simply beautiful. It was outdoors, lush and lovely. Watching my son Nathan turn to look at his stunning bride walking up the flagstone path to their future was restorative, cleansing and bittersweet. Then to cast my eyes on my other children, one by one: Patrick, Lauren, Sean—all sane, loving, well adjusted, wickedly funny, determined in their pursuit of all things non-penal, it was a life-defining moment for me. I felt blessed, proud and happy. Poor kids. Little did they know I'd be convening a coast-to-coast conference call come March to tell them my wild-ass idea to fly the coop with Miss Libby riding shotgun.

The autumn glow of the wedding wore off and winter set in hard. Christmas 2010 was shaping up to be a dark joke—well, except for Louie. Louie was a bright spot.

It was Sunday, December 12. I'd just returned from a trip to California with the man I was seeing at the time. George treated for the whole trip; it was his hometown, Santa Barbara, on opening night of a one-woman show by a painter he admired. He'd purchased a lovely painting and was proud to be one of her collectors. The show was wonderful, the trip great, until snow in St. Louis delayed our connection out of Phoenix. George grew cranky.

"Let's get a drink," I offered. We did. We had two hours to kill, so we had two, and we split a club sandwich—all for a mere sixty bucks.

"I'll get it," I whipped out my card when the check arrived, seeing how George had paid for the rest of the trip. Imagine my chagrin when Hector, the waiter, came back and said, "Sorry, declined."

I panicked; this was Sunday and I'd just gotten paid that Friday. George graciously covered for me as I was backpedaling in my head, embarrassed, flustered.

"This is really weird," I said. He was polite not to roll his eyes.

Thank God the Wi-Fi was slow that night at the Phoenix airport or I probably would have jumped out of the fucking plane. It wasn't until after I'd gotten home, past midnight, after a silent drive home from the airport on solid ice, that I discovered I had fourteen dollars in my checking account—fourteen dollars to last from December 12th to the 23rd. Talk about bad timing. In my haste to get out of town on Friday, I had paid all my bills but I forgot a couple of automatic payments. I hate it when this happens. You understand why I'm a writer and not an accountant, right?

That Monday morning, the 13th of December, dawn broke with hateful, icy roads and I had a 9:00 staff meeting. Stuck in traffic, all I could think about was, *I have fourteen dollars until Christmas. I have fourteen dollars until Christmas. What the hell am I going to do?* Patrick was coming from New York on the 23rd and that's when I was planning to "do" Christmas, you know, like, buy gifts and stuff? Such is the life of us wage earners who live paycheck to hot check. But it wasn't always like this for me. I used to have money! Well, at least some. There was even a time when I actually had savings, a 401K!

I wasn't worth killing that day at work. I two-stepped between self-pity and self-flagellation. I was more pissed off and miserable than usual, and it's not like I'd been Miss Congeniality before. I was truly distraught. It was one thing to put off Christmas shopping, but we needed to eat. Fourteen dollars wouldn't feed us for one day. Fourteen dollars wouldn't even fill up my gas tank or buy a fifth of vodka! I was completely fixated on this dilemma.

Until I got home. In a moment of weakness or hypnosis, a few days earlier I'd conceded to allow Sean to bring another dog into our lives. His girlfriend Amy wanted to give him a puppy for Christmas, a puppy whose mama was a full-blooded Chow and whose daddy was a purebred Mastiff. Can you say oops? Okay, I realize that not only have I admitted to being hateful, flipping people off behind their backs, and being a financial moron, but I am now confessing to being a certifiable idiot. Enter King Louie. All of my friends warned, "That dog will never leave your house! You're going to be stuck with him."

Oh, that I would be so lucky! Although I doubt Sean would ever part with him now as Louie and Sean have bonded like Super Glue, much like

Libby and I. That Monday night, that first night, Sean had gone to work to make pizzas and I was instructed to come straight home so Louie would not be alone for too long. I came in; the house was quiet. Libby lay by the door looking indignant, then anxious. Louie was in his kennel, which we'd set up in the family room. I leaned over to get my first look at him—a chestnut ball of downy-soft fur with a black tongue and a teacup tail. I scooped up a bundle of pure puppy love the likes of which I have never experienced except for all the other sacred times in my life when I've gotten a new puppy. He smelled like a puppy, he gave me little puppy kisses and nuzzled my neck. And of course, he had puppy breath, an aroma so intoxicating that if you could spray it over battlefields, soldiers would lay down their arms.

I sat down on the couch with him, not even taking off my coat. Libby, jealous, hopped up. I moved over to make room. With Louie cradled asleep on my left leg and Libby's head on my right, I didn't budge. We stayed that way for a solid hour. His whimpering subsided, giving way to his pudgy little belly slowly rising and falling as fear turned to contented sleep. Holding that puppy was the most important thing I'd done all day. It gave me purpose. He needed me. This tiny, irresistible ball of fur, which God or the universe or Sean had entrusted to my care, required me to be fully present to him, on this, the first night away from everything he had ever known. Just think about that for one second. What would it be like to be snatched up from every source of food, warmth and familiarity you'd ever known and placed with someone else, most notably *humans*, who gave you a towel, a toy, put you in a metal cage and left? I was his new mama now, species be damned. And within days, he would learn to navigate the stairs, not be startled by the vacuum, discover my blue shoes, eat out of Libby's bowl and in general come to reign over his dominion—hence King Louie. But at that moment, he simply needed me to sit still and comfort him.

They have no idea how they comfort us. I have had a dog in my life since I was nine years old—Bowser, Jenny, Maddy, Pete, Libby and now, King Louie. How many secrets have they heard? How many tears have fallen on their backs? How many comedy acts have they performed? They're unaware of how they coax us out of our misery and drag us like a sock into the here and now. That night, I worried not about my finances; like Scarlett O'Hara, I'd think about it tomorrow. I worried not about dinner; hell, I didn't even take off my coat! Sean came in about nine o'clock carrying a pizza. Dinner solved. He could see I was completely smitten. "I told you he was cute," he said with smug satisfaction, and got down on the rug with Louie. And in what would become a ridiculous evening devotional, we spent at least another hour playing with the puppy. Sean looked up at me from the floor where the puppy had crawled up on his back, king of the mountain, and said, "When you're having a poor Christmas, just get another dog."

Or draw your weapon. With fourteen bucks until Christmas, I had no other choice. I'm not talking about holding up a bank, although with all the bailout bullshit, if I thought I could get away with it, man, I'd seriously consider it. Me going to prison would be a bit much with one of the kids' parents already in the slammer. No, I got out my gun to *sell it*. I'd stolen it anyway.

Desperate times called for desperate measures in both situations: the acquiring and the discharge of said weapon. I don't mean it went off, I simply mean I discharged myself of the weapon. Of course it nearly went off, but that was thirteen years ago, when I was newly divorced from Rick and came into possession of this firearm. He'd been going through a rough patch of depression. It came time for him to load up the kids and head to Utah to visit his folks. They took this trip every summer. But Rick had sounded particularly despondent in the days leading up to their trip, although then and now— I assure you of this— he had never laid a hand on the kids in any way, sordid or disciplinary. He wouldn't even swat them on the behind, unlike myself, who believed this was an effective way to get their attention, especially if they were about to dart out in front of a car. I was working the early morning shift at my TV station and was chronically sleep-deprived, (a.k.a. psychotic) and I started fixating on his revolver. He'd always kept a gun and he always traveled with it under the front seat of the car. For years, this was our routine. I didn't have much say in the matter. His dad had been a cop and Rick had been a part-time deputy back in Prescott, Arizona during college. With each day closer to their road trip, I got more and more worked up over him being depressed, driving on a long road trip with my three youngest kids and having a gun in the car.

So, I broke into his house and stole it. One day, when I knew he was still at his TV station, I got a ladder, loaded it into my minivan and went to his house. I found an open window, which of course was on the front of the house with all kinds of traffic and any number of cops driving by at any given second, propped up the ladder, pushed up the screen and climbed in the window, landing with a thump on the floor. I went straight to the bed, where I knew from fourteen years of marriage, the gun would be stuck between the mattresses. It was. I grabbed it, crammed it in my pocket and went back to the window, only to knock the ladder over with the first leg swung over. I had to just drop from the window. Fortunately, my feet were only about four feet from the ground. I stood the ladder back against the house, climbed back up, closed the window, pulled down the screen and limped back to my car. I tossed the ladder in the back and made my getaway. I drove just a short distance down the alley before pulling over to see if the gun—a six-shooter service revolver—had any bullets. The fucking thing was loaded. Worse yet, I had accidentally cocked it.

My heart was thumping. I was already guilty of B&E and now I was driving down the street in a white Dodge Caravan with a loaded gun and the hammer cocked. Holy Mother of God! I called my friend, Gina. Her husband is the same detective who, two years down the road, read off the charges against Rick on the night he was arrested. As things turned out, me stealing the gun two years before his arrest and the subsequent ransacking of his apartment meant the police would have no weapon to confiscate. It most certainly would have eventually disappeared from the evidence room, destined to become a throw down. (Apologies to any police officers whom I may have offended.) Anyway, it would not end up in the cop shop because I held it in my hot little hand. Well, really, I had it lying on the floorboard on the passenger side of my Dodge Caravan. I didn't want to stick it under the driver's seat for fear the damn thing would go off taking my foot with it.

"Gina, call Mick," I told her, panic in my voice. "I don't want to get him in trouble, but I had to get a gun out of Rick's house and now I've got the damn thing cocked and I don't know how to uncock it."

Calmly, Gina says, "Okay. I'll find him." No questions asked. Twelve minutes later, Mick met me in a downtown parking lot and let the hammer down on an empty chamber.

"Put the bullets someplace away from the gun," he said and went back to work.

Rick didn't miss the gun for months. He and the kids took the road trip to Utah. He must have abandoned his custom of packing a gun on vacation because he never mentioned it. About a year later he asked if I recalled him getting it out from under the mattress when we split the sheets. I simply said I did not. That gun sat in my dresser drawer for thirteen years until I was down to my last fourteen dollars with fourteen days until Christmas. I had thought about selling it a hundred times before when short on tuition, car repairs, plumbing bills, airplane tickets, prescriptions, utilities, you name it. There had been time after time I needed to cash it in. But the gun in the drawer was like money in the bank. There was something very sobering about making that withdrawal. My back was against the wall this time. I sold it to a reputable dealer, got good money for it. I cried when I walked out of the gun shop with a check. Seriously. But I used the gun money for Christmas gifts, groceries, and the electric bill. Sucks when there's no lights on the tree.

We had our Christmas, the kids clueless as to the lengths I had gone to make it festive. I had my kids. That is all that's ever mattered. We were in one place. We had a roof over our heads and homemade Mexican food for Christmas Eve dinner. It's our family tradition. Everything was absolutely wonderful. Have you ever had to bottom-line stuff like that? I bet you have. I had done it so many times in the past thirteen years, it had become like running bases. Think about it like this: You're a little kid learning how to play baseball. You hit the ball, you run like crazy. You hear your coach yelling, "Slide, slide, slide!" You smash hard into that damn canvas-covered square and the fucker doesn't budge. You rip open a raspberry on the bottom of your chin and you feel like you've dislocated your shoulder, but you get up, brush it off, *nobody hurt*. Sure enough, you're hurting like a son of a gun, but you're not going to let anybody know.

I had developed the Evelyn Wood Speed Reading method of bottom-lining the crisis du jour: *"Is anybody bleeding? Is anyone in jail? Does anybody have any credit left? Do we have electricity?"* Compared to that, pulling off Christmas with a Colt .45 was a piece of red velvet cake. And the man I was dating gave me pearls! Never mind that we wouldn't last past the first week of January, never mind the very next week the fancy New York literary agent would spring forth like an angel from on high, then run away like a fickle Valentine come February. Never mind that the mad, mad, mad road trip obsession would sprout like the crocus in the early spring; all that stuff could wait. Because on this one night, this Christmas Eve salvaged with a gun, we were warm. We were together. We were laughing our asses off because we got another dog.

3

Somebody Broke In Here In the Middle of the Night and Stole My Sanity

Louie rules the roost. He's a stocky little dude, with a swagger, and a devilish gleam in his eye. He's an operator, reminds me a great deal of my late brother Garrett. He was rascally that way: cute and funny, slightly conniving, but never malicious. Garrett had wavy, dark brown hair, brown eyes, 5'8" tops. Picture Mark Ruffalo with a little Bill Murray thrown in. I can't watch either one of them without my heart hurting just a bit.

Anytime Garrett could not find something he had misplaced, he would holler, "Somebody broke in here in the middle of night and stole my...." whatever it was he was missing. Silly of course, but damn funny. And just like those phantom thieves who wreaked havoc in his life, such were the powers which swooped down on me in the spring of 2011, except these voices and signs from the universe would end up hijacking my sanity. I was ripe for their intercession, what with my winter blues and all.

The voices spoke to me on a miserable, drippy, cold day in March. I was in my office in the "Florida room." Why are they called that? They don't remind me of Florida at all, not that I'm a big fan of the Sunshine State to begin with. In fact, when I was planning my coast-to-coast road trip, part of my rationale was to revisit every single place I'd ever lived in my life, to pay homage to the people and places that molded me into the certified nut that I am. But I decided to skip Key West; it was a little out of the way and never on my mind. I had lived there only a short time during my first marriage to my hippie-turned-sailor high-school sweetheart. I was a young Navy bride; we were too broke to even pay attention. Funny how some things never change. The entire time we lived on Key West the only movie showing at the only movie theater on the island was *Jaws*. Talk about a disincentive for snorkeling. The one other cinema option was the drive-in. They played *Day of the Locust* all summer, which was bad enough; then the insecticide planes would fly over and dump mosquito-killing fog all over the island. This was particularly bothersome when you're at the drive-in with the sunroof open on your '72 Monte Carlo. The only redeeming thing about that three-month tour of duty in Key West was the Navy pier at sunset, where we could sit with a couple of tallboys (and I'm not talking other sailors), watch the sun go down, and then go back to our motel-turned-apartment and engage in rambunctious sex. We were newlyweds. There wasn't anything else to do.

But there is not one single thing about the view from my sun room on the back of this old house—which is both my sanctuary and torture chamber, because this is where I write, or think about writing, or think about why I'm not writing—that reminded me of Florida that day unless you're talking about a swamp, because it had rained steady for 9,000 days. The rain spilled over my clogged gutters and deepened the muddy pit in the front yard where Libby loved to lie. I think it was spite—not Libby, but the weather.

Midwest winters are spiteful sons of bitches. Like some budding starlet being smothered by a jealous has-been, winter comes back time and again, smashing down yet another layer of punishing cold and by the time the wobbly sprigs of spring are allowed to dance to life, they'd better be hardy because it's 90-degrees already.

Disguising my contempt for St. Louis weather is futile. You'll understand what fueled my resentment later, but for now, I just want you to know that I loved North Carolina; that's where we lived before we moved to the Midwest. It was our last stop in the journalism traveling road show with husband number two. I absolutely loved North Carolina and did not want to move. If I could have tied myself to the pin oak in our front yard in Winston-Salem, or the dogwood, or the weeping cherry, or the white pine, I would have done so. My roots had grown deep in six years. I remember standing in the front yard, listening to the rumble of the diesel engine of the moving truck idling in the driveway. I was confirming the new address in St. Louis with Daryl, the man who would be driving all my worldly possessions to the Midwest. I had handled all the details: the garage sale (where one toothless guy made an offer on the dog), repainting all the wood trim, re-screening the screened-in porch, getting it on the market, selling it, hiring the mover—the whole bit. It was the third time inside seven years; one becomes proficient in cross-country moves.

I was a morning-show news anchor at the time. It's always a great gig if you can adjust to getting up at 3:30 in the morning. But the sleep deprivation and associated emotional instability is a constant occupational hazard. Rick earned the bigger paycheck in those days as a news director and it was a big step up for him to come to St. Louis, a Top 20 market. He moved a few months ahead of me, while I settled our affairs down south. I gave the mover our new address.

"Meet you in St. Louie," he said as he climbed into the cab.

He put the rig in first gear and slowly pulled out onto Cavalier Drive. I was anything but. He drove away with my precious life. My life. Six years of making a home in North Carolina, six years of kids in school, soccer games, dance recitals, first communions, Moravian stars on the porches at Christmas and Single-A baseball in the summer. I'd drunk the sweet tea and was as happy as a Carolina coastal clam. People who live in North Carolina can afford to be nice; they know how good they've got it. I watched the moving truck roll down the road, around the corner, out of sight. I think I knew then that my marriage was dead, but I had to try to resuscitate it one more time with one more move. The kids were so young then.

They're grown now, though. Even so, I had my moments last spring when the road-trip idea first sprang up. I felt like I was abandoning them, thinking I'd be risking their future by going off the grid. How could I explain to them what was calling me? It seemed so illogical, so ridiculous.

"What? You're going to quit your job, with nothing but a few thousand bucks to your name, and do what? Drive across the country with the dog? And you're doing this because? And why are you taking the damn dog anyway? Wait, maybe that's a good thing. She has more sense than you do."

It was Libby's fault in the first place. On a sunny August morning the summer before, she unknowingly held up a mirror to my life. I have never been the same since. It was the day before my brother Don would give up his battle with cancer. I sat with Libby at my feet on my sun-drenched front porch, drinking coffee from my mother's bone-china, gold-rimmed white cup and saucer. This was my custom, a weekend gift I gave to myself: savoring a morning cup of coffee in a relaxed, genteel manner, far different from the slave-driving commuter mug from which I gulped caffeine Monday through Friday. I was thinking about the phrase "sun bathing," reasoning that I needed to absorb as much of this nourishment as possible to fortify me for the imminent dark days ahead. I knew I'd be receiving the death call at any moment. I was steeped in sadness that Don's days were waning and I had not been able to spend as much time with him as I had intended. All of a sudden Libby jumped up and took off like a shot, barreling across the yard, ripping open the morning quiet, rousing me from my grief-sodden stupor, barking like a rabid dog.

It was that damn cat next door. The neighbors had let out the black-and-white calico sandwich that Libby was dying to sink her teeth into. Libby detests that cat; so did Pete, our old dog, who hated that cat with a vengeance. They must have had some score to settle from a past life. Libby bolted across the yard and then slammed on the paws, coming to a screeching halt, stirring up dirt. The temptress was crouched under a boxwood bush not twenty feet away, but Libby went no farther. Instead she yelped and writhed in restrained misery. She lowered her head and stuck up her tail and paced back and forth along the driveway, but she didn't dare get any closer to the object of her most fervent desire because of her fear of the invisible electrical current that held her back.

"You poor dog, Libby," I mused, thinking it a bit cruel that she was being made a fool of. "If only you knew that barrier has no bite, honey; the battery in your collar is dead. It's been dead for months."

It's an unintentional trick I play on her; I simply forget to replace the batteries. But she is so conditioned by fear of the electric fence that she would not dare to cross the line, even though there was nothing, really, holding her back.

Then I saw it. I saw myself in her. I saw myself in my dog, a hapless mutt, with a powerless grip around her neck, within eyesight of the prize she coveted the most. Barricade, where is thy sting?

In stunned amazement, I sat there and watched this message from the universe unfold. It was a stinging indictment on my life: *What really stood between me and being a writer?* Here I sat, grief-stricken, absolutely brokenhearted over losing my big brother, wishing I had taken more time off from work to go see him, regretting that I had not listened to my gut to drop everything when he was first diagnosed with the worst kind of cancer imaginable and take him on a road trip to revisit the places where we'd grown up. Don was the oldest. Don knew the old stories. I needed him to share them so I could write them all down. He was the only person left in the world who knew about San Francisco; Garrett was already gone. Don was the only one left who knew about that *other* brother and where he might be. But now Don was dying and I'd lost my chance.

"Lib, come here." She bounded to the porch, nearly knocking the cup out of my hand. "Thank you." I lay my head on her sun-soaked, golden back. "Thank you so much."

The memory of that scene strengthened its hold on me over the next few months to the point of obsession. The daily question had become, *What is the hold on me, really?* I could barely look myself in the eye anymore; my reflection in the mirror had lost her patience. *You must do something about this.* Changing my life had become a moral imperative, because *if you don't do something, you might die.* I know this is dramatic, but have you ever felt like if you didn't do something drastic, you just might die? I had lost too much already: two brothers and my mother inside a few short years and therein lay the root of my bittersweet wanderlust. I had intended to go and see them. I meant to go more often. They all lived more than a thousand miles away. I went when I could, but it was never enough. I wanted to spend more time—free of demanding deadlines calling me back to work, incessant emails, conference calls in hospital corridors, weary plane rides back and forth, trying to straddle two realties. But the sad reality was we were out of time. I didn't get to see them as much as I needed to; I was never able to be fully present and nobody gave me an option for a do over.

But maybe, just maybe, I'd been given an opportunity for a *do better*, before it was too late for *me*. I had been lost in drone-like allegiance to all things mainstream—a nine-to-seven job, mortgage, car payment, kids in college, roof repairs, root canals, lawn care, elder care, health-care premiums, scrimping on clothes, scrimping on groceries, scrimping on my life, saving for that precious two weeks of freedom a year, saving for retirement and hoping it would arrive before I turned ninety.

Yeah, if I live that long. Who knows how long I have?

I fantasized about saying fuck it and simply walking out. It hung in the back of my mind like a sequined party dress in the closet. In the meantime, we had the funeral, we had the wedding, we did Thanksgiving, and we had the pauper's Christmas financed with a gun. We survived New Year's Eve. Both my daughter and I survived New Year's breakups. I barely survived being gutted by the literary agent, and then, on a cold rainy day in March, seven months after Libby's epiphany play in the front yard, the voices had their way with me. As surely as if somebody had broken in in the middle of the night and traced these words on the filmy windows of my fake Florida room, the voices told me:

Do the road trip anyway. Take the dog.

I was wearing Don's forest-green terry cloth robe. It's heavy. Quality merchandise was the hallmark of his shopping habits all his life. It's the one item I asked for out of all his things, my brother's bathrobe, to keep me warm. It works. My house is so old and so cold; it leaks like a sieve. Every time I tie the belt around my waist, I think of Don with gratitude.

But on this particularly dreary March morning, my rebound was sagging. I was flat-out pissed off, fed up, sad and mad at the world. Not worth hanging, as my mama used to say. I was standing there in Don's robe, looking out the window at the rain. I seemed to be doing that a lot lately—standing, staring out the window. I kept trying to shake the morose mood I was in to get back to the writing I was working on, when I looked down at my muse, my golden mutt, the girl who wouldn't let me forget. There was Libby, stretched out on the sunroom floor with no fucking sun, and it hit me. I longed to be in the desert again. I longed for mountain vistas, wide-open spaces, where a person can see for sixty miles. I didn't care if all I was looking at was mesquite trees or tumble weeds. I needed the sun. I needed the warmth. I needed the space. I needed to breathe. I had a few thousand dollars burning a hole in my pocket from my tax return, which most years went to things like past-due personal property taxes, overdue car registrations, mechanics, plumbers, tree-trimmers or pet groomers or, imagine this: vacations. This year it was going to be Jean's turn. My very own version of *Thelma and Louise*, but one of us would have four legs! I was giddy from the crazy irresponsibility of it!

Quit your job. Take off with the dog. Go see all those people you've been longing to see. Go back to North Carolina. Go back to Texas. Go back to New Mexico. Go all the way to California and find out if that *Lester dude really exists.*

I am telling you, the idea grabbed hold of me like an electrical current, the way it makes you shudder involuntarily, yet there's something curiously arousing about it. Have you ever had such an obsession? I couldn't sleep for thinking about it. I couldn't walk in my office every day without secretly dreaming about it. I dared not tell anybody about it as the concept was percolating in my manic mind. Well, except for my children, with whom I shared this crazy scheme no more than five minutes after it popped into my head. I banged out an action plan and sent it soaring through cyberspace to my co-conspirators, a.k.a. my children. My blessed brood, they understand me, or perhaps they simply humor me, but I do believe they're dreamers too. I'm the classic enabler—don't know if it's a gift or a dereliction of duty. I'll lean towards the former; after what they've been through, why the hell not?

The first time I ever went to New York City I was fifty-two. I'm embarrassed to admit it, but in all my travels all over the country, I had just never made it to the mecca. Patrick had moved up there to work in the movie biz. He was living with his girlfriend in a cramped apartment in Brooklyn (are there any other kind for struggling young film producers?). We were walking through Central Park, brown and gold remnants of autumn still holding tight to the trees, the high-rise buildings all around. As a first-time visitor, it's awe-inspiring. My mother had passed away just a couple of years earlier. I found myself thinking about her that day and how much she would have reveled in it, or at the least, enjoyed hearing all about it. I don't think you ever get over wanting to call your mama.

"Patrick," I said, "I just can't believe it! I can't believe you live in New York City!"

"It's because of you, Mom. You made me think it was possible."

What a gift, when our children become our teachers. Through the years, each of my kids have uttered phrases which have become emblematic to my life. Nate says, "Carry on," Lauren asks, "What do I have to be afraid of?" even Sean's, "Just get another dog," and now this: "You made me think it was possible." Well, okay, then. When fiery dreams burn up our beds and spring us to our feet on the cold floor, calling us to the window to look outside, to look beyond, but listen within, don't we have an obligation to do so? I had been feeling this way for years, this longing. Looking out the window, pacing, thinking that what I needed to quiet the voices in my head hovered out there somewhere. Out there, somewhere, at the edge of the lawn, at the beginning of the road, like a low-lying fog, which, if you could change the substance from vapor to cotton candy, you just might be able to grab a hold of what makes you whole.

Winter, summer, front yard, back—whether I stood in the bedroom studying the ice-wrapped holly branches, green, brilliant red, dazzling in their diamond luster cocoons in the low morning sun or humid, hazy, late-summer gazes out into the back yard, locusts buzzing, weeds mocking; how often I peered out beyond what confined me, lamenting that a good time to go would be right after I pruned the trees, painted the tool shed, cleaned up the dog poop and restored the flower beds to some semblance of decent order. *Then* might be an acceptable time to go after what I longed for. Where does it come from, this longing? How I envy those who are not afflicted.

And it wasn't just the voices; it was those damn signs too. I wasn't always into cosmic crap like this, but now I'm a believer. I don't eat a lot of Chinese carryout—not that I don't like it, but I can't handle the calories or the expense. But for months, *months*, my fortunes read like the prologue for this trip. I have my fortunes taped to the kitchen wall, just in case you ever want to come by and verify for yourself:

"Depart not from the path to which fate has you assigned."

"Remember: it's the journey and not the destination which counts."

"Your fondest dream will come true this year."

"Take your dog on a road trip across the country."

Okay, I'm lying about the last one, but there were many others such as "You desire to discover new frontiers. It's time to travel." That one I swear is true. Still, I was going through the torments of the damned trying to make a decision once the road trip idea took over my life. Oh why, oh why, oh why had this idea come into my head? First of all, I'd be broke. Flat broke by the time I got home, maybe flat broke by the time I reached Nevada. That's a hell of a place to wind up penniless, although thousands of people do it every day. I had that tax-return money squirreled away, but it wasn't enough to get me from the Midwest to the East Coast, to the West Coast and back again. I understand this is crazy. Secondly, I wouldn't have a job to come home to, and third, *I was going to be driving all across the country, a woman alone, with just a dog.*

Why the whole country? Because I needed a defibrillator as big as a nation and you know what they say: "Go big or stay home." I had children on both coasts and a shit ton of past lives I needed to look in on and scores of neglected friends and family at all points in between. So that was it. I had to do it up big, had to be willing to walk away, give my notice, have my boss fall out of his chair in disbelief and then tell people behind my back that I'd lost my mind AND I had to write about it as I went. That was the deal. That was the whole package. All or nothing, going for broke and every other imaginable high stakes cliché you can think of. I had no backup. I had $3,800 to my name.

You begin to see the magnitude of my madness. I would be leaving home without enough money to get there and back. How fucking crazy is that? I didn't volunteer all of these particular details to just anybody. I kind of danced around the issue when well-intentioned friends would ask, "Now, how, exactly are you going to do this?" I shrugged off their probing questions because I had a plan. The plan was to place my faith in my writing. I called it a *"book in motion."* I'd write every day about my experiences as I traveled and ask for backers to help me finish the project and get back home. I would use an online creative-funding platform called Kickstarter. The rules are pretty simple. You pitch your idea; if the Kickstarter folks think it's good enough, you get the green light to plead your case on their site, exposing your creative endeavor to millions of people who peruse the site. It's called crowd funding, a popular new twist on the age-old concept of patronage. The trick is, it's an all or nothing proposition. The writer, painter, musician or filmmaker decides what his or her project will cost and how long the fundraising drive will be, and if the goal isn't reached within that time frame, they get nothing: zero, nada, zilch. Nobody who pledges has to pay a dime if the artist doesn't reach 100 percent of his or her goal. Now, *most* people launch their Kickstarter campaign and wait to see if they raise the money before starting their project, but not old Jean. I was going no matter what. I had to. I made a video pitch and started the thirty-day clock on the Kickstarter site and took off. It's somewhat like being a politician. It's filing day. You have to declare your candidacy. You state your intentions and hope to hell you can get enough money to get you to election day. I just needed to get enough money to get back home on. I backed out of the driveway, the meter started running and I started writing. My words would become my currency. It was a complete and total leap of faith, placing my future in the hands of the jury. My testimony? Blog posts from Motel 6s from the east coast to the west.

Even though this may sound like a snap decision, I actually had plenty of time to agonize and talk myself out of it. I told a few close friends, told the kids, all the while qualifying my comments with phrases such as, "if I take this road trip," or, "if I do this thing." I don't think they believed I would really do it. To tell you the truth, I often thought I was kidding myself. I was *the Mom!* I was the person who was always there. I was the one who took phone calls from my kids from London to Bangkok. I was the one who took out the trash, fed the dogs, turned off all the lights. But man, I'll tell you, there'd been a lot of a lot in our house in ten years. That was another of Garrett's famous phrases: "a lot of a lot." He used it to describe a string of bad stuff. He knew from whence he spoke.

I just hadn't convinced myself I could really go through with it. There would be so many defining moments: giving my notice at work, packing up, saying goodbye to my Sean, the only kid still at home. I started losing weight! The sheer turmoil of this irrational obsession was giving me what years of Weight Watchers had failed to do. It was wonderful!

So there I am in the throes of full tilt angst, and I'm walking back from lunch at work one day, doing my normal routine—park close to the gate, race to beat it closing so I can avoid my co-workers at all costs—when, *bam!* Right before my eyes, lying in the middle of the sidewalk, with nobody else walking toward me from any direction, face up on the sidewalk is a single playing card, a seven of spades. I found this interesting. There hadn't been a tornado or even high winds the night before to send one lonely playing card flying out a nearby window. I had seen no children playing Go Fish on the sidewalk that morning. There it was: one tattered seven of spades, face up. How random is that? And considering that my antenna was tuned specifically to all things supernatural, I found it more than slightly curious. I picked it up. I buzzed Janelle up on cellblock three to let me in and I headed straight to my office to Google "seven of spades." What I found out blew my mind. It was a far sight better than the fortune cookies had been. Tarot Teachings told me that, essentially, the seven of spades, or seven of swords, (same thing) represented being caught in a state of "in-betweeness."

Hell, that's the definition of Missouri! The Seven of Swords depicts a solitary traveler, with seven swords in his pack, walking one direction but with his eyes looking back over his shoulder. It asks the question, *"Why is he moving in the opposite direction of where his senses are pointed?"* Tarot Teachings went on to advise, *"There is no hope of finding our true path if we give no consideration to the direction we are taking first. Do we take the path of orthodoxy? The tried and true way? The way yielding expected results? The path we know is safe? Or, what if we take the dreaming mind's path? What if we hold the thoughts of hearth and home in our consciousness while closing our psychic eyes and conjuring up creativity to be our sole guide on the journey to exotic realms?"* Can you believe this? I mean, really! The summary statement sealed the deal:

"The high advice of this card is: Be not of two minds."

I thought I had uncovered the DaVinci code of my own life. How could I not listen now to my gut, telling me I had to do this, telling me I could not justify one more day staying in an unfulfilling job, doing work I did not believe in? How could I silence my writer's voice, calling me out, challenging me to have the courage to say, *This simply is not working for me anymore*?

I had learned the hard way the folly of ignoring that inner voice. I knew how doubt could sit in the bottom of your gut, growing like a malignant tumor. I was practiced in the art of deception, knowing that you can train yourself for years to hide the black spots, to reduce that tiny speck of doubt to a pinpoint. You can cover it up for decades. But, honey, I am here to tell you it's like a hole in a condom: that seed of doubt will come out. It will sprout and grow into a painful, tragic thistle, in the cracks of your sunny-sidewalk life—that doubt, that gut check which goes unchecked.

Our wisdom is remarkable in hindsight, isn't it? Twenty-eight years ago, when I was a young reporter with one divorce already under my belt and a cherubic five-year-old boy in tow, I let that little mustard seed of doubt lie fallow. Rick was a rising star among New Mexico journalists and we both worked at the same television station. He was the whole package: Ryan O'Neal wholesome and handsome with a nice build, blond, and shiny blue eyes. I've heard that sexual attraction is as much audible as it is visual. Rick had a wonderful voice, which he plied to perfection. They don't call them broadcasters for nothing. And he was the epitome of success: a great job at the top news organization in the state, lots of friends, made good money, had two cars, had just bought his first house, wore Brooks Brothers suits and Grey Flannel cologne. In the days when "Type A" personalities were considered attractive, a single man at thirty-one was nothing to be suspicious of. He'd been focused on his career, already amassing a long list of accomplishments as an up-and-coming newsman who'd traveled around the globe and was the darling of the country club set and rubbed elbows with politicians, lawyers and cops. He had a standing racquetball date with the chief of police every Wednesday night. How the irony becomes richer in the fullness of time.

And Rick was crazy about me! I felt like the luckiest girl in the world. When he'd pull me close and wrap his arms around me, I felt safe and loved and protected—finally protected. It's only through the wisdom of hindsight, that makes me realize what we were really seeking was legitimacy. We wanted to feel normal, mainstream, acceptable, distanced from the fringe. He would rescue me from the shame I couldn't even acknowledge; I could help him make up for lost time. We both kept climbing the journalistic road to success and I started having babies—three kids inside four and a half years—to add to the one I had already brought to the party. It became a topic of conversation, what with me waddling around crime scenes on live TV with yet another bun in the oven.

We were walking through a department store one day, after Sean was born. Seeing two kids trailing along beside us and two babies in strollers, a man comes up to us.

"Hey, Rick," he said, pointing to our kids. "Don't you know what's causing that?"

People would say the most inappropriate things. They assumed because you were on TV, they not only knew you, but had the right to say anything they pleased. The gall. Rick took it in stride. "Yeah, we're about to get it figured out," and let it go at that. I wanted to tell the guy it was none of his fucking business, but I was feeling a little testy already, even then. Because after I quit having babies, the bloom started falling off the rose.

Rick was unhappy. He was picking fights with the wrong people at work. He'd raise a stink about insignificant things; he got his name in the paper for a pissing match with a reporter across town. The long-term contract dried up. The station where we were both working promoted the new guy instead of Rick. He was younger, more handsome, more hair and Hispanic, which was good for the Albuquerque market. Plus, he played guitar and sang, always a plus. The general manager told Rick it was nothing personal, that the station was "moving in a different direction." Rick looked in a different direction too. We went through the monthly ordeal of sending out demo reels and hearing nothing back. He got exasperated, saying he was done with TV news. He decided his life's ambition was to be a doctor. If he worked really hard, he could get through med school and finish his residency by the time he was forty. We rearranged our lives. He changed his schedule to work more nights and weekends so he could go back to college. It was during this back-to-school phase when I got a little history lesson.

It was as if my gut rang the doorbell and said, *Why did you leave me out on the doorstep all these years? I'm here and I'm loud.* It actually occurred over the phone, the gut call. Nowadays, a person has so many other options: text or call the person's cellphone, but never call the house! What an idiot! This poor guy must have been desperate.

"Is Rick home?" a young man asked on the other end of the line.

"Um, no, he's not." I was in the laundry room, matching up pairs of baby socks.

In three words, "Is Rick home?" I knew this was the manifestation of dread my gut had been forecasting for years. When Rick and I first started dating, I'd always wondered why Rick never talked about any other women in his life. Maybe I was trying to appease my own indiscretions. I'd certainly had a few. I had been divorced for three years from my high-school-sweetheart-turned-husband. I was going to school full-time to finish my journalism degree and waiting tables at night to make a living. Even with that, I had time for a fling or two. That's what folks in their twenties do, right? Apparently not Rick, at least not any he was willing to talk about. He deftly changed the subject when I probed about his past loves. Nowadays, dating again in my fifties, it's "Don't ask, don't tell," but when you're young and planning a life together, *voir dire* is fair game.

"So, have you ever been in love?" I asked him one night after we'd been making out in his car in the parking lot at the TV station. Years later, a friend would tell me she thought it strange that he didn't whisk me away to his apartment just a block away. Now, I understand why.

"I've been in lust," he said. He told me he'd been so focused on his career that he didn't have time to fall in love "until I met you." We dated only six months before we got married.

Five years later, three more kids and baskets of laundry to fold, there's this guy on the phone. How is it that a stranger's voice over the phone can remove the muzzle you've kept on your inner voice for years? I knew instantly, with uncanny certainty, that this was someone who knew Rick in a way I did not want to know about. It's not that Rick wasn't showing up for dinner, or wasn't accountable almost 24-hours a day, but he was up on that college campus a lot. This whole business of going back to school and changing careers, what was that about? Like a videotape of our life, in my mind I was shuttling back and forth, forward and back, through everything Rick had ever said to me, even while the guy was on the line.

"Rick won't be home until later," I told the caller in a thinly disguised accusatory tone. "Can I tell him who called?"

"Matt," said the man on the phone. "Tell him Matt called. I'm, uh, a friend."

Rick was out of town; he'd flown to be with his sister, who was bringing home an adopted baby from China. He called to check in before he boarded his flight. "Someone named Matt called tonight," I told him after we'd talked about the blessed event. "Who is that?"

He couldn't even muster a good save. The pregnant pause was long enough to fly in a nursery school full of adopted babies. "A guy, uh, a guy at school. In some of my classes."

He would later tell me that if it wasn't so condemnable to wish this on a plane full of innocent passengers, he kept hoping the plane would crash rather than come home to face me. But he did. Thank God the kids were asleep by the time he got home, because I wanted to know straight up who was this Matt guy. He told me he ran into Matt at the university. He was someone he knew once, back when he *thought* he might be gay. He came to realize that he was probably bisexual because when he met me, he started liking women. Well, I'm one hell of a woman, but you can't unpaint a fucking zebra. It's not that I have a prejudice bone in my body about people who are gay or bisexual, I just don't care much for liars. He cried; he begged me to believe him.

"If you're going to doubt me for the rest of our lives, I just don't know what I'll do," he said in his pale-blue pajamas with the navy-blue piping, shifting the burden to how I would screw things up if I held it against him. It was hours after the inquisition had begun. Exhausted and facing a work day in which we both had to look perky on TV, we were going to bed. At least we'd sleep in the same room; we didn't want to alarm the kids.

"The day I met you it changed my life," he said. "I love you more than anything in the world and I don't want to lose you or my family. Please tell me you'll stay."

I got up to brush my teeth and turn out the lights. I walked down the hall, quietly going into each of my children's rooms one by one. Star Wars toys, baseball gloves, Legos, *Goodnight, Moon*—this was what my life was made of. Lauren's little pink tricycle with the streamers on the handle bars. Sean's wind-up giraffe which played "It's a Small World After All." Jenny was our dog back then; she slept on the floor of the babies' room every night. I stood in the door and looked at their cribs, side by side, my innocents, sleeping, contented and safe. We had four children under the age of ten. We were nestled in the bosoms of both our extended families, all just one big, happy bunch. I hosted a houseful of people for Thanksgiving every year. We had friends. We were on TV every night. We *were* somebody. If I left him, where would I go? How would I explain it? If I told, it would ruin his career. Coming out in 1985 wasn't a good career move. How would I make it then? What would it do to my babies?

This barrier had bite. I couldn't cross it. I pledged, and kept my word for years, trying to work through it, trying to trust him. He worked at it too. There was a *Time* magazine cover story that grabbed my attention at the checkout stand a few days after Rick's revelation. It was about a movement that was gaining momentum at that time, whereby gay people would renounce their sexuality and "learn" to become heterosexual. I snatched it up. I needed all the voodoo I could find. I took it home and showed it to Rick. He said he thought it was completely plausible, that in fact it was precisely what he was doing and he was happy to leave that "other" life behind. He never went out alone, never strayed from work, kids' sports, church, our small circle of friends and family, a routine which kept him on a short leash. He was aware of what lay beyond the perimeter of his invisible fence, the object of his true desire. It was still there, crouching, taunting him, just beyond his reach, but for years he never dared approach it, never got close to the boundary between himself and his temptation.

By last summer, none of that ancient history mattered one whit. That was a lifetime ago and I was contemplating what I needed to make the most out of the rest of this one. My boundaries were crumbling. I had a calling. Something was calling me out, mocking my lame excuses for leaving my longing unattended. I longed to see the places which had nourished my life: lush, sweet North Carolina, the wide open skies of Texas, the fiery sunsets of the New Mexico desert, California. Oh, California, coming home. I wanted to write about it. I needed to stake a claim to my own life. Mostly I just wanted to uncover the person I forgot I liked. I didn't know who I was anymore, but I sure as hell didn't like who I'd become. I was weary, tired of being the troll under the bridge. Besides, there had been the seven of spades on the sidewalk! What more proof could I need?

Try the Metropolitan Museum of Art in New York City. I was in New York for a meeting in May and I stayed over for the weekend. My son Patrick had to work during the day, so I went to the Met. I trotted up the stairs and right there, smack dab in front of me was a huge banner with this painting by Caspar David Friedrich, "Woman at a Window." I ran to see the special exhibit, "Rooms with a View: The Open Window in the 19th Century." I came upon the signature painting from which the banners had been designed. There it was, a painting of a slender brunette woman, her hands draped poetically inside the window sill, leaning slightly forward, looking out. It stopped me in my tracks. "Woman at a Window"—I studied her. I studied the world outside her window. I felt I knew her. I felt an affinity to this woman that spanned the centuries between us. I wanted to touch her, to pat her shoulder, to feel the texture of the soft blue sheen of the folds of her long dress. I felt myself breathing, I mean really breathing, as if I had not drawn a deep breath in months. I felt a connection to this painting, this artist's message, his slender model, this mythical woman—a connection so powerful the cavalry could have trotted through the gallery and it would not have disturbed my rapture. I consumed all the background material in the gallery about the artist, Friedrich, and learned that he was Germany's most important Romantic painter at the time. He was fond of placing pensive figures in the foregrounds of his landscapes. The "Woman at the Window," the graceful young woman in this painting, was gazing out over the river Elbe, *exemplifying her yearning for something, someone, out there.*

How comforting to know I wasn't the only one.

4

Merge

It was a peephole, not an open window, through which I looked quite pensively come mid-July. Libby and I were in a Motel 6 in Toledo and I had my eye pressed against the door peering into a long, dark hallway. The fish-eye view on the other side was like a scene from an episode of *Cops*, and I was the one who called the law.

Toledo was our third stop after getting a late start on our journey. It took me that long to finally commit, launch my Kickstarter fundraising campaign, gather my wits and Libby's vaccination record and get my act together. Perpetually a day late and a dollar short, the day after Independence Day seemed fitting for our departure. It coincided with the fifth anniversary of my mama's departure, when she boarded her train bound for glory.

It was shaky those first few days, like getting my sea legs under me. Libby too. She still looked bewildered, to the degree a person can label what's really going on inside a canine noggin. Maybe it's a mistake to give much thought to dog thoughts, although there's a whole book on the subject now. All I can say is she looked pretty puzzled from Illinois all the way to Texas. By Dallas, she was like, "Just get me out of this damn heat." That night in the Motel 6 in Toledo, on Day Four, she was ready to rip somebody's arm off, with each "boom, boom, boom" reverberating through the walls. Libby stood on the saggy bed and barked like a banshee with every downbeat. How fitting that the song was "House Party." Google it, you'll see what I mean.

I had chosen Motel 6 because it's cheaper than anyplace else, not because Tom Bodette was leaving the lights on. Plus, they're dog-friendly. Not so much though when the boys down the hall are having a rager. Libby and I had checked in around sunset. This was becoming my pattern. I'd drive until about a half-hour before sunset, then find a place to stop for the night. I'd leave her in the car while I checked in, her head stuck out the back window. I'd walk back to the car, waving the key, which would make her go nuts. She'd leap out of the car, bound up the stairs or run down the hall, depending on the motel, and promptly jump on the bed the same way little kids do. It took a few stops to perfect this little routine. It seemed she always needed to pee desperately by the time we'd stop and so did I. Since I couldn't go outside (I would by the end of the trip) and she couldn't go inside, sacrifices had to be made. Hers. We eventually became a well-oiled hotel checkin' in machine.

That night, still affectionately referred to as the "Holy Toledo" night, we rolled in, and the place seemed safe and clean enough, so I got us a room. We checked out the bouncy bed. I went to the bathroom, then took her out to the grass in the back. We crossed the parking lot with me carrying a "traveler," a vodka tonic in a red plastic cup. We ate outside at a pizza joint across the wide expanse of concrete, home to the Motel 6, Lucky Strikes Bowling Lanes, a Dollar General store and Pizza Baron, which came highly recommended by the desk clerk. Aside from the zebra-striped, dive-bombing mosquitoes, which I was a bit concerned were carrying the avian flu after I accidentally ate one, life was good.

A cute kid, probably the age of my daughter Lauren, who is 24, was the pizza deliveryman and busboy on duty. He pulled up, presumably fresh from a delivery, to see Libby and me enjoying our al fresco dining experience—wrought iron tables and chairs chained into the concrete. That's something you learn early on traversing the country with a dog: dinner is always on the patio.

"Nice dog," he said, getting out of his car wearing an apron, a white tee-shirt and faded cutoffs. He had one of those magnetic pizza delivery signs on top of a beat-up old Mazda, which had seen the best of its zoom-zoom. "It's nice to actually see somebody eating out here. Nobody ever does."

"Well, we kinda have to," I told him, hoping he wouldn't bust me for my BYOB. "We're traveling across the country."

"Really? That is so cool!" This is the universal reaction I received from people everywhere from Philadelphia to Flagstaff last summer. I took this to mean that there are millions of malcontents across the country tugging on their leash to be free. My own research notwithstanding, evidence abounds that there are swarms of people who fantasize about chucking everything to hit the road. It is fun, I wouldn't argue that, but not as glam as you might think.

"Where are you from?" He had come over and was petting Libby now, who was rolled over on her back. She's loose like that.

"St. Louis," I said. I hate saying I'm from St. Louis. It's such a temporary thing, like for fifteen years now.

"Wow, long way." We talked about dogs and travel and school. He was still in college. He had, I think, about six earrings in one ear and tats galore; his curly, long hair, like Carrot Top's, was not only red but pulled back into a ponytail. "I have a dog. Had it ever since I started college. It's kind of a hassle, cause I always have to figure out where I'm gonna live, you know, with the dog. But he's like the best part of my day, know what I mean?"

I said I did. He started sweeping.

"Dogs are so sensitive. It's like, they always know if you're upset, or something's wrong."

Yeah, like when twenty-five people are packed into a Motel 6 motel room with paper-thin walls and some guy out in the hall is yelling into his cellphone, "Hurry up, motherfucker, we are going to par-tay!" By the time I'd said goodnight to the pizza boy and got back to the room, it was unbearable. The nice young men who'd rented the suite at the end of the hall invited all their friends from far and wide, who yelled into their cellphones and stomped and ran all night long, up and down the hall.

"You are one stupid motherfucker." It was the same guy on the phone again. Must have been the same guy on the other end of the line too, because he was repeating the directions for at least the fifth time to his buddy, who, apparently, was lost. I was ready to go out in the hall and grab the phone and say, "You are a stupid motherfucker! How many times does this guy have to give you the address!"

But I didn't. I would have been mugged because by then I had dialed 9-1-1. The noise had gotten completely out of hand. I had dialed zero a number of times but it seemed nobody was manning the front desk. As it turned out, the front desk clerk was out smoking reefer in the parking lot. When the chatter went from, shall we say, colloquial to homicidal, I called the po-po. Before a real policeman could arrive on the scene however, a knock came at my door.

Pound, pound, pound.

Libby's hysterical by now; I've already been threatening her with certain death if she didn't stop barking at the boom, boom, boom down the hall. Now the bastards were pound, pound, pounding on my door! I crossed to the peep hole. A handsome, athletic, young black man, holding a Starbucks in his hand, with his sunglasses hung backwards on his ears, was standing five inches from the door.

"What do you want?" I demanded.

"Security." He flashed a fake looking badge.

Well, honey, I wasn't born yesterday.

"So, what do you want?" I demanded again.

"Did you call 9-1-1? Are you okay in there? We got a report that somebody called 9-1-1 from this room."

I told him I did. I told him I thought a fight was breaking out at the party down the hall and I didn't want any stray bullets to come flying through the walls. I told him I was not going to open the door.

"Okay, we're on top of it."

They weren't. This went on until three o'clock in the morning. By then, I'm lying in the bed, huddled up with Libby, who would fall asleep and then wake with a start about every fifteen minutes. It was ridiculous. I was trying to just hunker down, because after the rent-a-cop came to the door, two nice young ladies came and banged on my door and called me a bitch for calling the police. Way to protect your snitches, you sorry-ass rent-a-cop.

When an all-out assault broke out directly in front of my door, however, it was time to take off the gloves. I called 9-1-1 again and told them I believed a woman was being murdered at the Motel 6. I wasn't exaggerating, much.

A man and a woman had gotten into a shouting match out in the hall. They were standing at the top of the stairs, just outside my door. The woman was saying, "Give me my cellphone back, you son of a bitch," and she took a wild swing at him with her purse. He pleaded with her, "Just come back inside, baby. I won't be jealous, I swear! I just want you to be with me." Yeah, like I'd be all over that. She screamed, "How can you say you love me and want to marry me when you accuse me of cheating? I can't even talk to other guys!" It went downhill from there. More like down the stairs. She shoved him, he shoved back. They slammed up against my door and then they fell down the stairs. I called the cops, and, yes, rent-a-cop showed up again.

"I am not opening this door for anybody until I see real live policemen from a real live police department," I hollered through the door, with Libby barking in the background. I pity the poor fool who would try to come in and get me.

A few minutes later, sure enough, uniformed policemen arrived on the scene. They stopped a guy, a different one this time, right in front of the peep hole, where I was glued.

"Where's your baby mama at?" the cop asked him.

I promise you this is true. Dude told the cop something like "he don't know, he thinks she gone." The cop tells him to go on home, the party's over. Meanwhile, I overhear that the quarreling lovers are now sitting in squad cars in the parking lot. Turns out the woman has an outstanding warrant. Probably for assault with a deadly weapon: her purse. Within about ten minutes, the place is cleared. It's quiet. It is 3:45 in the morning. I never did unlock the dead bolt, until about nine o'clock when I rolled out, marched downstairs and demanded a refund. I actually got one.

Wow. So this was it, huh? *This* was exactly what I was longing for? Really? If anybody who had heard my misty-eyed vision about the journey of a lifetime had been a fly on the wall that night, seeing me spooning with Libby, my nose to her back, they would have killed themselves laughing. I'm telling you, it was pitiful, truly pitiful. And truthfully, it wasn't even the first time I'd had one of these motel moments. The first one was my very first night on the road.

It had been an emotional two weeks leading up to "D-Day" or Departure Day, once I'd given my notice at work.

"Today's the day." I stood out on the seven-of-spades sidewalk, on a conference call with my kids over my cellphone. The sidewalk was the only place I had decent reception and I didn't want my co-worker in the cellblock next to me to overhear. "I'm giving my notice at two o'clock." I had arranged a cellular family meeting, since my kids were spread from NYC to LA to DC to STL. It's hard to explain how this felt, telling my children that I was on the brink of doing something almost indefensible. Can you imagine? Telling your four grown children that you're simply checking out? Telling them that you're not quite sure exactly where you're going, you don't really have enough money to get there and back, but you think you've got it figured out, and you're going, no matter what? You're not really asking their permission; it's more like asking forgiveness, the way you'd ask a true friend to understand why you're having an affair.

"I just need you to understand," I said, choking up a bit. "I don't want this to be hard on you. I don't want you to worry, I'll be fine. I'll be safe. I just have to do this." They made it easy because they are four of the funniest, most irreverent people I know and after all, we're thick as thieves. In all candor, they were a little bit more interested in talking to each other than talking to me, since it was becoming increasingly rare for the four of them to converse en masse. They talked some smack to their mama too.

"Don't do anything to get arrested, because none of us has any money."

And then, "We're proud of you, Mom." Those were the words I needed to hear.

Because I was getting ready to call my own bluff. I was already on the record. I'd painted myself into a social-media corner by publishing a blog post the night before titled, *"We're Going."* I told the whole world I was quitting my job, hitting the road with my dog to travel across America and, incidentally, write a book. Now, I had no choice; I had to go. I'd be made out a liar if I backed out. Sucks when that happens.

But let me share something that happened within that same 24-hour period which would be as important as a blood transfusion to a hemophiliac. It would become my encouragement, the extra backbone, comfort and purpose I would need in the weeks ahead. It opened my eyes to a common emotion I had never had the opportunity to understand. It was late at night when I let the cat out of the bag with the blog post about the road trip. Within minutes, literally minutes, after I published the first entry about the road trip on my website and Open Salon, comments came pinging in from France to California. Complete strangers were saying they'd walk away from their jobs and hit the road in a minute, if only they could! People I do not know, people whom I've never met, with whom I had never corresponded were posting comments on the blog:

"I'm riding right along beside you."

"You're going for me."

"I have always dreamed of doing this."

What does this say about our lives? I had apparently struck a nerve.

The next morning, seeing how I'd blabbed all over the Internet and had shared the link with a few folks at work, which was dicey considering I couldn't get in to see my boss until 2:00 p.m., *everybody* in the whole building knew! I was getting winks and emails and a steady stream of people popping into my office, closing the glass door behind them and pouring out their hearts to me as if I was a priest or the office shrink. The same people who, just a week before I'd lumped into the category of being stand-offish—all of a sudden I understood they were just like me. I felt like such a jerk! I felt ashamed of how closed-off I had been, how judgmental. It was a humbling lesson in not making assumptions. They echoed the very words that were in my heart; they felt as burned out as I did. Many of them wished they could be doing something different. Some had big dreams they'd set aside, some of them didn't know what they were longing for; they just wanted to feel happier. But they had so many responsibilities, so much riding on their jobs, they couldn't let go. They told me I inspired them. Me? Really? For this? They gave me money for my trip. They told me they'd be reading every post along the way. I was stunned at the outpouring of support and generosity, and completely blown away. I will never forget it. Truly.

From that moment on, it stopped being about me and it became about them. It ceased being my moral imperative and became a commitment to all the people who felt the same way I did but couldn't do anything about it. And I understood. I had been that way for years. Fear keeps us trapped in bad marriages. Fear prevents us from pursuing our dreams. Fear keeps us isolated: crouched inside our bunkers, scurrying to our cars, dutifully driving to and from work every day, mowing the grass, raking the leaves, shoveling the snow, many of us thinking that we simply cannot wash and repeat for one more season of our lives. Yet we do. The staggering fear of free-fall, cut loose from the mainstream, the daily commute with coffee in the car and conference calls a waitin', which not only pays our mortgage, but also dictates our health and determines our children's futures, keeps us trapped. Everything is riding on the holy grail of automatic deposit, along with some pittance of security in our old age, which is squeezed out of the diminishing dollars, if there are any left to squeeze, all of this, pitted against the constant fear of losing it all, makes us toxic. It makes us less human. It makes us the backbiting, small people who sit inside our offices and snarl at folks walking by. I should know; I was the worst of the mongrels.

But now, on the verge of getting off the chain, of going up to the boss's office to tender my resignation, I would be leaving the devil I knew for the devil I didn't. The second hand on the plastic wall clock in my office ticked straight up. Two o'clock: no going back. I walked up the stairs, past the glass cubicles where my compatriots worked on graphics or audio, copy or complaining clients. I walked into the inner sanctum from which there'd be no return. My boss was very approachable.

"I simply must to do this thing," I continued after I'd opened up with, "I'm letting you know I'm leaving. I'm quitting to drive across the country with my dog to write a book."

Now, my former boss is a certified genius and he knows everybody on the planet. He immediately launched into a story about some uber-rich guy he knew who did the same thing, except the guy he knew was a former CEO who bailed out from running his multinational company to drive around the country with a dog in a brand spankin' new AirStream to give away money, lots of money, to strangers. Kind of like the old *Millionaire* show.

"Do you have a dog?" Ken asked.

"Of course I have a dog!" I laughed. "She's a big part of the inspiration for this little trip."

"Well, this guy didn't. He had to buy one."

Now, if I had a lick of sense, and clearly we have established the questionable nature of that, I would have vigorously followed up on the split second thought I had of finding the uber-rich guy to see if he'd be interested in funding my trip across the country, seeing as how he was fond of giving away money, but of course, I didn't. I just gave my notice and Ken said,

"Wow, you really do have to do this. I can tell how passionate you are. Your face just lights up when you talk about it."

He drew the line on his magnanimity when it came to my unused vacation time, however; he wouldn't let me take it at the end of my employment, so I lost my vacation days. I'm sure he was crouched in fear over a mutiny if word got out that I'd been allowed to break the rules. Okay, rules are rules. I had four days from my last day on the job to my first day on the road, *four days!*

The night before I left, I went around the house, performing some unorthodox version of laying on of hands. Except it wasn't people, it was things I was blessing. Insignificant things seemed precious to me now: the spidery crack in the bathroom sink, the pencil marks measuring the kids' height on the kitchen wall next to the pantry, my mother's paintings in the living room. I went down to the basement and patted the washing machine. "Don't break down now, you hear?" I watered my clematis vine and thanked her for her beauty. I talked to the roses. Lord knows they're my taskmasters. I told them I'd be back. But leaving Sean, now, that was the hardest. Backing the car out, watching him stand there and wave, with Louie sitting at his feet, was the hardest thing to do. He was the only kid still at home, between his junior and senior year in college, waiting tables at night. He would be the only kid left at home. My babies, Sean and Louie, guarding the castle.

I didn't let him see me cry. I waved and smiled and held my chin up while Libby's ears flapped out the back window. I still wonder how it felt to him: being left there all alone, siblings strewn from coast-to-coast and his harebrained mother traipsing around the country with a dog. After all the stuff we'd been through, there I went.

That first night, I didn't get far, seeing how I got a late start. Instead of pulling out at the crack of dawn, I was on TV at the crack of dawn; it was a slow news day. Some of my buddies in the news biz actually did a story on the journalist-cum-writer throwing off the corporate shackles to hit the road. They fantasize about this too. Trust me, I've been there. Being on TV again was great! There was only one problem: I'd picked up a nail somewhere, so I had to get my tire fixed. Plus there was the matter of that little oil change I'd put off. It was near sundown when I finally pulled out.

Here's where I'm going to give you a little traveling tip: Do not drink a margarita on your way out of town. We have this great Mexican restaurant here in St. Louis where you can get a margarita at the drive-up. Honest. I was in a celebratory mood, I had finally gotten the oil changed and the tire fixed, I was jubilant over my exciting adventure about to begin, I figured I could have a margarita and stop for coffee later. I drove through and got a couple of tacos and a marg to go. Bad idea. I didn't even make it to my first planned stop. I was too sleepy. I pulled into an aging Red Roof Inn in Springfield, Illinois and called it a night. I lay on top of the cheap floral sateen bedspread which my blog readers would recoil in horror over later. But I didn't care. I could have climbed onto that bed with the people who had just finished having sex on the bedspread with a simple "Move over," I was that tired.

Really, I was overwhelmed. I was so afraid I'd set myself up. I had told, basically, the world that I was going to drive more than 8,000 miles and visit every place I'd ever lived and reconnect with everybody who'd ever meant anything to me and try to locate the rumored half-brother. Hell's bells, I didn't even have a clue if this guy was alive, much less where he lived!

"Libby, what have I done? What have I done?" I was sobbing.

Then I thought about Sean. Something that happened three years earlier, when he was a freshman in college in Kansas City. He was going through the motions at school, keeping his grades up, keeping up appearances, putting on a brave front until he just couldn't do it anymore. Talk to anybody who has panic attacks; they'll tell you how bad it can get. Wrapped in anxiety, curled up in the stairwell of the dorm, my youngest son called me in the middle of the night.

"I have to come home. I can't do this. I feel like my heart is going to explode out of my chest."

Jean Ellen Whatley

He'd had these episodes before, even when he was a kid. He had worked through it. He had chosen to be a football player, for Christ's sake. Talk about fear! My first instinct was to jump in the car at three in the morning and race across the state to talk him off the ledge. But I wouldn't be able to do that every time. Instead, I steered him toward some answers. He confided in his roommates, who were great. He talked to a counselor at school and we found a wonderful therapist close to campus. Turns out anxiety runs high among art students. Go figure. Sean tried to sleep at night and get through classes while he waited for his appointment, three more days, then two, then one. When you're struggling, hours feels like days. I get a call at five o'clock in the morning on the day of his first therapy session.

"It's bad; it's worse. I want to come home."

We'd made a deal. If his anxiety got so bad that he felt like he couldn't make it through another day, all he had to do was get a ride to the train station where there were two trains a day to St. Louis.

"You've got an appointment at eight this morning with someone who can help you," I told him. "That's three hours. Three hours. Get through just three more hours and go see the doctor. And if you still want to come home, there's a train at ten o'clock."

I didn't hear from him for hours. I went to work. The waiting was awful. Finally he called. He'd gone straight to class after his appointment.

"I liked him; he's a good guy," Sean said. "I feel better."

He told me months later how it had been raining that morning in Kansas City. The only way he could get to the shrink's office was on a bike. Sean got on his bike during an early spring storm and rode through the driving rain in search of his healing. I remembered that lesson from my son as I lay on the bed in a crappy Red Roof Inn on the first night of a journey that would lead to my own.

"It's just me and you, Lib," I whispered, my tears subsided. "You have to stay close, you hear?" Libby sighed one of those deep doggie sighs, as if saying, "What choice do I have?" I fell asleep in my clothes.

It got progressively better with each hotel—well, except for Toledo. Libby and I felt less and less like refugees. Each day, I seemed to get my confidence up a little more. From the stand point of physical safety, a person can plan for the obvious dangers—travel during the day, park close to the doors, don't wander around at night. The emotional landmines, though; they were hard to avoid.

It was that goddamn Cracker Barrel. I was waiting for my take-out order on a Sunday in Youngstown, Ohio about a week into my trip. I had been writing all day; it had been a productive one. Earlier that morning, I had made the decision to stay over. There was no reason I had to travel every single day, especially when I was writing about it. Libby and I had met a bunch of bikers from Buffalo in the parking lot at the EconoLodge, our deluxe accommodations, two nights in a row. They were the coolest guys, most of them Puerto Rican. I took pictures of them with Libby standing in front of their bad-ass Harleys, after which she and I went hunting for something to eat. Hmmm, okay, how about Cracker Barrel? It was a known entity and seeing how it was Sunday, felt like Sunday dinner. I was sitting there rocking in one of those stupid-ass rockers, people watching—women and men in their Sunday best, fresh from church, in dresses with hats, creased slacks and dress shirts with neck ties, grandmas and grandpas with their grown kids and their babies, blue jeans and flip flops, all walks of life, in and out of the Cracker Barrel. Then there was me, alone, a voyeur in Adidas sweats, an old grey tank top, no makeup, my hair in a ponytail on top of my head. I looked appalling. But what did I care? Who was going to see me anyway? Alone, except for my dog with her head out the window, parked over in the shade. *What was I doing out here on a Sunday afternoon on the outskirts of Youngstown, Ohio, where I didn't know a soul, where it appeared that everybody else in the world was with somebody? What was I doing on a sunny, summer afternoon all alone?* I felt a bit conspicuous, as if the voices in my head were audible, to the point that the other diners in their ladder-back rockers would soon say something like, "Hey, quiet that shit down!"

They called my number. I got my food. Libby was excited because there was chicken.

The parking lot at the EconoLodge was empty when we got back. Absolutely empty. Ours was the only car. They'd moved on, the bikers. It made me feel strange. They'd moved on, and I was left behind, off the track, off my pace, not moving forward, *off the grid.* How could I miss a bunch of Puerto Rican bikers I had met just thirty minutes ago? I was left with too much time to travel to those spongy spots in my mind which have never really been fully drained of all the hurtful pus that kept me feverish. I had nowhere to go to get away from myself, sitting there in a run-down motor court, eating out of a white plastic box with white plastic utensils, next to a cracked swimming pool with a foot of stagnant water and a sign that says "closed for the season" knowing full well it'd been closed for much longer than that.

It's like this: you're thinking about the seasons in your life. You've taken a dive off the deep end by abandoning your old life because you're afraid that time is running out on the only one you've got left and your faithful pup, the canine who keeps you from toppling over the edge of insanity, is just hoping you'll drop even one, tiny morsel of chicken on the grubby rug as you're asking yourself, *how in the fuck did this happen?* These are the necessary things, these questions. These are questions I asked myself when nobody else was in the room, when the sun was going down, casting hard-edged shadows on the cheap, blond, pressed-wood TV armoire where my silhouette was splashed in vivid black and white: my nose, my cheekbone, the shape of my hand which held my head. I raised myself up and took a photo—a self-portrait of the shadow of my doubt.

I righted myself with the sun. I said, "Come on, Lib, we're getting out of here," and we took a Sunday drive into downtown Youngstown. It would have been a ghost town if not for the biker concert in the Veteran's Park where these guys still mourn their MIAs just as I mourn mine. A good-looking guy with a salt-and-pepper ponytail, crackling sharp blue eyes and a red bandana tied around his forehead asked if he could pet Libby. Of course, I said. We chatted about dogs and he smiled so wonderfully, he was like Robert Redford as a biker. The guy next to him nodded approvingly at the dog and me. Both men were so decent: no come-on, no menace, no threat.

I feel better. Not quite so alone. This is what saves you. You join. If you can't go back to the family you once were, you join the family you're with.

You merge. You wake up early the next day and get back out there again. You get back in the flow: first gear, second, third, fourth, taking your turn on the on-ramp with the truckers lined up for a quarter-mile, coming out of the Travel America hub across the street from the empty EconoLodge parking lot. You merge. And in a once-in-a-lifetime moment of providence, you flip on the radio to check up on the world, with the annoying static of the AM dial sounding like "War of the Worlds," the radio scans for a clear signal. It finally lands on one, just in time to hear the preacher say: "You are not alone. Your scars will not defeat you. You will survive to tell your story."

You merge. On a bicycle in the traffic in the pouring rain, you merge to find your healing. You merge to tell your stories. You merge to share what makes you human. In Philly with the boys drinking tallboys inside paper sacks, with the mom at Pop's Deli who made my cheesesteak and gave me a pamphlet of scriptures from St. James, you merge. With the couple I sat down next to at a sidewalk café in New York City, both of them recovering alcoholics, who are rehabbing a house in Brooklyn to help others rehab in a different way, you merge. You merge to tell them thank you, to tell them about your little brother who almost died from drinking and how you pray for him every day. You merge into the pace of a young man's life New York City, gliding into the current of his life, the view from his windows, his routes, his rhythm. We're like synchronized swimmers, stroke by stroke, sometimes miles, sometimes minutes, sometimes lifetimes, until we swim apart.

On this night, two days after Youngstown, step-by-step, my son and I are walking with Libby. It's my first night in the city and we're going to a taco stand around the corner. We get our food and take a seat. Strangers pass by, pat Libby on the head. There's a revival going on, a real one. Across the street, there's a big white tent in a vacant lot where the faithful have gathered on a blistering night. Patrick smiles his winning smile, an epic charmer, shaking his head. "I've been living here for four years and I have never seen a tent revival in Brooklyn, ever."

I laugh and shrug my shoulders, so open now to the wondrous things which will come my way. You merge with what lies in front of you. All you have to do is be open. All you have to do is be ready to receive, just like the people under the white tent across the street, their hands and hearts upturned. The service is coming to a close and they're singing the invitational:

"Watchfully, tenderly, Jesus is calling, calling for you and for me. Come home, come home. Ye who are weary, come home."

The Jamaican preacher, in the slowly waning heat, when the concrete lets go of what it's been clinging to all day, offers salvation.

"Come and be saved."

His voice carries from across the street like a sweet, caramel current through the dense city air.

God bless you brother, I already am.

5

Blue Ridge Transfusion

From the time I was a baby I have been yanked all over the country by one man or another. Not by my hair or anything, just uprooted against my will. It was unsettling, in the most literal sense of the word. The first time I was just a toddler. My mother and I boarded a train in San Francisco bound for Texas when I was just three, leaving behind my real father whom I would never see again.

"I want my Daddy!"

In the tiny hisses of information that my mother was generous enough to leak out, like spurts of gas from a helium balloon at the approximate rate of one factoid per decade, she casually admitted to me, once I was grown, that on the day we left San Francisco, I pitched a fit at the train station. I tried to crawl out of my mother's clutches and get back into the arms of my father. Funny how, some fifty years later, here I was, still rooting around for some trace of him. All I can say about my mom leaving San Francisco for a man in Fort Worth is that she must have really been in love, or that long, tall Texan was mighty good in bed.

So at this juncture, if you'll indulge me, it might be a good time to give you a little history, Plus it's the method to my "mapness" last summer, the rationale behind the route.

I was born in San Francisco and moved to Texas when I was three so my mom could reconcile with the man she was still legally married to. Jim Whatley's name is on my birth certificate, even though he was nowhere near the scene of the crime at conception, or birth. But out of respect for the four Whatley brothers I grew up with, and for brand consistency, I carry his name to this day. Alas, my mother's happy reunion with Jim lasted only six years—long enough for her to produce another couple of little brothers.

By now, I'm nine. That's when she took up with the Mexican. I don't say this in any pejorative sense, merely as a way to identify him. In 1963, it was quite controversial, a white woman cavorting with a Mexican. Fort Worth, Texas was very segregated. We had only one kid with a Hispanic surname in our entire high school: Frankie Alvarez. I still remember because his was the first picture in the yearbook. All the Hispanic kids went to school at North Side High and upwards of 90 percent of the Hispanics lived on the north side, too. That's where my stepdad's parents settled after they fled San Luis Potosi in north central Mexico during Pancho Villa's time. The situation in Mexico was about as lawless as it is now. The story goes that Pancho and his banditos took over the Garza hacienda after the Garzas split, wading across the Rio Grande to safety and eventual civil-service employment. My mom and Mexican stepdad both worked for the Federal Aviation Administration and he was offered a promotion to move to Albuquerque. I was a sophomore in high school and not happy about it. I had tons of great friends to hang out and smoke pot with at Trinity Park. Why oh why would I want to leave to go live in the backwater town of Albuquerque?

I had no choice. I sulked all the way from Fort Worth to Albuquerque where I started tenth grade, met new friends to smoke pot with in Columbus Park, and, at nineteen, married the longhair I talked into being in the school play with me because he could play the guitar and memorize long lines of narration. He also just happened to live around the corner.

We got married in the Catholic Church, a High Mass; half of the groomsmen were also high. Later at the reception they spiked the punch with Everclear and the Mexican rowdies, who were also our friends, "abducted" me from the ballroom. It's a quaint Mexican custom, hijacking the bride and holding her for ransom while the "kidnappers" shake down the wedding guests for cash, which is then given to the newlyweds upon the bride's triumphant return to the reception. Best-laid plans gone awry. Marty Salinas' burly brother-in-law, Chuy the ex-con, got only halfway down the fire escape stairs with me slung over his shoulder before some big hippies stopped him on the landing, shoved him against the wall, with my updo-adorned head sandwiched between his back and said wall, at which time I was released from Chuy's gunnysack hold on me, set back down on my white sandals and returned to the dance somewhat dazed. You begin to get the picture. Albuquerque was rough around the edges at this time. It was 1974.

The golden-blond tresses (he had *great* hair) were shorn when husband number one joined the Navy. It was our ticket out of Albuquerque and a way for a young couple to gel as a self-sufficient unit and not an appendage of either of our families, who, living less than half a mile apart, expected us for dinner on alternate Sundays. So I followed him from New Mexico first to Key West and then Virginia Beach where my son Nathan, "The Virginian," was born. His last duty station would be our undoing, though. The Navy discouraged the presence of wives and babies on the remote island of Midway, which I don't know why they call it "Midway" since it's really about a *third* of the way from Honolulu to Tokyo. A brand-new mother at twenty-three, just two weeks after giving birth, I moved back to Albuquerque with newborn Nathan, to live with my doting but demanding mother, aforementioned Mexican stepdad and my increasingly delinquent youngest brother, Paul. Good times. Navy Man flew off to spend a year with the gooney birds on Midway Island. By the time he'd finished his one-year tour, I was an experienced mom, chomping at the bit to get out from under my year-long imprisonment with the family natal. He came home an inexperienced father who had a tough time assimilating to civilian life, coming back to a full college load, a wife and toddler. We tried. Well, he tried best as he could. I tried at first, but used his hesitancy to get on with the program to justify a wandering eye toward a more mature man. The fling didn't last; neither did the marriage. We fought. I won. I broke his heart. Let me give you some advice: Don't leave too many of these behind in one lifetime, it weighs on you. He got the stereo, I got the kid, the house and all the debt. You'd think by the time I did this the second time around, years later, with Rick the newsman, I would have gotten smarter. Not so much.

Divorced at the ripe old age of twenty-six and with a toddler in tow, I headed back to college. I needed to support a child and myself now. That's when I got into journalism, which, thank God, federal grants and a Scripps Howard scholarship led to a solid career which fed my family for twenty years.

I met Rick when I landed my first reporting job. He was the Kelsey Grammer to my Sally Field (only taller). We married just months after we met. Five years and three more babies later, the honeymoon was over and Mr. Rick went to Washington to become a Capitol Hill press secretary. The family gave chase. Just about the time I'd unpacked the last wardrobe box in our suburban D.C. rental we moved again, this time to North Carolina. Winston lasted six blessed years, long enough for me to perfect my accent. That's when he came home and said, "I just got a job offer in St. Louis!" I acquiesced with a tacit understanding that this, indeed, would be the "last chance" move to the Show Me State where I have remained in a state of denial ever since. Fifteen years; I never would have dreamed it.

So to review, California, Texas, New Mexico, Florida, Virginia, D.C., North Carolina and Missouri—every time I have ever moved in my life it's been to follow some man. There is one notable exception: my last move. I changed neighborhoods to get my kids out of the white bread suburbs in which we'd been deposited when Rick scouted out our St. Louis location. I sold the blue, vinyl-wrapped, corner-lot-on-a-cul-de-sac house and bought an 80-year-old bungalow in an older part of St. Louis where there are actually some people of color (what a concept!) and put a stake in the ground, proudly proclaiming, "On this rock I will rebuild my life!"

And that is precisely what I'd been doing: births, deaths, sex scandal, imprisonment of the child-support payer, poverty, and all. I'd been rehabbing my life for ten years. I was tucked in, nice and snug, until those damn voices called me out last spring. Here's the irony, though, girls and boys: the voices were telling me to go back and visit all the places that some dude had dragged me to in the first place! Who would have thought? It would be churlish of me not to say, "Thanks for the ride, fellas" at least for the first go-around.

But this time, the trip would be on my own time, on my own dime, and for my own peace of mind. There's cruelty in having lived so many places. Each location calls you home. How do know which one to tend to? How can one choose? These backdrops, these stages upon which our lives have been acted, these locations, are almost like our children: each one endearing and annoying in their own way, each one clenching a chunk of your heart, where the memories run deep.

Well, sometimes the memories are only as deep as a plastic dog dish. How does a person get choked up over a silly water bowl? I made a blubbering fool out of myself at the Outpost Café, in Brooklyn on Fulton Avenue, where Libby and I had spent five happy days being a gypsy writer with her gypsy dog at a hipster coffee shop. I was sliding my laptop into my backpack when I caught a glimpse of Libby's empty, red bowl. The owner of the coffee shop filled it up for her every day. Seeing it there, on the uneven bricks of the patio, and knowing that countless other people with their dogs would come and go after we were gone; it just got to me. I welled up. The Outpost had been *our* outpost for five days. I had gone there to write, because Patrick was piggybacking off

Jean Ellen Whatley

some other tenant's Wi-Fi and I had to sit in the upstairs window sill to get a signal, so the coffee shop around the corner was much less dangerous. The minute I sat down to write, David Bowie's "Jean Genie" was on the stereo. I felt at home. After five days, I had recorded some history there, but now it was time to go. I hoisted my backpack on my shoulder , grabbed Libby's leash, kept my head down and my sunglasses on to hide my tears. What a boob! I wrote an entire blog post about leaving a little piece of my heart in that scummy water bowl. See how it is when you're out on your own? It's raw. My stomach was in knots at the prospect of saying goodbye to Patrick. Brave as you might think I am, each time I'd drive away from a city in which I had a child, I felt lonely and scared. It was that feeling of just being out there. I was so fucking *out there*.

With a daughter in D.C., I didn't have too long to be lonely, though. Lauren was doing an internship on Capitol Hill and I would get free lodging; well, not free, since I paid for her dorm, but Libby and I would get to benefit from my investment by my staying with her on campus at George Washington University. Sneaking an 86-pound dog in and out of a sorority house isn't real easy. Getting her out in the middle of the night when she's barking like a seal, that's even harder.

Libby had somehow contracted kennel cough. In a way, it was lucky it happened when I was in a big city like D.C. as opposed to a few nights later when I'd be holed up in some small mountain town in northern Virginia. I arrived in the District after an ungodly traffic backup on I-95, where we saw the first of three fatal car wrecks we would encounter on our journey. I hugged Lauren real tight when I saw her. We had a nice dinner at the outdoor café across the street from her dorm. We had a glass of wine. Libby sprawled on the brick patio next to our table and everything was cool. As luck would have it, Lauren's roommate had cut her D.C. summer short, so there was an available bed with a butter-yellow Ralph Lauren down comforter on top. Oh, happy day. All we had to do was cross through the lobby undetected to get upstairs.

Here's how we would sneak Libby in: Lauren went into the sorority house, scanned the lobby and hallway, and then motioned for Libby and I to follow. Libby and I would tiptoe in (okay, dogs don't tiptoe), make a hard right and immediately go up the stairs rather than taking the elevator. We made that mistake only once. We pushed the button for the elevator and when the doors opened on the first floor, some poor little girl screamed her head off at the site of a big dog standing there calmly waiting, no fangs. I am just amazed by people who are such pussies about dogs. But, not wanting that to happen again, we took the stairs the rest of the time, which Libby considered a fitness challenge. She bounded up the stairs, the sound of her nails clicking on the linoleum tiles, and then, when I got to the fourth floor (yes, four flights) I opened the door, scoped out the hall, and if it was empty, I'd let her run down the hall sniffing every door until she found the one which led to her girl. Took her only two tries to find the correct door, but my daughter was annoyed.

"Mom, don't let her do that!" she scolded.

When Libby woke us up at three o'clock in the morning sounding like a kid with croup, Lauren was scared, not only that something was terribly wrong with the dog, but also that she'd get kicked out of the building. Libby sounded terrible, really, really terrible. She was coughing so hard she was throwing up. The sound of her barfing was more frightening than the cough. I was beside myself because I thought she had a goddamn chicken bone lodged in her windpipe. Let me tell you why.

The entire United States is littered with chicken bones. I do not understand this for two reasons. Number one, I do not understand why people who eat fried chicken in public parks or on public sidewalks believe it is okay to throw the chicken bones on the ground. Number two, I do not understand, with all the evidence to suggest that it's probably not that good for you, why fried chicken remains so popular to this day. In every major city to which I traveled, from Chicago to San Francisco and all urban areas in between, plus many rural, Libby managed to sniff out somebody's dirty old, discarded chicken bones: in parks, on sidewalks, in the streets of New York and, yes, even on a corner in Winslow, Arizona. I swear to God, I had to yank her drooling muzzle off the sidewalks, many times too late, and then attempt to pry chicken bones out of her clenched jaw. This is dangerous. I hope a million people read this book if only to jump-start a "Put Your Goddamn Chicken Bones in the Trash" movement all across America. My fear of rapists or murderers paled in comparison to the dread of a chicken bone getting caught crossways in Libby's windpipe or bowel.

Meanwhile, I didn't know why she was coughing and throwing up in Lauren's room. I was scared to death. "Let's just get her outside," I said and threw on some clothes. We grabbed keys and phones, and I gently led her down the hall, down the stairs, and outside to the hot, moist air of a D.C. night in July, much like a vaporizer in and of itself. I had no idea if she was choking, or had eaten something which made her terribly sick, or maybe she'd contracted some kind of respiratory infection—by this time, we had been in six or seven dog parks from St. Louis to Washington D.C.

We ended up sleeping in the car. After one failed attempt to get her back upstairs and settled, where Libby fell asleep only to wake up again barking like a seal, I gave up and brought her down to the car where she seemed to be more comfortable. It was a long night. If you ever take your dog on a long car trip, two things to remember: make sure they get the vaccine for kennel cough because you never know if they'll be exposed to it, and understand that the car is their absolute favorite place to be on the planet. It's their kennel on wheels, the only place which smells familiar to them when everything else is changing. Libby was comfortable and happy in the car. It smelled like home and seemed to calm her down. Lauren and I took turns, one sleeping, one standing watch for muggers.

We were very fortunate. A lovely veterinarian in DuPont Circle was able to see Libby by noon the next day, and on a Sunday to boot. Sure enough, it was kennel cough. One hundred and forty-eight dollars later, a prescription and a quick photo op on the front steps with the doc, we were on our way. We stopped at a sidewalk café, had Bloody Marys, loaded Libby up with cough medicine and went back to the dorm and crashed.

I hid out in Lauren's room for a few days, writing and letting Libby rest. When you're traveling with a dog on practically no money, it tends to exclude a lot of things from the itinerary. This wasn't a vacation tour. There would be no Smithsonian or National Gallery visits, no dinner at Ebbott's Grill or sipping Tullamore Dew at the Dubliner. My car was my island and increasingly I felt like a spectator, an outsider, looking in on the museum of normal. Funny how quickly one's perspective can change, from windows pacing to windows passing.

The first time this happened was on a Saturday night in Akron. I was jubilant after finding a very hard-to-locate dog park. This was part of the bargain; in exchange for Libby's company, she got to run free in some of the best dog parks in America. I found Cascade Valley Park tucked way back at the end of a long, winding residential road which took me past homes both palatial and modest. It was about an hour before sunset: warm, not unbearable and slightly breezy. The dog park was perched on top a hill overlooking subdivisions in the distance, with freshly-mown grass and shade trees and park benches for the parents to sit on and chat about their doggies on the playground. No lack of material there. It was lovely, really. It was also the first time I tried to record an interview with someone I'd met on the road. The first time out, I hit pay dirt with a bittersweet story of a man who'd lost his life partner to cancer the year before and how he'd given up the ghosts, literally, to move cross-country, back home to Ohio. He had inherited his partner's dog, had one of his own and came back home to Akron to tend to an ailing family member. (And here I'd been thinking I had it rough.) Mike's story was sad, yet amazing, because while our dogs lay panting in the dirt, worn out from running and playing all over hill and dale, here we were, complete strangers, sharing intimate stories about the people we had loved and lost. The sun was going down. I shook Mike's hand and got back in the car with Libby, feeling satisfied and humbled. I backtracked through the streets under a canopy of trees, the low-lying sun throwing long, twilight shadows. I drove past the country club where fancy-dressed folks carried white-wrapped boxes, the girls in clicky heels and low-cut dresses, boys in suits with skinny ties: a wedding, of course. It must have been a wedding on a lovely summer evening. At a four-way stop a couple crossed in front of me, walking their dog. A half-block down, two adolescent boys on skateboards, laughing, rolled past a jogger logging his miles before dark. Lights popped on here and there: table lamps, porch lights, street lights, the blue light from TVs spilling across kitchen counters and coffee tables. Through the sheer curtains, I could see eight o'clock, Saturday night in Akron, Ohio coming on. I couldn't help but wonder: were the lights turned on back home? Was Louie on the couch with Sean? What were my friends doing in St. Louis on this lovely summer night as Libby and I passed through an Akron neighborhood, inconsequential interlopers, transient, invisible?

On a hazy morning in D.C. I felt that way again, except it was the rest of the world in motion and Lib and I were sitting still. I had just dropped off Lauren on the Hill and was sitting on a park bench sipping coffee from a paper cup. Libby was watching squirrels. I was watching people.

Just weeks before I had been participating in the reality of which I was now a mere observer. I had been a card-carrying member of the Monday-through-Friday drones, always in a hurry, texting while they walk, talking while they text, texting in cabs, never even looking out the window, constantly on the phone and constantly looking serious. People who work in D.C. look so damn serious; must be the burden of all that public policy. I didn't envy them. But even while I derided them, my un-tethering was beginning to tell on me. I felt self-conscious, irrelevant, borderline bag woman, more and more on the fringe. I looked across the mall to a huge office building—the white marble kind, as so many are in D.C., where, on the second floor, there was window after window, with picture-perfect blue velvet drapes pulled back uniformly, with tassel-laden tiebacks. It looked very Louis the XIV. It was all so perfect, so symmetrical, so imposing.

I had been in fancy offices like that. I had taken a seat in plush lobbies with thick carpets, fresh flowers on the table, sipping designer water, my business card , drawn and ready. I had held a seat at the table in some of the most elite conference rooms in the country, giving advice to power brokers, politicians, pundits and stars … sometimes all wrapped up into one. I had been there, was taken seriously, was highly regarded. And I had found it laughable.

On this particular morning, though, I found it unnerving, in the way cold medicine makes your head feel disconnected from your body. It's weird being off the grid; it tends to make you feel shabby. You lose your position. You lose your access and access is power, cachet, juice. Life is easier when you've got juice.

Of course it didn't help that I was petrified that I would run out of money before I ran out of miles. Ten days into the trip but fifteen days into my fundraising campaign, I was less than halfway toward my goal. I was beginning to get some traction; total strangers were kicking in twenty, thirty, thirty-five dollars, but it was coming in slowly. Each time I'd hear the "ping" of an auto-email from the Kickstarter site informing me of another "backer," I'd get all emotional and have to wipe my eyes to keep the car on the road, praying and driving, driving and praying.

D.C. was stressful; a lot of memories there, good and bad. I'd had a toehold here once; I'd worked for C-SPAN for a while, had a lot of big-name PR clients in later years. On this day, though, here I was in the park, on a bench, with my dog. Now some of you may be saying, "Why in the hell didn't she just relax?" I was trying to. Honestly. Zen-filled moments did break through the angst, like the time when I met the Jehovah's Witnesses witnessing in a park. They were amazing, just adorable. Two old duffers, one black man, one white, one of them blind, one leading the way, came to the same pocket park on West Capitol Street every day, across the street from a bunch of restaurants where congressional staffers would frequently walk into telephone poles as they texted on their way to lunch. These two fine gents would sit on the bench and hand out copies of The Watchtower and cite Bible verses, trying to save the souls of high-minded wonks. I stopped to talk to these two, true believers when I was walking Libby around the park. We got into a deep conversation about life after death. They let me take their pictures and record a video. They were so sweet and so secure in the courage of their convictions, they inspired me.

But slowly the glow of fellowship from this brief human exchange and the general agreement about not needing to worry about the hereafter began to fade. I was brought back to the here and now and my insecure little psychodrama. I'm sorry; I realize this is becoming tedious. But just imagine when you don't have anyone to talk to. You're out on your own, completely alone, hundreds of miles from home. You've put up this big, brave front and you really don't have anyone credible saying, "it's gonna be okay," just a dog who looks at you sympathetically. So you just roll with it. You allow the dark feelings to bubble up long enough to say hello, then you shove them down to the bottom of the duffle bag of your psyche. But it was often a battle. I was wearing six-year-old shoes, eating granola bars and peanut butter sandwiches to save money; I hadn't even bought a flippin' bagel at the coffee shop that morning, knowing there was cereal back at the dorm. Lauren had been eating ramen noodles all damn summer, so I dared not complain. I had split my fortune with her, my brown-eyed girl. I gave her part of my tax refund to intern in D.C. and I took the bigger chunk to roam around the country. We'd scoff at the trust-fund brats she was rooming with at the dorms—a reverse kind of snobbery—holding ourselves in some kind of moral superiority for our financial inferiority, even while we *loved* their clothes. Lauren walked home from Capitol Hill to the GW campus every day after work to save the metro fare. The things we do. But we were in the nation's capital! She was kicking ass and taking names and we were together! We found a cheap Italian Thai place—yeah, that's right, Thai and Italian: what a combo. Libby scared the hell out of the tiny Thai woman who carried out our noodles in the 90-degree-plus heat. Nobody else was partaking of the patio dining but us. We had a cocktail. We ate our Pad Thai and the next day I had to head on down the road.

It ripped my guts out, though: different city, different kid, same emotion. I waved goodbye to my daughter who was standing out in front of the Longworth Office Building on Capitol Hill, watching her in the rear-view mirror as long as I could. Oh, man, I wanted to go back. I wanted to turn around and hug her one more time. I wanted to go back and crawl under the butter yellow blanket on the twin bed in her dorm room across the four-foot swath of cold beige linoleum and watch her sleeping just one more night. But that's not how I roll. I had to keep going, even if the traffic out of D.C. trapped me for two hours. The fucking gridlock on I-66 westbound made me want to never go back.

By mid-afternoon I'd be meandering along a picturesque mountain highway with a lone Ford F-150 riding my ass. This pretty well sums up my entire experience in Virginia. Forget the official state slogan: Virginia is for haters. Amazing that I could feel safer in the heart of Brooklyn, or a D.C. park at night with homeless people on every bench, than I felt out on the bucolic two-lane highway I took from D.C. to Waynesboro. They drive like maniacs on these roads because they know them like the backs of their fisted hands. They tailgate. Even though you're doing 65 MPH on S-turns, the first opportunity they get to pass you, they do. Even though you can see the car in the oncoming lane and your sphincter muscle is closed so tight you could hold back the Chesapeake Bay because you're afraid the truck will crash head on into the oncoming car and fly through the air and land on you and your dog, they pass you. They don't fucking care.

I pulled over a couple of times to get the hell out of the way, to explore a little bit, up some gravel roads. There was one in particular leading way up a hill where I parked next to a pasture, with yellow wildflowers growing close to the barbed wire fence and hay rolled up like cinnamon rolls dotting the freshly-mown field and the blue mountains in the distance. It smelled so wonderful, as if the sun was fabric softener infused in the dirt. The soft slope and hues of the landscape were beginning to cover me with a layer of calm. I felt happy. I was happy like I didn't have good sense. Out in the middle of nowhere in Rappahannock County, Virginia, close to the Shenandoah River, parked on a gravel road that was probably posted with "No Trespassing" signs, with bugs buzzing in the tall grass, over the heads of slithering snakes, with my faithful mutt who didn't question a single thing I did, I just sat in my car and admired the view. Mostly I breathed in all the summery goodness of that sweet spot on the globe and I felt peaceful. It was a cleansing breath. And I'll tell you what; there wasn't a single solitary gnarly old chicken bone in that whole damn pasture.

After a quick walk down the road, we hopped back in the car. I was really into taking my time by now, as these were the first real mountain roads and vistas I'd encountered so far. To that point it had mostly been big Midwest and East Coast cities. Just consider: St. Louis, Chicago, Philadelphia, New York, Washington, D.C. I had done a ton of hot, noisy freeway driving, and now, just two hours away from D.C., I was in the beautiful Smoky Mountains. I spotted a barn and a country store and pulled over to take a few pics in Hope Mills, Virginia. By the end of my little encounter there, I was hoping to get out alive. Okay, I'm exaggerating, a bit.

Libby and I pulled over at this quaint little Hope Mills Country Store. The Mid-Eastern owner was quite nice—the redneck woman in the pickup, not so much. I had stopped for gas and a bathroom break and the view from the fillin' station was magnificent. I hopped back out of the car to take a few photos and I'm standing there, minding my own business, my back to the single gas pump, when a pickup rumbled to a stop behind me. The driver cut the engine. I had pulled out of the way of the solitary pump. I looked over my shoulder briefly but went about my business when I heard this woman's voice, a Dixie Carter kind of drawl.

"Folks 'round here don't like people takin' pitchers of their barns."

I turned to see a leathery-skinned blonde woman leaning out the passenger window, smoking a cigarette. This made me nervous anyhow, being around gas pumps and all. Her male companion was filling up the truck. He looked at me hard.

"Say what?" I offered up in a friendly, non-confrontational way, as I pivoted ever so slightly, focusing my iPhone away from the barn, aiming now at the panoramic view to my right. When I turned around, she was still glaring at me.

I asked, "I'm sorry, is this your place?"

"Nope." That's all, just nope.

"I'm from Missouri, traveling across the country with my dog. This was just such a beautiful spot. I've been taking pictures of stuff I see along the road."

I was thinking if I said something nice it might win her over.

"Yeah, it's r-e-e-e-l nice here. And people don't like other people coming around takin' pitchers."

"Well, okay then. Thanks a lot."

The only stupid-ass thing I didn't add was, "Have a nice day!" Like WTF would I be telling her to have a nice day for? And why in the hell was I thanking her? For being a jerk? I got in the car, with their eyes burning a hole through my license plate, and I drove on down the highway with that narrowly-missed-being-hit-by-a-bus shudder. Only in this case, it was more like narrowly-missed-being-shot-in-the-ass.

Imagine my delight when, about ten miles farther south, what to my wandering eyes should appear but a shiny yellow vinyl banner with huge red letters: "REVIVAL." It was like an oversized yard sign for a politician. In many

Jean Ellen Whatley

ways, it's the same principle. Down the hill at the bottom of a gravel driveway leading to baseball diamonds, soccer fields and a concession stand was a huge white tent with two peaks, big enough to cover several hundred worshippers in case a mountain thunderstorm should crop up. Instead of a postage-stamp-sized asphalt lot with cars and people and dogs and taxis and the sound of the subway singing below, with its aromatic updrafts of packed dirt and engine oil, this revival was nestled in a wide-open field against a backdrop of Appalachian green and the heavenly aroma of French fries in the deep fryer at the concession stand. Libby and I (I could tell by the anxious look in her eyes) were glad to pull off the highway to shake off the jitters from the mountain mama who had not welcomed us to her country home. I needed a big dose of Jesus by now. I drove down the hill, pulled in between a Dodge Ram pickup and a Chevy S-10, got out and sat on the roof of the car with Libby sniffing around in the grass looking for corn dog crumbs. The music was moving. I soaked in all the abundant benevolence I could absorb, in stark contrast to the hair-raising malevolence from just an hour before. And yes, I got video, from a distance, not wanting to invade their spiritual space. The drummer, noticing me and my dog, gave a friendly wave with his drum sticks and never missed a beat. I wish now I'd gone in. I really do. But it was getting late and I still had a good sixty miles of mountain road between me and my bed for the night. Early on I had learned not to push myself too far past sundown; the road took on a threatening vibe and after I found a hotel, I'd be forced to walk Libby around in the dark, which was dangerous in itself.

Lauren had called ahead and booked a room for me in the luxurious Royal Inn in Waynesboro, Virginia. It lived up to its name. The first thing I noticed was the smell of curry wafting up through the cash drawer the Indian motel owner pushed toward me from behind the bulletproof glass. I dropped in my credit card. Seemed strange needing bulletproof glass out here in the mountains, but they've probably got a meth epidemic like just about every other rural community in America right now. My suspicions about this would be validated by the time I got to Pearl, Mississippi.

"How big is the dog?" he asked after I'd admitted I was traveling with one.

"Not that big, maybe fifty pounds," I replied, knowing there was some arbitrary cutoff at sixty pounds. This is ludicrous. So what happens if you're traveling with a Newfoundland hound? I played their little "guess the mutt's weight" game with every motel clerk from New York to California. What were they going to do, put her on a scale?

He was nice enough, charging me the customary ten dollar cleaning fee for the dog, and that was that. Except it would be the last time I'd fess up about the mutt for the remainder of the trip.

The second thing I noticed, as I walked Libby around the back of the motel, after we checked in, was the barbecue grill, the worn-down grass in a 360-degree circle with a dog tie left out in the middle, gnawed and muddy chew bones and little kids' cars and trucks abandoned right in the spot where they'd finished playing. These rooms were far away from the office and the front parking lot, rooms with economy-sized bottles of shampoo and conditioner sitting on the window sills, visible through the frosted bathroom glass. These were the rooms behind which there was a flat-tired motorcycle with a tattered tarp and car-length grease spots in the empty spaces, where grass sprouted through the cracks in the pavement, evidence of the beater cars that carried somebody here. God only knows if those beat up old cars carried them to the next place.

People live here.

I tugged on Libby's leash to keep her from licking the blackened, crusty barbecue grate leaning up against the dilapidated Flame Glo grill, so old the wooden knobs had been worn down to metal.

It was the perfect contrast. The front of the hotel, with its meticulously groomed Bermuda grass and straight-edged boxwood shrubs, had a large nursery right next door. The two business owners probably had some kind of trade-out. Who knows? Maybe the guy who owned the motel owned the garden center too. The landscaping in the front of the Royal Inn was quite nice: upscale, like so many fancy entrances to apartment complexes, hotels, country clubs and gated communities tended by Mexicans all over the country. Yet in the back, it was a hovel. The difference was startling, depressing, but mildly reassuring because I figured if I ran out of money, there would almost assuredly be another little town farther down the road with another motor court where I could get a good weekly rate, stash Libby in my room, and, I hoped, not have to chain her to the tie out in the back while I waited tables or worked at the drive-up.

Of which there was a plethora to choose from in downtown Waynesboro, Virginia. There were at least ten drive-thrus within walking distance of my motel room. I fully believe that this is the utter demise of our country and I promise you faithfully, because I have the pictures to prove it, there were at least ten fast-food joints inside a half-mile radius at the major intersection of

Jean Ellen Whatley

Main Street and Vendette.

After Libby finally found a suitable place to squat out behind the motel where the poor folk live, (bearing in mind this was early in the trip; by the time we got to Texas, she was far less discriminating) we got back into the car and drove to find some food. I would have walked, but, of course, in these friendly mountain towns, there are no sidewalks and people drive ninety-miles per hour in their pickups. I went to A&W. It seemed less gross than Burger King, Long John Sliver's, (yes, "Sliver's") McDonald's, Taco Bell, Arby's, Dairy Queen, Pizza Hut and even "eat fresh" Subway. I was sick of sandwiches. Plus, the A&W was the only place still open. I took my Kiddie Burger, Libby's Kiddie Burger (okay, all you PETA people, I gave her plain hamburgers from time to time), a small order of French fries, and went back to the motel and made myself a drink.

I needed one. The next day would be the day of truth. It was Kickstarter deadline day. I was down to $2,000— total—to my name. If I didn't make my funding goal, which was "Plan A," I'd either have to turn around and limp home, the humiliating "Plan B," and hope to hell I could find a new job right away, or go to "Plan C." I didn't really have a "Plan C," to tell you the absolute truth. It was kind of nebulous.

Up until then, the funding pledges came in fits and starts. I'd post a particularly oddball or gut-wrenching story and, sure enough, money would come in. Pledges would show up, ten, twenty bucks at a time. Thirty five guaranteed the funder a copy of the book, (this book) in exchange for their patronage. These are the rules of engagement with Kickstarter: there has to be commercial exchange, "You give me this, I'll give you that." My backers were people I had recently worked with, people I'd worked with more than thirty years ago, former husbands and boyfriends, former high-school friends, friends of my kids, friends of their friends, and people I'd met on the road already and who'd been reading my daily posts, plus, of course, my family. Still, I was short.

I posted an update on my blog from the Royal Inn, wadded up the hamburger wrappers, made a three-pointer in the waste basket, brushed my teeth and turned out the light. Libby and I lay in the dark and listened to our neighbors.

There was a road construction crew in the two rooms next to us. When I'd pulled up, the men, no doubt worn out from a long day on asphalt in record-breaking heat, which I'd tried to avoid by heading to the mountains to no avail, were doing what working men do. They were sitting out on the porch in their socks, their steel-toed boots pulled off and set inside the door, leaning back in their plastic chairs against the cool, red brick of the motel exterior. They were drinking beer, smoking cigarettes and talking as Tejano music spilled from the radio in the cab of their truck. They were fine. They'd smiled at Libby and I, watching somewhat curiously , but not so much as to be nosy, as I pulled up and engaged in the unloading ritual: dog, backpack, overnight bag, yoga quilt, dog food, water bowl, ice chest. Maybe they wondered, "What's this *juera* doing out here all alone?" Hell, I don't know. I said hello. They nodded and said hello; that was it. I must say that is one benefit of traveling with an 86-pound dog, whom you've just told the motel owner weighs only fifty; people don't fuck with you. By the time we got back from our fast-food run the doors were closed, the curtains drawn, the trucks backed into the parking spots so the tool boxes would be four feet closer to the windows, lest some permanent resident of the back of the house needed cash for next week's rent. They needn't have worried; Libby's nothing if not a damn fine guard dog. The music had been replaced by the low hum of sexy Spanish dialogue from the *telenovelas* they were watching on TV. It wasn't unpleasant; in fact, it was oddly comforting to me—a snapshot of the working class in our country: the Indian guy and his wife who ran the motel and the Mexican road crew next door, with a crazy white woman thrown in the mix, whose road trip might soon take a turn for the worse.

They were gone by the time I woke up. Road crews start early. I forced myself to go to the lobby for my Styrofoam java. That's what I was calling it by now—the brown liquid they passed off as coffee. Then I took Libby for her morning constitutional before I fired up my computer to see if I'd have enough money for the rest of the trip.

I was hyperventilating. I truly was. Before I went to sleep the night before, I'd told the story about the crazy lady in Hope Mills and then ended my nightly post with what you might call a direct appeal. I laid it out that I had just one more day to raise the money to finish my project and it was an all-or-nothing proposition. I was not in the habit of asking anybody for, well, anything. It was uncomfortable for me. I believed so much in what I was doing, though, that I felt like maybe, just maybe, the stories I would mete out from the road might make a difference in somebody's day. Maybe I could make them laugh. Maybe I'd piss 'em off, or make them cry. Or maybe, just maybe, they might not feel so alone. I felt in my heart that there was some value there. And, what the hell, they'd get a book out of the deal.

We came back into the air-conditioned, drape-drawn darkness of our Royal Inn suite. Libby hopped up on the bed and stretched out, figuring I'd be chained to the computer until the maids came and banged on the door. Such was our routine. The altar of my Mac hummed to life. I was strung out by now; like, seriously, that little Mac wheel could not spin fast enough. Blip, blip, blip. I clicked on the Internet connection. Drat! I had to enter the damn hotel code again! It was a full twenty-second delay, as I was welcomed by the lovely landing page of the Royal Inn and its well-appointed hotel lobby and bulletproof glass. I agreed to the terms of service and then, finally, clicked on the link to Kickstarter.

Holy Mother of God, I was within twenty-five dollars of my goal.

"Oh my God, Libby!" I jumped, pushing back the rickety, straight-backed chair with the sagging cushion so fast that it tipped over and startled her, making her leap off the bed and cower on the carpet, like she'd done something wrong. She's a Catholic dog, you know.

"No, no, come here, Lib!"

I sat on the bed, patting the heap of covers. She hesitantly hopped back up and I threw my arms around all eighty-six pounds of her.

"We made it, we made it, we made it!"

She was wagging her tail with her butt in the air, her nose buried in the blanket, as excited as if she'd just discovered a piece of steak.

"Oh my God, Libby, we're gonna be okay."

I was laughing and batting at her one minute and bawling, curled up in the fetal position the next. She stuck her nose under my hands which covered my face and I pulled her up close to me, my body cupped around hers, wiping my eyes on her silky ears.

Only twenty-five bucks to go and I still had until midnight to get it. I figured I could rustle that up. My friend Steve, who's been my partner in crime for some fourteen years now, had been holding out on me. He wanted to be the backer who took me over the top. And he did. In the short time it took me to do the reverse load-out; dog, dog food, water bowl, overnight bag, yoga quilt, ice chest, and then, one more quick check of the tote board on Kickstarter, I was literally, over the top. Over the top but out of time.

"You need to get out of the room so we can clean!"

My friendly Indian host was rapping on the door with his sari-wrapped wife standing behind him and the cart, looks of aggravation on both their faces. I had pleaded for leniency, "Just ten more minutes." I'd stuck my head out the door at 11:00 when she was next door cleaning the mud off the carpet after the road crew. I guess that had set her off. Christ Almighty, it was only 11:29! At the Motel 6s where these gals are working for minimum wage, I learned a little secret: they always go to lunch at 11:00. I'd throw a bunch of stuff in the car and wave, and then go back in and write for another hour. At the Royal Inn, with Mom and Pop running the joint, whole 'nother story.

To tell you the truth, I cannot remember ever feeling so completely grateful to a collective group of people in my life. Seventy-two people, many of whom I have never seen, and probably never will, had thrown in money to help me write this story. I felt, and still do, that I owed them something really precious in return: my absolute, rock-solid best, my unflinching honesty, and with any luck, a decent story. You are now the judge of that.

I got in the car, Libby looking expectantly, as she always did. "Where we going?" But I didn't back out. I wasn't quite sure where I was going. My next stop was supposed to be somewhere just over the North Carolina line. I might have even been able to make it to Winston-Salem that day, but a little side trip was nagging me.

I dialed the number in Culpeper, Virginia with some hesitation. It had been nineteen years since I'd see my former brother-in-law, Pat. *Why in the hell would he want to see me?* I was his former sister-in-law, the outlaw, the one who'd divorced his little brother. But it was his little brother, my first ex-husband, the high-school sweetheart, hippie-turned-sailor cum commercial-real-estate guy, who encouraged me to call his big bro Pat in the first place: Retired Navy Captain Pat, to be exact. I was only sixty miles or so from his horse farm. How often does that happen?

He immediately put me at ease. "Come on, we don't get much company! But I warn you, I may be mucking out stalls when you get here," which was exactly what he was doing when I arrived. His wife Beckie and four dogs greeted me at the end of a driveway which looked like it came straight out of a movie: a movie about the landed gentry in the rolling hills of the Shenandoah Valley, where horse farms thrive and former CIA agents write memoirs. Having never laid eyes on me, Beckie welcomed Libby and me straight away, apologizing for Pat being tied up in the barn. She fetched me a cold drink and Libby a fresh bowl of water. The dogs sniffed each other out. Then Beckie's four dogs retired to the garage, where they lay in the cool protection of shaded garage with a half-raised door with fans and giant bowls of water while Diva Libby was allowed in to the luxurious confines of the air-conditioned house. Recall, last year's heat wave was widespread and long lasting. It was 100-degrees plus, even up in the mountains.

"Do you like ribs? Patrick said he'd smoke some ribs later," said Beckie, hopping around the kitchen, putting an orange pound cake in the oven.

She is a very pretty woman: thick long blonde hair pulled into a neatly coiled-up bun on the back of her head, with intelligent, intense blue eyes and not a scrap of makeup because she spends her days into the evenings tending to thoroughbreds. Her complexion reminded me of the Ivory soap commercials way back when. She has the distinct accent of a Northern Virginian, which, if you've ever spent any time in the Commonwealth, is a unique blend of southern drawl and English aristocracy. Just ask someone who comes from Roanoke to say "water" ("wah-tuh") and you'll hear what I mean.

It would be a good half-hour before Pat made his way up to the house from the barn, plenty of time to hear the endearing story about how Patrick (as she refers to him) and Beckie met. Pat, a fairly recent widower and a sorely out-of-practice suitor, was wearing a sweat-stained cowboy hat, driving a banged-up truck, pulled into her driveway one day in Suffolk County (Suffolk, that's another good word to ask Virginians to say) looking for his misbehaving, one-eyed dog, Rooster Cogburn. Beckie was in the finishing stages of building a home there in Suffolk County, in the Tidewater area, on some property adjacent to her brother and sister-in-law's. She was in need of being close to family at that time. Rooster, the dog, was in need of leftovers discarded by Beckie's construction crew. It was a fast-food run, right up the road, at which Rooster had become quite adept. Pat would become more adept at the courting, as it turned out, over time.

And raising horses. After a thirty-seven year naval career, his last duty station the Pentagon, Pat did something that was a complete departure from anything he had ever done in his life. He bought a horse—a pregnant horse. In fact, it was Pat's urgent messages left on Beckie's voicemail, after she had moved in to her new house, with him imploring "When are you coming back?" that she considered a bit inappropriate since they had shared only a few casual exchanges following their introduction over the stray dog. Beckie had been out of town for Christmas and came home to Pat's multiple messages on her machine. "You've got to come over as soon as you get home!" He sounded like a kid hiding a puppy behind his back.

Instead, it was a foal. While Beckie was visiting her daughters in Virginia Beach, Pat's first mare bore her first foal. Like a proud papa, he could not wait to show the baby to his special lady friend up the lane. Now, you tell me, girlfriends, what in the world could be more irresistible to a woman than a blue-eyed Irish sailor in a chilly barn, bustin' his buttons over his new baby horse, waiting impatiently to share his happy news with the pretty filly he was hoping to corral?

The magic worked. Ten years, two different farms, and more than a dozen horses later, Pat and Beckie would be the first to admit that raising race horses is a hell of a job for retired folks. Sitting at the dinner table that night, eating well-cooked ribs, (Pat had received a call from an old Navy buddy who was looking to buy his first horse and forgot about the grill!) but a delicious dessert, I was captivated by their passion for the life they've created together. They told me stories about midnight watches in the birthing stall, death-defying emergency trips to horse hospitals and how they'd have to lift the laboring mare, using a winch and a giant sling, to get her into a horse ambulance to save her life. They told me about the heartbreak of stillborn foals and the thrill of seeing one of their babies cross the finish line first. It was contagious, their love and devotion to their horses.

I'd never been a big fan of horse racing, truth be told. I always feel sorry for the horses. I get nervous; my stomach balls up. I'm always afraid the horse will falter or the jockey will get hurt. But I'd been to the races a lot as a kid, at the State Fair and Santa Fe Downs. As a journalist, I had done many a story on the horse-racing industry in New Mexico, but I'd never experienced anything like this. It changed my view.

On the night I stayed over, I rode out with Pat and his grandson Andrew to feed the horses at sunset. As he was looking out over the picturesque green hills, I asked Pat if he ever missed the sea. It took him a minute to answer. I cannot describe what his mind's eye sees, but he explained to me, quite vividly, what it's like to push out, to leave the base behind: the wives and kids waving from the dock, the birds, the view of the gunmetal gray of other ships growing more and more faint as the land disappears and one's eyes are filled with nothing but ocean.

"Yeah, I miss it. There's this saying: 'Once a man has been to sea, he is not fit for land'," he chuckled in his rich, resonating voice. "But I'll tell you, the first time you see a foal being born … now that's something."

Here is a man who begged his parents to let him join the Navy when he was only seventeen, a desert rat from the *pachuco* North Valley of Albuquerque, who defied the odds as a "mustang," (meaning he crossed over from being an enlisted man to being an officer), a man who has fought in every conflict since Vietnam, who acquired the rank of Captain, responsible for entire cities on the sea with crews numbering in the thousands. Here's a guy who, after a storied military career, completely reinvented himself and loves what he does. I think this is pretty damn awesome. Now, I know, because they told me, that there are some days when Pat and Beckie say, "We must be crazy" because they work from sunup to sundown running this forty-acre farm on their own. They could be truly retired. But horses are their healers.

When Pat met Beckie, her hair was only about an inch long. Her head had been shaved because of an operation to control her tremors. She takes my hand, places it on the top of her head saying, "Do you feel that? There's a piece of metal there." She was recovering from the surgery when cowboy Pat came amblin' up the driveway to fetch his runaway dog and to check out the new girl in town. Pat was recovering too. His wife Jan had died suddenly just a few years earlier, complications from what was supposed to be minor foot surgery. Pat and Jan had married young, had three boys and a good, solid marriage. Jan followed Pat all over the country. They were quite the pair: legendary, actually, among the clan and the scores of military couples they had befriended in crappy base housing from California to Virginia. Pat's sons had urged their father to do something different after their mother died, to quit working so hard, move out of the house, leave the ghosts, start something new. The eldest son asked him, "What would you do if you could do anything you wanted?"

Pat replied, "I've always wanted to have a racehorse."

Pat and Beckie have twelve now. They are all adored. But there was one colt that I met last summer that holds a special place in their hearts. This colt jumped the fence during a spring thunderstorm to get closer to his mama and, since then, he'd been allowed to stay with the mares—a privilege the other male horses were not granted. That's probably changed by now, but last summer Steve-o's owners indulged him in some adolescent reassurance. Steve-o is a source of delight and comic relief, "like a clumsy teenager" Beckie said, kissing him on the nose. They named him after Pat's son Steve, who died from leukemia about four years ago. Steve was the middle son, the impetuous one, the goofy one, a bit of a slacker while he was growing up, full of mischief and off-handedness, but cute; oh my God that kid was cute, with freckles splashed across his cheeks, devilish green eyes and eyelashes like a movie star's—a lot like his mother. Steve-o, as of course he had also been called, fought that damn leukemia for years. His older brother Greg took care of him until he died. I'm told they played bagpipes at Steve's wake.

People who've experienced loss like this will tell you it can be as vast as the sea. It swells and rushes in, covering you up, defenseless in its tide. Loss was my constant companion on this ride, every mile, every day: my brothers, my mother, and the life I thought I'd have. There ain't no throwing that loss out the window; you focus on the road and keep moving.

Pat and Beckie tend to their horses. Beckie says it is a powerful force, this bond between humans and animals. She still faces challenges from the tremors; her first surgery didn't quite take. Doctors wanted to try again but she and Pat didn't like the odds. She didn't opt for a second operation and she's weaned herself from the nineteen-pill-a-day regime they prescribed to stop the trembling. She believes her purposeful work of loving and tending to these magnificent animals and the abundant blessings she derives from being their caretaker is what keeps her steady.

"It heals me."

To which I say, "Amen."

Pat says it takes three years from the time a foal is born until you know if you've got a horse that will run. Three years of love and attention, care and feeding, vet bills and horse stalls to muck, before you know whether that horse will take off at the starting gate.

I have an abiding affection for folks who are willing to take their chances. Kindred spirits, one might say. I did it when I backed out my driveway, against the odds, betting on the come. On this day, on a stifling-hot afternoon which belied the suggestive emerald cool forgiveness of the nearby hills, as the ice in our cocktails on the patio melted faster than we could sip our drinks, my ship came in: the bounty of renewed affection from a sailor whom I'd loved like a brother, the promising friendship of a beautiful, intuitive woman, and a wad of cash from people who were willing to take their chances with me.

6

Where the Kudzu Wraps Around
You in a Loving Embrace

"Can you come tonight?"

It had been years since I'd spoken to my neighbor Betsy. Her Carolina accent was as sweet as Moravian sugar cake. She picked up on the second ring. Thank God she still had a landline; it's much harder to track down long-lost friends when they've given up the house phone. I mean, you'd hate to just show up on the doorstep. It would have been fine with Betsy, though.

"Oh my God! I can*not* wait to see you!"

Do you have any idea how wonderful this makes you feel? After a decade? Especially when you're on the road alone, to know somebody's actually *waiting for you* with a meal on a plate not out of a box, with a coffeepot that brews real coffee, in a house that smells like a real house, with the dishwasher humming everybody to sleep each night instead of some stale, cheap motel room where the last sound you hear is the cold metal click of the deadbolt. I was excited. One day after I was relieved to learn that I'd have enough money to make it all the way to California and home again, I was now free to focus on retracing my life. North Carolina would be like salve on a wounded soul.

There is no logical reason why North Carolina feels as comforting to me as a pair of flannel pajamas which have been hanging on the back of the bathroom door with the heater vent blowing on them, which you eagerly step into to cover your chapped ass after being in an ice storm. That's how wonderful North Carolina feels to me. It is somewhat inexplicable, what with me being a Westerner and all. I've always theorized that I must be a descendant of the Lost Colony. Or maybe it's the light. Maybe it's the pine trees lining the highways that crisscross the state like so many tunnels through a kudzu-draped maze. Maybe it's the stark contrast of the rounded, blue-grey contours of the Blue Ridge and the way the fog nestles in low, resembling a grade-school art project crafted out of construction paper and cotton balls, gentle and forgiving compared to the shouting, jagged, formidable mountains of the West. Maybe it's the way spring comes gradual and sweet, misting the azaleas and rhododendrons like pastel bumper pads hugging brick Colonials; where dogwoods, white and pink, pose erect, lithesome ballerinas under the canopy of towering hardwoods. Hell, maybe it's the pig pickin' slathered with slaw piled on a bun. All I know is that this California/Texas/New Mexico girl has a tar heel tattooed on her heart.

And now, I was headed to Winston. That's what the natives call it. Not Winston-Salem; that's a dead giveaway that you're an out-of-towner. Nope, it's just Winston: the town tobacco built. I remember the first night we slept in our new house in Winston back in 1991, with moving boxes stacked like cardboard fortresses in every room, the mystery of the desperately-needed frying pan buried deep inside over-wrapped kitchen goods. You'd think the movers were being paid per sheet of paper. The top story on the ten o'clock news that night showed a crowd of angry demonstrators jostling signs and chanting "Don't tread on me" in front of Baptist Hospital. They were protesting the hospital's new policy of banning smoking in patient rooms. Visitors and patients would now have to use the smoking lounge. The very nerve! R.J. Reynolds Tobacco had, for decades, been providing a steady stream of customers to the hospital pulmonary and cancer wards. Indeed, my eldest son graduated from R. J. Reynolds High School, which was also the benevolent corporate father to any number of buildings, parks, museums, and gold-plated downtown building facades. You name it, cigarettes funded it. Most decent folk had a tough time biting the tar-stained fingers that fed them. It was simply woven through the tobacco-sack fabric of that community; they held their nose and took the cash. I grew to love it. We'd had some good times here, our Winston days, back in the early '90s, back when the kids were still little, back when we were all still so innocent.

In these situations, where it had been many years since I'd seen someone, it always made me a little anxious to call them up again. It's not as if I couldn't tell them what had gone down. It would be dishonest. I couldn't sit at the kitchen table, going down the roster, reporting on Nathan, Patrick, Lauren, Sean and simply skip over Rick. I mean, he had been their neighbor too.

When we first moved into our house on Cavalier Drive, life was good.

Rick had landed a great job at a TV station. He was glad to be back in the biz. He was the boss, the News Director, the person who ran the newsroom. He had the dubious pleasure of hiring and firing people. Truthfully, it's a thankless job. The News Director is the person everybody loves to hate. If the talent sucks, if the ratings are bad, if a photographer crashes a jeep, it's all the News Director's fault. But they wield a lot of power. Rick was into power. He needed to be the big dog again. He'd been at the back of the pack for a couple of years.

Earlier, back in Albuquerque, the medical school gig didn't last one semester, especially after Matt had blown Rick's cover. He dropped out. He was still restless though, but said he was burnt out on the news business. When the younger guy, the airhead with a full head of hair, got the top slot that Rick had been groomed for, that was it; he was done. He jumped at the opportunity for a communications job on Capitol Hill. We needed a fresh start. We both thought it would be a great adventure. I saw it as a chance to get out from under my in-laws, who were cloying, Republicans on top of it! Rick and I thought moving away would make us closer as a couple. Mostly, it just made us tired. Trying to live and work in D.C. with four young kids, two still in daycare, is expensive and hard. One Halloween I got stuck in traffic on I-95 North frantically trying to get to Springfield because the babysitter was tapping her foot and my kids were distraught. It had already been dark for half an hour, trick-or-treaters were already showing up in batches, and my children were still stuck at the sitter's, didn't even have their costumes on. These are the moments of failure that haunt mothers for years.

Homicidal commutes and high cost of living notwithstanding, the novelty, the bragging rights ("My husband works on the Hill, I work for C-SPAN") was unlike anything we'd ever done. Despite everything which came later, I still look back with fondness on the layover we did in D.C. before we moved to N.C., only four hours south.

It did feel a little bit like being in the military, though, moving twice inside of one year. We had barely found a doctor, a haircutter and a passable Mexican restaurant in the D.C. suburbs when Rick came home one day and said he had an opportunity to get back into the news business, this time as management. Enter the Mayflower truck. Good thing, too, because he hated the D. C. rat race already.

My Winston neighbors knew nothing of what happened once we left Carolina. They had heard that Rick and I had divorced after we landed in St. Louis, but that was it. I had sent the customary Christmas letters and told everybody that the kids and I were getting along fine after the divorce. Actually, we were. There was so much less tension after he moved out. It was as if some heavy, brooding mass of molecular malcontent had been ripped up like dirty carpet.

I decided to stay put in St. Louis after the divorce, in order for the kids to maintain a relationship with their father (oh, the irony ...). I found a small house in an inner-ring suburb called Webster Groves. It was the first house I'd ever bought by myself. I was, and still am, very proud of it. The kids got into great schools, Sean in seventh grade, Lauren in ninth, Patrick a senior, waiting to hear if he'd been accepted to film school. We had all made new friends. We had our village. I had no idea then how the friendships we were creating would come to sustain us later.

Things were perking along just fine until the day Rick was arrested. It happened in early December. I didn't send Christmas cards *that* year. Or the next. Or the next. Before I knew it, I'd lost touch with my old Winston friends. Even though both the older boys went to college there, any time I would visit I'd slip in and out of town, not looking anybody up. I just didn't feel like talking about it. It got to the point where we skipped Winston on our trips to the Carolina coast. For many years after we first moved to Missouri, we made the long road trip to North Carolina every summer, spending a week in the same beach town we'd grown to love when we'd lived close by. Year after year, we'd trek the twelve hours from St. Louis to Winston, spend the night with our friends, and then drive the remaining four hours to Wrightsville Beach. It felt like home to us. It became a tradition for our new family, our closer family, our stronger family. Wrightsville Beach, just east of Wilmington, is where the Cape Fear River flows into the Atlantic. There's a lot of history there, from Blackbeard's pirates to Confederate blockade-runners. The beaches are wide, the sand is warm, the water is swimmable and the hush puppies are mighty fine. The comfort has always been worth the distance traveled.

I think people go a long way seeking comfort. Sometimes a person just needs to go back to places to make sure they still exist. When everything else is changing, there is something profoundly satisfying about having at least one thing remain constant, or at least the appearance of it being so. Your first whiff of the ocean from the bridge over the waterway becomes a healing vapor. Your first glimpse of all things familiar rushes to your heart; the marina, the seafood market, the bike rental store, the pink stucco souvenir shop, the hotdog stand, and the lights on the pier at night. The sight of white roofs against the backdrop of endless grey sea reassures you that there is order in this world. When everything else feels upended, disrupted, torn up and painful, laying your eyes on familiar sights is optical tonic.

Hearing familiar voices is a lot like that too, for a woman alone on the road. I called when I was about thirty minutes away. This time, Betsy's husband answered the phone.

"John! What are you up to?" I asked excitedly.

"Waitin' on you," he answered.

After ten years, *"Waitin' on you"* with steaks on the grill, a bottle of wine and pound cake with maple glaze for dessert. I felt like visiting royalty, sitting around the kitchen table: not family, just a neighbor, who'd been largely MIA for ten years, whose youngest son had been best buds with their youngest son, whose dog was catching scraps from the table, who soon would be obliged to 'fess up about what the hell had made me go missing for so long. As much as I dreaded it, I felt safe telling them the truth. They deserved to know what happened. I spent fourteen nights with fourteen different families over the course of this odyssey and I did not go through this drill with all of them. No need to. But these folks had been my neighbors. There's an intimacy with neighbors that you don't have even with your best friends. You see neighbors fetching the paper in their boxers in the front yard, their kids show up at your house with sticky fingers and dirty faces which you automatically wash. You see husbands and wives kissing each other goodbye in the driveway, you borrow eggs and oil and sugar. You spot the old man sneaking a cig on the back porch, teenagers crawling in at the crack of dawn, fights you're not supposed to hear over TVs turned up too loud, and through the crack in the living room drapes, you notice the old man asleep in his chair, all the lights still on, with nobody telling him to come to bed. You hear beer bottles clanking in the recycle bin on Saturday morning, pots banging in the kitchen come supper time, the scent of their laundry, wafting across your yard from their dryer vent. There's an intimacy in being neighbors. Betsy and John had been good ones.

God love them. Here we sat in their kitchen, with its white lacquered cupboards, everything in Betsy's house neat as a pin, and they're looking at this crazy woman, whom they had not seen in nearly ten years, who's quit her job and is driving all over the country with a damn dog, who had called with just two days' notice, to say she'd be in town. And they, without hesitation, had said, "Come on." By the time we got to the pound cake and coffee, I had already told them about losing my brother Garrett, my mother, and my brother Don. Now we were moving on to the night Rick was arrested.

"So, I jumped out of the booth and I took the call from the parking lot. I didn't want to answer it in front of the kids. And then I had to keep it together until we got home. Nate was here in Winston." After I told my neighbors what had happened, they were disappointed that I hadn't asked them to look in on Nate, whose campus apartment wasn't ten minutes from their house. "I had to tell him over the phone. It was horrible. I couldn't fly down here—I had just gotten home the day before from Garrett's funeral! And I couldn't leave the younger kids. It would be all over the news any minute, you know, so I had to level with them."

"Oh, my Lord." This is Betsy's favorite expression.

Telling the kids was the hardest thing I have ever done. Rick had steadfastly refused to talk to them about being gay. Eight years after the phone call from his former good buddy Matt, eight years after begging me not to leave him, with many a denial and me throwing up my die-hard doubts to a shrink in the meantime, after eight years Rick finally admitted that he was "still" gay. Funny how finding pages and pages of long-distance numbers on a phone bill, back in the day when it cost extra, will arouse a suspicious wife's curiosity. One night in the newsroom, on a slow news night, I called up a few, and sure enough, it was all young men on the other end of the line. These were not fishing buddies. Did Rick think I wouldn't notice? Was this his cry for help or an invitation for a foot up his ass ?

After I got over wanting to kill him, we worked out a peaceful exit. I had encouraged him to be honest with the kids. They were older by now, they would understand. Hell, *Will and Grace* was a big show by 1998; gay was in prime time. This honest explanation was a lot more plausible than the lame excuses we had cobbled together: "We've grown apart" and "We've tried to work it out," followed by the hollow, yet obligatory tag-line that divorce manuals advise parents to recite: "It's not your fault." But as things would reveal themselves a few years later, it wasn't that he was gay. How I wish that's all it had been. That would have been easy. No, this was something entirely different.

How in the world to explain it to my kids? They sat big-eyed, full of dread, like sacrificial lambs on the couch in our paneled den, waiting for me to come out of the bathroom where I was swallowing hard and praying for fortification. How, exactly, does a mother explain to a thirteen-year-old boy that his dad has just been arrested for having sex with a thirteen-year-old?

To this day, I shudder to think about how Sean must have felt. He was only in the seventh grade. With Patrick and Lauren in high school, they would have a harder time socially, since their friends would be more aware. To her everlasting credit, Patrick's girlfriend, Polly, tried to protect her boy. The day after the story broke, Polly went to school early and raced through the library, snatching up the newspapers with Rick's mugshot on the front page, just below the fold. She gathered them up and threw them away, trying to spare Patrick the humiliation. This was one among many, many kindnesses extended in those first few days.

On that first night, when it was just me and them, I started out with, "Your dad is in a lot of trouble." My innocents. They asked a lot of questions, "Will he be okay?" "What are they gonna do to him?" "When will he get out?" Patrick immediately wanted to go to the jail, but of course, they would not have let in a seventeen-year-old. Only lawyers were allowed to see someone fresh from booking. My attorney friend went to the jail right away, but some other lawyer had already beat him there, dispatched by a friend of Rick's in the newsroom. The folks at the TV station were hoping it was some kind of trumped-up charge. Little did they know. My goal was to make sure *somebody* was keeping an eye on him, because all the reporters were wrapping up their stories with this: "Jail officials say the accused is on a 24-hour suicide watch."

Thank God I'd convinced the kids to go to bed before the news came on. Thank God. It was an out-of-body experience seeing Rick's mugshot on the TV screen. It was simply impossible to grasp, as I sat on the footstool in the family room, inches away from the screen, the volume turned down low so the kids wouldn't hear, trying to spare them, for just one more day, from seeing their dad on the news as an accused pedophile.

Who was this person? I studied his hollow eyes, searching for anything familiar, for some trace of the man who'd been my lover, my husband, my colleague and confidant. Here in this sad and shameful photo of the man with the downcast eyes was the face I'd memorized with my lips, the smooth spot on his cheek bone just under his eyes, the cleft in his chin, the morning stubble. This was the face of the man I had loved, the same man who, when we first fell in love, held me in the quiet of a June night, a tear tracing from the corner of his eye. "I wish we'd met sooner," he said. "Fifty years is not enough time to spend with you."

Who was this man? The man in the mugshot had been an adoring husband who danced with me at the symphony ball the night before our daughter was born, my pregnant belly pressed against the cummerbund of his tuxedo and him whispering, "You are the most beautiful woman on the dance floor." The man in the mugshot was once a new father who eagerly, instinctively cradled each of his newborns: no hesitation, pure joy. This was the same man who rushed with fear and dread in his eyes to the newborn ICU with a team of neonatologists, our newborn in arms, when our youngest child struggled to breathe. You should have seen the commotion when we finally brought Sean home from the hospital!

My God, how many pictures do I have of that day? And Christmases and baptisms and birthdays, soccer games and Little League tournaments, dance recitals and thousands of ordinary days in between? Ordinary days I now see as precious. Ordinary days, like the hazy twilights of the summer in D.C., oppressively hot, when, after work, after he'd changed out of his Capitol Hill wardrobe, when the heat was finally letting up, we'd take the kids outside for their favorite game, a game he'd made up one night after I dumped a load of mulch on the roses. "Climb in you guys," he'd say and would commence carting the kids around and around and around the yard in the wheelbarrow. They were just babies then, delirious with laughter at every deliberate bump and turn he'd make. They would climb out of the rusty, yellow wheelbarrow, dizzy and rubber-legged, begging to go again on Daddy's version of *Mr. Toad's Wild Ride.*

Who was this man? I studied his pitiful image on the screen. Was he thinking about our children when he looked away from the camera at the instant the shutter closed? The house phone rang and I jumped a foot.

"Jean?"

That voice. The golden voice that had launched his broadcast career, the voice on the pillow next to me for so many years, his voice was now raw, anguished, fearful.

"Jean, are you there?"

"I'm here."

"I'm so sorry." He broke down on the other end of the line. "I never meant to hurt you or the kids. I am so very sorry—"

It was impossible to formulate words, as if Novocaine had been painted on my brain. Then I seem to recall rallying, with some measure of control. "Did you ever touch any of our kids?" I asked flatly.

"No, no, never, I swear to God. Please believe me, I would never do that, Jean. Please believe me. You can ask them."

I didn't say anything. He went on. "I want you to know, and I'm not saying this to defend anything, I know I've fucked up. But I swear to God, Jean, he told me he was eighteen. He's a big kid, like, six-three. He is very mature for his age. I had no idea he was thirteen."

As if that teenage boy being eighteen, the same age as our middle son, would have somehow made it morally defensible for a fifty-one-year-old man to be meeting him in a public restroom at a high-school football field.

"And I need to let you know," his voice now hushed and urgent. "There's gonna be more. When they see what's on my computer, I'm a dead man."

I didn't need him to paint me a picture. I could only imagine what those poor cops would have to catalogue. It made my skin crawl.

"What do you want?"

"I need you to tell my parents," he managed to get out in between sobs. "I only get one phone call. I know it's asking a lot, but it would be so much better coming from you instead of the cops. This is going to kill them."

Calling his elderly, conservative, head-in-the-sand parents in Utah to let them know that their only son was in the clink was, to put it mildly, the last thing I wanted to do. I had no earthly idea how I was going to break it to my own mother. It wasn't particularly good timing for her to cope with her daughter and grandkids getting dropped in the grease, considering she was still in shock from losing her son just days before, as in *days*. Garrett's funeral was Saturday and this was only Tuesday.

"I don't really want to call them, Rick."

He told me I was the only person who could do it. He would not be able to make another call until the next day. This man, my former husband, who at one time had a standing racquetball date with the chief of police, who'd had the Governor of New Mexico show up for his going-away party, who once had dozens of friends, had nobody else to turn to now.

"Jean? I'm out of time. I have to hang up. Tell the kids I'm sorry. Tell them I love them, okay?" Then he paused again, his voice flat, his words barely audible. "I'm going to make it easy on everybody. I think I've figured out a way to kill myself. Everybody's better off. At least you'll have the insurance money."

He would have been dead wrong. Insurance doesn't pay out when someone hangs himself in prison—it's not as if I tried to call the insurance company that night, tapping my fingers together like a maniacal Fred Burns from *The Simpsons*. Given that it was 10:45 at night and I'd been buffeted by this shit storm for a full eight hours, which felt like a week already, his life insurance policy was the last thing on my mind. I was too shell-shocked. I was too worried about what I'd wake up to read in the paper the next morning and have to explain to my children. Worse yet, to have to tell them their father was dead.

I swear to God though, at that moment I would have handed him the rope. It's not that I didn't have compassion; of course I did. We humans are not robots. Our emotional wiring is far more complex than what can be diagrammed in a four-color schematic. There are far too many shades that don't fit into a single hue. I cried with him over the phone, "I am so sorry this has happened, Rick." Even as I allowed myself a momentary consideration of his subterranean existence, in which normal people had been like subway cars, coming and going in the dark corridor where he resided, where the time in between trains leaves the person who remains there too much time to inhale the dankness, too much time to observe the rats, even as I began to contemplate the addiction to which he'd succumbed, with even the slim chance of him killing himself, or any other egregious deed which might ooze from his rancid being, even with all that darkness clouding my mind, I seized upon one red-hot coal of truth which would burn in me from that moment forward. Now I knew the magnitude of the collateral damage he could exact. So I made a decision, a decision that would be my strength and the light on the hill leading my family out of this disaster. I knew I had only so much energy and so much time. From that moment forward every waking second I possessed would be spent helping my kids survive. It was simple. Cell by cell, the anesthesia of disbelief began to wear off, converting to full-on maternal rage that coursed through my veins like fucking jet fuel.

"How dare you? You spineless sack of miserable shit! How dare you?" It was now an hour after his jail cell confession and I was sitting in front of my computer, the online story already filed. "How dare you risk my children's lives and happiness like this? How dare you throw this stain on them?" I hissed at the screen. "I will beat you, mother fucker. I will beat you. You will not bring them down. You will not ruin their lives." This would be the seminal moment in the battle to protect my kids, from which there would be no turning back.

Tactical operations kicked in at dawn when the media reported that he was indeed still alive and also facing federal charges for possession of child pornography. Didn't take those cops long to whiz through his computer. I called the parents of my children's friends to learn they'd already quizzed their kids about whether or not Rick had touched them. Thank God he had not. I called my children's teachers, their counselors, the family shrink. Poor Nathan, in a subsequent call after I'd broken the news to him, I added, "We've got a family therapy session the night after you get home."

"There's no place like home for the holidays," he'd responded with a rueful smirk.

I bribed them with Chinese at our favorite place in exchange for humoring me for just one session. In one of the most telling expressions of love I've ever received from my children, sitting there in the therapist's office that night, the room crowded with four kids on the couch, me and the shrink in armchairs on either end, in the silence which hung in the air after the counselor asked what was on their minds, I believe it was Nathan who opened things up: "To be perfectly honest, I'm more worried about my mom right now than anybody else." Each one them, like birds on a wire, nodded in unison. They were worried about the toll this would take on me. I was worried about the burden it would place on them.

But there was no preventing it. For all the ranting and raving I would do in the privacy of my car, crying and screaming and pointing an accusing finger at the God whom I was now cross-wise with, there wasn't a thing in the world I could do to spare them this pain. It would become like a drop of ink on clean, white linen. You cannot undrop it. One fiber at a time, strand by strand, the pristine, intricate, absorbent grid soaks up the ink, then stops once it's drunk the drop. There is no rubbing. There is no bleaching, nor cutting it out, because doing so would destroy the entire cloth. And so it was with my children. I couldn't stop it. The stain was there, whether I liked it or not. After time, and ever the negotiator, I swapped contempt for contriteness.

"Please, God, please let them be okay. Please, God, please don't mark them for life. Please, God, please help me."

For seven years this was my prayer. For seven years, this was the cadence, the inner drumbeat to which I marched. "Please, God, please" over and over and over again. Through countless nights waiting for a teenager's car to turn into the driveway, seven years of nail-biting financial stress, college loans which were like giving birth, seven years of crappy cars and midnight tows, trips to the emergency room, the police station, and houses where your children were *supposed* to be in for the night, for seven years I chanted my chant, "Please, God, please," to keep us moving forward. On some days, it was beyond the pale.

When the enormity of circumstances piled up on me, typically while

I'd be folding piles of laundry in the basement, I would call my mother in Albuquerque to ruin her day. Not that I did it on purpose. Hell hath no fury than a mother whose daughter has been wronged. She'd jumped on the righteously angry bandwagon with me from day one when I'd called her to let her know what happened. It grieved her to see the extra strain on me and she worried for her grandkids. But my mother was nothing if not resilient and she took great pride, and all the credit, for raising me to be the same. She was also my "Get Out of Jail Free" card. I knew I could call her and unload. We both knew she couldn't fix it. She couldn't mend the gaps with a solution or a blank check or a cure when I'd pause on the other end of the line and she knew my silence meant tears. I would take a deep breath and try to keep talking without completely breaking down, but the burden of what I was dealing with at that given moment traveled instantly across four states, like a pus-filled lump in the phone line. She couldn't pop the blister and she couldn't fill the void; her heart was simply broken for me, as mine was broken for my kids. She would say, "Go ahead, honey," and I would keep talking. I could say things to her that I could not say to anyone else, not anyone. When I was through, emotionally spent, calmed down, the pressure valve relieved enough to get a hold of myself to make it through the next hour, or day, or week, she would remind me, "You can't get tired now, baby."

One foot in front of the other. It's how I roll. Like the day I called out my demons. The morning after that night of Rick's arrest, I went for a run. After I'd broken the news to my mom, after I had phoned Rick's mother (his father had the beginning of Alzheimer's at this point, so when he picked up, I asked for her because Lord knows I did not want to repeat it) and she just kept saying, "I just don't believe this," to which I wanted to reply, "Get a grip, sister" after I'd called the counselors, the parents, the shrink, and, oh yeah, my client, the CEO of a huge telecommunications company, for whom I was her crisis communications consultant (hilarious, right?), after I'd put all that shit in motion, I went for a run. These days, I would simply have a drink.

I watched the noon news, and with each newscast there were new, titillating follow-up reports, such as the obligatory interview with the next-door neighbor: "He was the shy type, kept to himself." Then the enterprising interview with the manager of the Little League association for which Rick had been an umpire, who spouted, "That man will never set foot on this ball field again!" Which made me think, *well, no shit, dude. He'd have a hell of a hard time umpiring adolescent boys once he graduates from the sex offender program.*

Jean Ellen Whatley

The banality of it was making me crazy. After years of standing in front of burning houses, fatal car wrecks, the police station, or the court house doing live reports on the worst days of other people's lives, I knew in one instant how it felt to be singed. I snapped off the TV and threw down the remote. I had to get out of the house. I laced up my running shoes in the pre-op ritual in preparation for the healing. It was December 4th but unseasonably warm as I stepped outside into the noonday sun. It reminded me of hundreds of clear winter days in the past: the early days back in Albuquerque, in Washington, in Winston—days I would duck outside for a quick jog, to chase away whatever needling fear or suspicion might have been working me over that day.

For years I had tried so hard to believe him. Long before the night when the stranger named Matt called and Rick begged me not to leave him, I had reason to be uneasy. Early on—married just over a year with a new baby already—someone had called the TV station. We had just finished the ten o'clock news. I was walking out of the newsroom with him right behind me when he went back to answer the phone. I couldn't make out the words, but his voice sounded strange. He hung up abruptly. He was quiet as we walked out to the car. As we were driving to my mom's to pick up our boys, I glanced over and noticed his forehead beaded with sweat. "Are you all right?" I asked him. His shirt collar was damp. The heavy sweat mixed with his on-air makeup, was dripping clay-colored stains onto his blue Oxford shirt. "Rick, are you okay? Are you sick?" I was scared he was having a heart attack.

"I'm fine," he said, as we pulled into my mother's driveway.

Thank God it was dark inside. We scooped up our sleeping kids and got back to the car in a hurry. We got them home and settled into their own beds. By now, it was midnight. The wind-up clock chimed twelve. Rick washed his face, and sat on the couch, grabbing the remote, turning the volume down low, so as not to wake the boys.

Nathan was five when Rick and I got married. He was so excited to move into Rick's brand-new house, where he got a bunk bed of his very own, the red chrome kind. He was fascinated with the rabbits on the lawn, early in the morning, when they'd dash across the grass after the automatic sprinklers shut off. Rick taught him how to ride a bike that summer. I still have the photos of him running alongside Nate when they took off the training wheels. Within nine months Nate had a baby brother in the room down the hall, sleeping in the spindle crib with the matching quilt and bumper pads I'd ordered out of the Lillian Vernon catalog. I loved that catalog. The pictures were of happy people in well-kept homes with monogrammed bathrobes and neatly coiled garden hoses. Neat, orderly, normal, perfect, just like the life I'd finally found. The baby's room was perfect. He was a perfect baby, a blue-eyed baby boy, adored, perfectly adored, down the hall from his perfectly adored big brother. Life had never been this perfect for me.

"Rick, what's wrong?" I sat down next to him on the couch.

We were sitting in the living room of his starter home in which we had blended our lives. I had packed up the leftovers of my youthful gallop to get married, travel around the country, have a baby, only to feel the sting of broken commitment, then having to slug it out as a single mom, back in college, starting all over. Rick was more than I ever dreamed of. I sold my older home in the city, which I'd leveraged to the hilt and took in boarders just to keep a roof over my head. I sold it off, paid off my debts and started over: a model life with a model husband in a model home, with its custom draperies, wallpaper and landscaping already in place. Stir in a new baby and you've got a dream life.

"I don't want to talk about it," he said, agitated, clicking through the channels.

"Talk about *what?* What in the world is wrong?"

"Nothing's wrong. Everything is okay." He clicked off the TV, got up and walked out of the room, leaving his shirt draped over the arm of the couch. I didn't get up to Spray n' Wash it just then.

I just sat staring at Rick's news trophies on the shelf in the living room. Apricot. The accent wall was apricot, with custom shelves brimming with his mementos, his life, his family, except for the desert watercolor in the copper frame on the center shelf. I had bought him that painting for Christmas, when we'd first started dating.

Rick insisted we keep that under wraps for a while. Even when we got married, he wanted to fly to Las Vegas, just the two of us. "Let's keep our private life private," he said, but his parents and I held sway and we got married at the courthouse instead. When news of our marriage showed up in the gossip column in the paper, he was slightly annoyed. This was the kind of thing that triggered the clamp down, as certain as slamming down a gate on the outside of a pawn shop, when the metal hit the concrete, there was no getting in. This would be a clamp down night, despite me pleading to know what prompted him to break out in a cold sweat.

"I love you and you love me and that's all that matters," he said in the same raw and anguished voice I would not hear again until the night he called me from jail.

He went to bed. I sat there for a long time, staring at the floor to ceiling shelves of our picture perfect life. *I am like that painting. Perfectly centered, plugged in. I'm a prop. And now I have two children. We're props in the life of a man keeping secrets.*

Until those secrets busted loose nearly twenty years later in a cold, dark restaurant parking lot, as my detective friend read off the charges, *"three counts of statutory sodomy"* while my innocent children sat inside in a booth. My fears had been vindicated.

So, that next day, I went for a run. It had been my drug of choice for years, my salvation, the only way I knew how to smack down my demons. When the howling voices of doubt and suspicion were burning in my brain, I doused them with endorphins, followed by a shot of guilt—guilt because I doubted him, aided and abetted by a master manipulator.

"I come home every night! I don't go anywhere for fear you'll suspect I'm up to something. What is wrong with you?" He always showed up for supper. He accused me of being irrational. He told me I needed therapy. So I ran. I ran to muzzle the demons that dared to gnaw on the glossy pages of my catalogue life. I ran to untie the knot of uncertainty I had carried in my gut for years. But on this day, the breaking news day, I simply said, *bring it.*

"Come on all you fucking demons! Come on out and ride on my shoulders for the entire world to see. Everybody knows now! Everybody knows!" I was running and crying. It's a wonder I didn't trip and fall in the street. I was screaming now, punching the air. "Come on out, all you demons. You can't hurt me now! I've got nothing left to hide."

It's like that drop of ink, indelible, infused into the fabric of our lives, undeniable now. But its stain is not ruinous. We simply fold around it.

I folded my napkin and laid in on the cake plate, not a bite left. Our butts were sore from sitting at Betsy and John's kitchen table for so long. We'd moved from the sordid tale of Rick to Nathan's wedding photos.

"Oh my Lord!" Betsy declared. "They're all grown up!"

It's the same way I felt when I saw her sons. People change a lot between the ages of twelve and twenty-two. Josh, the oldest, plans to be a minister. The younger son, Taylor, is a musician and a chef. Both of them are smart, kind, engaged, loving, interesting, wonderful human beings. All grown up.

It's ten o'clock at night by now. I'm exhausted from purge; my neighbors are worn out from listening. Betsy sets the timer on the coffeepot. John takes Libby out for one more walk. Such a luxury! We all go to bed.

Do you remember what it felt like, when you were a child, and no matter what kind of chaos might have been going on in your house, do you remember how good it felt to go to sleep knowing there were grownups at home? It was comforting to know there was another buffer between you and disaster. There was somebody else to get the dog in, lock the door, turn off the lights, call the fire department if the drapes caught on fire or the pipes burst. There was somebody else on duty to walk the floors waiting for a tardy teen, somebody else to plunge the toilet, reset the circuit breaker, take out the trash, or scoop the dead possum off the grass before the dog rolled in it. I'm sure a shrink could have a field day with my apparent residual psychosis of being a single parent for more than 4,200 days and nights. I'm just saying it was a luxury, a throwback to my quasi-protected youth, falling asleep with somebody else manning the guard shack. I slept like a baby that night, with Libby hopping up on the bed sometime in the middle of the night. I woke up to the soft light of a Carolina summer morning.

Betsy and I took Libby to the Washington Dog Park after breakfast. It was awesome: shady, dirt paths, even a stream where the dogs could romp. We met a couple who had three giant rescue dogs: a Golden, a Great Pyrenees and a Burmese Mountain mix. We're talking serious slobber. That night, Libby and I went out for cocktails with the young bloods at Single Brothers on Trade Street. A friend of my son owns it. They like dogs there. I ordered one of their "hand crafted" (which makes it sound like a leather purse) signature tequila drinks with grapefruit juice and agave nectar, which was truly delicious. Libby ordered water. A couple of other members of Patrick's posse showed up, making me feel genuinely welcomed. Besides, the story of a fifty-six-year-old woman who goes semi-berserk is a plot line that film-school kids can wrap their heads around. I left feeling loved and cooler than shit.

I got back to Betsy and John's late and let myself in quietly. I picked up where I'd left off on a blog post from earlier in the day and filed my story. I am, after all, a correspondent. I heard music somewhere in the house and Libby was missing. I walked out of my room and followed the music. Taylor was sitting on the living room couch in Betsy's perfectly decorated, southern traditional living room with cherry wood tables, stripes and solids, valance and drapes, maroons and golds—playing the guitar. He is a classically trained guitarist, plays beautifully. Libby is a classically trained sprawler, as big as a throw rug. I sat down in one of the winged-backed chairs, not saying a word. Wouldn't have mattered. Taylor was in the guitar-player's trance. If you've ever dated a musician, you know what I'm talking about. He smiled a bit, but kept to his business. I was the lucky one. I was a fortunate concertgoer with a front row seat, just he and I, the rest of the house asleep. He was playing real good, for free, reminded me of that Joni Mitchell song. I was moved, so moved.

He leaned over his guitar when he was through and we began what ended up being a far-ranging conversation about—well, it was about pretty much everything, human to human, no gender difference, no generational boundaries. He told me about what life was like as a young gay man in the provincial little town of Winston-Salem. He told me about when he first knew, how he told his parents, how hard it was at first. He told me how his big brother, the other half of a quintessential sibling rivalry, rose to the calling of being his advocate. Josh stood up for him, stood by him, helped to open the doors of understanding between a young man who needed support and a mother and father who needed time. They weren't planning on this eventuality on the day they brought little brother home from the hospital. I mean who does, really? It's not top of mind, our children's sexuality, in the quiet of the night, in the hospital room, when you look in amazement at the miracle God has just bestowed upon you, swaddled in a striped-cotton receiving blanket, in a glass bin with a pink or blue index card taped to the inside. Pink or blue, girl or boy, done and done. Was it Josh's divine calling from the time he was "baby boy" to one day rise to the very definition of brotherly love for the other baby boy? Blessed be the peacemakers.

When Taylor came out to his parents, Josh was not a seminary student; he was your typical college kid, going to Appalachian State in Boone, NC and working on the ski patrol. He was also an Eagle Scout. So maybe that was it. Maybe it was the combo of Boy Scouts and God. "Be prepared because you *are* your brother's keeper." Taylor told me that things were pretty much okay now. Everybody had settled in, learned to accept it, come to terms, which of course makes it sound like he has a disease or something. And of course, that's not the case. What they told him is "We love you," not in spite of, not because of, but *just because.* Just because is the brand of love which stands the test of time, the kind of love which evolves, surrounds, chides, abides, is tested, strengthened and adaptive.

I was struck with the thought of how differently things might have turned out for Rick if he'd been given that chance. Perhaps the fissure of a dark addiction which grew like a dangerous, jagged tree root to a poisoned pond, how maybe, just maybe, with some support and understanding, it might never have sprouted in the wrong direction. Rick's father was an L.A. cop, tough guy, and World War II Navy medic who went to work for the Los Angeles Police Department after he came home from the war. I am told when Rick was a little boy, his father would sometimes come home and brag about "beatin' up the queers." And then for reasons I do not know (as if somehow a motive constitutes justification), for some reason, Tough Guy had beat up on his son as well. Was it his emerging sexuality which provoked those blows? Imagine the terror of a young boy who thought he was turning into the very thing his father despised. Rick's father died while Rick was in prison. His family was too cheap to pay for a sheriff to travel with him so that Rick could attend the funeral. He wanted to. He loved his dad.

My second day in Winston, I drove by our old house on Cavalier Drive. The redbrick, split-level Colonial with the white Williamsburg cornice over the door still looks good. The yard is as big as a park. We had seven-eighths of an acre. Seven-eighths. If we'd had a full acre could we have made it? It was a good place for my babies and me. The swing set is gone but the toolshed we made into a playhouse still stands by the drive, the basketball pole with the kids' handprints pressed into the concrete pad still standing. The crepe myrtle is twice the size it was when I planted it; the weeping cherry I planted as a sapling is too.

From the street, transfixed for a moment, I peered into the basement windows, remembering a man at the computer. He used to be my husband. He used to take the kids to soccer practice and baseball games and on spins around the yard on the riding mower and read them stories at night. He was far better at homework than I, and putting together bikes and trikes and dollhouses. I suppose he tried to fight his demons, but little by little, they reached beyond the flicker of the computer screen and pulled him into a vast abyss of addiction. Here in this house, where we were so innocent, he began his choking descent.

On a steamy July day many years later, though, I was back. I had returned to my beloved Carolina to reclaim what I'd lost: memories that the kids and I had made here—birthday parties, snow days, vegetable gardens, that one Easter Sunday with the kids racing to get ahead of Maddie, our chocolate Lab puppy, to find the Easter eggs before she did. The kids and I had surprised Rick with a puppy for his fortieth birthday. *We* had been here, my children and me. This was sacred ground that I would not allow to be desecrated by his demise. I came back to honor it. I came back to scoop up the remnants.

Just as I did on the day I cleaned out Rick's apartment. His landlord had called me a few weeks after the arrest. He was matter-of-fact, civil, even apologetic. He'd gotten my phone number from the lease agreement. I guess Rick had listed me as an emergency contact. The landlord said he doubted Rick would be out of jail anytime soon; he'd seen news reports that his bond had been set at a quarter of a million dollars. The landlord needed to clean the place out, get it ready for a new tenant, said there was a lot of work to do after the cops ransacked it and the cat was left unattended for days. I had actually tried to catch that stupid cat. In a moment of weakness, or I guess compassion, the day after his arrest and my demon-cleansing jog, I went to check on the cat and get Rick's glasses to take to him in jail. Since he'd decided not to hang himself, I figured the least I could do was help him see. I could not catch that cat to save my life. It was wild. The kids said the cat had never been tamed. I left a giant bowl of cat food and a giant bowl of water and got the hell out. The place gave me the shudders. Three weeks later the landlord called and told me to come and get anything I wanted to keep, because everything else was going to charity or the dump. It sure as hell wasn't my job to clean out his shabby duplex, but there was something in there I wanted.

Returning to the scene of the crime was both eerie and depressing. The cops had scattered stuff everywhere; stacks of papers, magazines, DVDs, lay where they'd left them, doors ajar, drawers still open. Dirty dishes in the sink had been there a month. The stuffing from throw pillows, which the cat had ripped to shreds, was strewn all over the floor. The mattress was still on its side, leaned against the wall.

More telling was the disarray that had resided there from the beginning. The diseased half of what had been two lives joined as one, had taken up a very shallow residence there. Boxes he'd packed on the day he moved out of our house, four years earlier, remained taped up, stacked in a closet, behind hangers bent by coats and slacks. In the front part of the closet, a working wardrobe of khakis, a handful of dress shirts, and neckties I'd helped him pick out, knotted and hung on hooks, stood by the ready. This was a man who had owned his own tuxedo once, a man who had a house account at Brooks Brothers with his measurements on file. Rick's personal shopper would have everything waiting in the dressing room for his star client to try on. "Looked nice in that charcoal blazer last night," he'd flutter and fuss over Rick like a prized cow. But now the silks and tweeds and worsted wool had been relegated to the back of the closet, his other life, his past life, his pretend life. He'd narrowed his choices now: quick on and off, khakis and a dress shirt, quick on and off, so he could get back to the computer, his new life. He had narrowed his choices to the front half of a tiny closet in a dark bedroom with a thin mattress and a Goodwill nightstand. Journalism awards, scrapbooks, an expensive oil painting he'd purchased in Santa Fe, years before we married, hung on the wall like an afterthought. On the refrigerator, tucked under car-insurance magnets and pizza coupons, were team photos, yearbook pics, sketches from Sean, Post-It notes—"I love you, Dad!" from Lauren—even Patrick's report card, hardly worth bragging about at the time. Amid the stacks of clutter in the living room, my children had been watching him from framed photos on every table and shelf, unwilling witnesses, now refugees. I gathered them up, these remnants. I refused to allow them to wind up in a dump. I boxed them up and brought them home to honor them.

Before I left Winston last summer, I took Betsy and Taylor out for lunch. We went to a landmark BBQ joint called Little Richard's. It sits down low off Country Club Drive with a steep hill behind it. The smoke chugs up to the sky and the kudzu vines wrap their snaky tendrils around every single tree on that lot, forming giant, fantastical, green-draped creatures which makes the whole scene look like a page from a Dr. Seuss book. We ordered it all: pulled pork sandwiches with slaw and that good, sweet and vinegary North Carolina BBQ sauce, plus hush puppies and sweet tea. It was worth the ten-year wait.

As I was driving out of town feeling abundantly full and abundantly grateful for this renewed friendship, it occurred to me that maybe my Winston neighbors felt just as good about this whole reunion as I did. It's a two-way street, I reckoned. There's a rush that comes with the arriving and a rush that comes from waiting by the door. At the end of our lives, we just want to know we mattered. As I had already learned in spades, with more yet to come, to put off going to see someone you love is folly. Go today. Go this week. Book your ticket tonight. Go see them. Tell them they mattered.

7

When You're Feeling Low,
Buy a Cowboy Hat

I love the open road. I've figured this out now. It makes me happy. It brings me a quiet, revered and deeply held bliss.

Especially close to my heart is the Act of Acceleration. Far from an Act of Contrition, this is balls-to-the-walls, thrill-seeking delight. It became a ritual of sorts. After driving through hundreds of small towns, many of them little more than a wide spot in the road, after I'd slowed down for the requisite speed traps, or stopped to get lunch or gas, or let Libby pee, I took great pleasure in the Act. The minute I cleared the last of the 35 MPH signs on the outskirts of town—man, I'd let her rip. That's the cool thing about driving a stick shift, you get to pretend you're a race-car driver: first gear, second, third, fourth, wind it out, wind it out, wind it out, then ease that baby into overdrive. It's almost sexual. You're in charge, moving forward with a surge of speed, purpose and freedom; the car, your perfect lover—generous, responsive, cradling you and slamming you against the seat at the same time, taking you where you want to go. And whoo-eee baby, there ain't no place like the wide open Texas highways to get your thrill on.

It felt good to be back in the West, something I had dreamed about for years. The West was where my history lay; the West is where I had unfinished business; the West is what would restore my soul. But nobody, including myself, could have predicted the range of emotions that Texas would pump out of me, like oil coming to the surface, black as tar and just as valuable.

I'd forgotten about the grasshoppers, though. They're miserable sons of bitches and they're everywhere. Libby and I stopped just inside the Texas line to grab a BBQ brisket sandwich at the fanciest truck stop I'd ever seen. There were bronze sculptures of cowboys and longhorn steers erected on the massive lawn, which was no doubt the cause of the water shortage for the rest of the entire Western United States last year.

It was vast and still a verdant green, even in August in the midst of a 100-year drought. Not so green over in the pet exercise area though, where the grass was the same color as the hoppers: brown. Made Libby jumpy. She padded across the crackly grass, much like walking on crispy chow mein noodles, and snapped at the grasshoppers when they landed on her back. I jumped ten feet when they landed on mine. I hate those damn bugs. They're fucking noisy. Their incessant drone from the tall, brittle prairie grass next to the gas pumps transported me back in time to a terrifying chapter from my Fort Worth days of innocence at the hands of one Charles Lee Coates.

Charles Lee was a tow-headed, rag-tag, next-door-neighbor kid whom I played with when I was a very little girl. He had all the signs of being a Death Row inmate even at the tender age of six. We played Army and I was always the nurse. My duty? Fixin' mustard and mayonnaise sandwiches for the soldiers. That's right: no turkey, no ham, no bologna, just mustard and mayonnaise on Rainbow bread. In addition to relegating me to a subservient role in the hierarchy of pretend war, Charles Lee also delighted in throwing grasshoppers on my back and watching me run like I was possessed by the devil.

Truth is, that little fucker was Satan's spawn, seeing how he nearly cut off my thumb and forced me to set a house on fire. It wasn't my fault. When we got bored digging tunnels in the vacant lot to hide from the enemy and running around yackin' it up on walkie-talkies made from beer cans, we'd hang out in Charles Lee's garage, digging through spider-ridden, musty-smelling junk. It was one of those small, detached, one-bedroom garage-type apartments and the place was overrun with decades worth of *Look* magazines and *Forth Worth Star-Telegrams* stacked in bundles four feet high. Charles Lee, who possessed some kind of mature-beyond-his-years ability to influence women to do completely illogical things, talked me into playing with matches. Everybody knows the cliché: if you play with fire you'll get burned. And I did. So I threw down the lit match and the whole place went up in flames. It's a miracle the house didn't blow up, what with gas cans and paint thinner and all manner of combustible materials sitting around. I still remember the sound of the fire trucks rumbling down the street, lights and sirens blaring and me hightailing it down the alley ahead of them, through the gate of our cyclone-fenced backyard and straight into my room where I was so scared I promptly fell asleep. I recall waking up to the sound of angry adult voices in the living room. It was my parents, sounding defensive, with his. I got up, sleepily shuffling out to the living room, where I threw down with my team. I completely rolled over on Charles Lee because that blond little bastard, with the cowlicks all over his buzz-cut head, had threatened to pull my pants down! He told me he'd pull down my pants if I didn't strike a match! Tough spot, you know—bare ass or house on fire—but to me, really there was no question.

I don't recall if his attempt to cut off my thumb occurred before or after the house fire incident. We were playing Army in the vacant lot. Must have been time for me to fetch some more mustard and mayonnaise sandwiches and maybe I wanted to be the gunner for a while; I can't be sure. I *am* sure that that skinny, mean-spirited Charles Lee, who never wore shirt nor shoes from May until September, did hand me a piece of red glass: a big chunk of jagged, red glass from a broken taillight off a car. We had such pristine playgrounds back then. Who knows? Maybe I accidentally cut myself on the razor-sharp edge, maybe he took a swipe at me. (If you read this, Charles Lee, and can get a letter out of prison, let me know.) All I do know is that it was bleeding like a son of a gun, lots o' blood. I ran screaming next door to find my mama. She just about fainted when she saw it. She wrapped a towel around my bleeding left hand and we ran like the wind to the car, me climbing up into our Mercury sedan—the kind with the fold-down seats. My mom told me to keep applying pressure. She couldn't do it herself because the Mercury was a stick.

They whisked us right through the waiting room, straight into the examining room at Dr. McCarroll's office. He did everything for our family, from delivering my two little brothers to getting my big brother Garrett into rehab. I remember like it was yesterday, Doris the nurse in her crisp white uniform, smelling like AquaNet hairspray and rubbing alcohol as she unwrapped the bloody towel to see the deep gash at the thumb joint, saying to me, in a sweet Texas drawl, "Now, Jeannie, I'm gonna need you step up on this little stool so we can wash that cut out."

Doris turned on the faucet. There was a little red wooden stool tucked under the sink. She pulled it out with her foot, holding tightly to my wrist. My mom looked pale. I looked up at Doris. I looked at the water. I looked at the wound.

"I'll do it myself," I said and stepped up on the stool and stuck my bloody hand under the warm, running water. Doris was mildly surprised. My mom had to turn her head. I recall, beyond the shadow of any doubt, thinking it was better to take care of *my own business my own self* rather than letting somebody else take care of it for me. I also distinctly remember my mom saying she'd buy me a candy bar on the way home if I'd hold still for the stitches. I bawled like a baby when they sewed me up, but I got the Baby Ruth anyway.

The only testament to that traumatic event is the scar I have to this day. Everybody who was there that day is gone. There is an emptiness that comes from losing too many people too young in life. There's nobody I can call and ask, *"Do you remember that time...?"* We're left to fill in the blanks ourselves and often, we come up empty. It's the same way I felt when I arrived in Fort Worth: empty. Everybody I once knew had either died or moved away. It makes a person sad. But at least I would not have to spend the night in a crappy motel in my former hometown. For the first time on the road trip, I stayed with someone whom I did not know—the sister of a friend of the family. And even though I had probably met her at a birthday party or baby shower thirty years ago or more, I did not remember her, nor she me. But ever grateful for a free place to stay, I was game. Besides, she had a pool! When I opened the car door on the griddle of her driveway at 6:00 p.m. and still 111-degrees, Libby looked at me like, "Are you fucking kidding me? First the grasshoppers and now Dante's inferno?"

Staying there, however, would have a chilling effect on me. I was getting tired. I had been on the road for exactly one month when I got to Texas. Three thousand miles behind me and about 5,000 more to go. *Five thousand more miles to drive.* Wrap your head around that! I couldn't even think about it at that moment.

My hostess was quite cordial, could not have been nicer, and very kind to take in a woman and her dog on very short notice. But the downside to being a house guest is, you have to be cordial too, and sometimes you just don't feel like it. You're so worn out it's hard to muster the energy to talk, much less listen to some new person's stories. But you do, and Kathy had some stories to tell. She'd been widowed quite suddenly two years earlier, leaving her with a teenage daughter and a frail father-in-law, who had nobody else to take care of him. Kathy inherited all the responsibility, but also the legal authority and the money to handle his affairs. She bought a house around the corner from her house, moved him into it and hired a full-time nurse who just happened to need a full-time charge. It was perfect. She was also able to pay off her own house where she worked from home as an accountant, also perfect. Kathy had steady clients, a dependable income, a house that was paid for and she was home when her daughter got out of school, plus she was just around the corner if the nurse or her father-in-law needed her. I think she'd be the first to admit that if there was any good luck to be found from a devastating turn of events, she had found it. Still, you could tell she was worried, pretty much worried all the time. I understand this, although I can't say I've ever been widowed, have ever lost a husband I loved, who was fine one day and gone the next. I can't imagine what that feels like. All I know is how it feels to have the rug pulled out from under you when your child support gets sent up the river for seven years, just before it's time for the kids to go to college. But I did not share my little tale of woe with Kathy; it would have made me feel small.

I crawled off to bed. Kathy was gracious enough to give me her room with the king-sized bed, where her husband's slippers remained tucked under his nightstand. She had taken to sleeping in the guest room, said it was cooler there. Normally, I would write before I went to bed, but on this night I was just too exhausted. Maybe it was the heat. Maybe it was because I felt a bit embarrassed. For the first time on this journey, I was seeing myself through the eyes of someone who I really didn't know. There wasn't the automatic benefit of the doubt. It's not that she was judgmental—actually, far from it, she was quite generous. But I suddenly felt a little exposed, my situation hard to defend. I listened to her talk about how she was planning for the future, trying to hedge her bets on her job, her daughter's education, her ability to keep everything afloat. I could relate, nodding with intellectual understanding, but at the same time thinking about my total assets of about $4,000 to my name. Compared to my dicey situation, this woman had much more security than I had, the grief of widowhood notwithstanding. Then, of course, I immediately felt like a shit heel because I understood it's all relative. It is all relative to our life experience and what allows us to sleep at night. I was so tired, by the time I closed the bedroom door, I felt like I'd been beaten with a stick. I group-texted the kids, "In for the night, Fort Worth. It's cooled off, only 99-degrees. Love u, miss u." I kicked off my loafers, split open on the seam, stepped out of my faded Levis with the yellow paint drips. Hell, maybe I'm just cheap, but I couldn't bring myself to toss them, just because of a little paint, and I always figured, "Who's going to see me on the road anyway?" I kissed Libby on the head and crawled under the cool sheets, feeling threadbare.

Morning was worse. My quest no longer seemed brave or adventurous after there was the "reading of the bills," not to be confused with the "reading of the will," which in my life to date had meant more debt than inheritance.

Lauren had just returned to St. Louis from her internship in Washington, D.C. I'd asked her to gather up the bills and to give me the amounts so I could pay them online. And even with the Kickstarter funding, it became painfully clear that I'd be broke by the time I got back home. I know you're probably thinking, "Well, what the hell did you expect?" but please try to understand the fever I was under to get away. But on this day, in this woman's home, it reminded me of everything I had put at risk, and it didn't feel like such a great escape. It felt like a mistake.

After rattling off the amounts for utilities, insurance, car payment, plus all the household stuff, Lauren added, "and I'm $3,000 short on my tuition." I wasn't prepared for there to be a hitch in her financial aid for her last semester of college. This time around, her super senior year, we'd planned for Lauren to pick up the balance of what her scholarships and grants did not cover. We'd talked it out; she was fine with it, since I'd already helped out the first four years. But the purse-string holders at her college were keeping a tight grip, saying she would not be allowed to take out additional loans on her own. And I knew bad news for her would mean bad news for Sean, entering his junior year. We thought we had it all worked out. We apparently did not. It was my Achilles' heel.

The fight in me told me we'd figure it out. I always had before. I'm the one who'd drilled into their heads, "Never take no for an answer!" I knew damn well there had to be provisions for "extenuating circumstances." Jesus Christ Almighty, Extenuating Circumstances R Us! I could write those fucking hardship letters in my sleep. I knew the kids could apply for more loans; we could plead poverty and try to get a grant to make up the difference. The street fighter in me was lying just under the surface, ready to pounce on any two-bit bureaucrat who tried to stand between them and their education. But, the hardships of the past had been legitimate, not of my own making. This time, the rule makers had caught me lying down. They caught me being a bad mother. A mother who had abandoned her duty station to go chasing some self-indulgent dream. How utterly selfish, I kept thinking over and over again. I could battle any meddling authority with a vengeance, from mortgage bankers to cops, to get what I needed for my kids, if I was fighting from a position of moral high ground. But now I'd be in the position of indefensible negligence. Jeopardizing my kids' college? What in God's name was I thinking?

"Lauren, don't worry," I rallied the voice of assurance of the mom I used to be. "We'll figure something out."

I hung up the phone. It was about 8:00 a.m. Libby needed to pee but I needed to hide. I could hear Kathy grinding coffee. I wasn't ready to be sociable, wasn't ready to walk out and be the ridiculous, sorry-ass schlub of a pitiful parent who'd put her own crazy scheme in front of her daughter's last year of college.

"Libby, you're just going to have to wait, honey." I bent down, the tears already tumbling. To her everlasting credit (and this is why I love this dog more than life itself on some days) Libby just looked up at me with a patient and sympathetic gaze that said, "Okay, I can see you're having a meltdown," and she promptly jumped up on the forbidden king-sized bed. She had me on the ropes.

Do you remember the scene in *The Big Chill* when Glenn Close is sobbing in the shower because she was secretly in love with the guy who wasn't her husband, the guy who'd committed suicide? That was me, same shower scene, brunette instead of a blonde, with smaller breasts. I left Libby on the bed, went into Kathy's immaculately clean bathroom with plush towels and an array of shampoos, soaps and fragrances. I stepped into the shower, closed the door, turned on the water, and then began sobbing, head down, the stream of water a cascading shroud of shame around my shoulders. I buried my face in the thick terry washcloth to muffle the sound, crying so hard I had to steady myself by holding onto the faucet. I felt like a fool. I felt like everything I'd worked for to keep us on track all those years, was going down the drain. What was wrong with me? And what the hell was I going to do? And my kids? My God, I swore when Rick went to prison I would not allow them to pay the price, and yet here I had jeopardized everything I had accomplished to prevent that, in pursuit of some crazy-ass yearning to feel alive again. I hadn't realized until that moment how perfectly the guilt had kept pace with me.

I had to get my act together before I walked out to the living room. I dried off, blew my hair dry, put on a little makeup and put up a good front. She'd set out a cup for me. The coffee was good. I took Libby outside. It was 99-degrees already at 9:00 a.m. "Why don't you leave her with me today?" Kathy asked when I came back inside. She knew I'd be tooling all over Fort Worth, searching old neighborhoods, in and out of the car, taking pictures. It was hard to leave my dog for even a few hours. Libby was my rock, my partner, my co-conspirator, but it was beastly hot. I knew she was better off inside the cool confines of the three-bedroom brick ranch, lying at the feet of the lady of the house.

I thanked her and set out to revisit the streets and the houses I'd known as a kid. Hadn't seen these places in more than forty years. For many people, the street they grew up on is right around the corner or just the other side of town. But when you've lived all over the country, to go back, as I did, to every street I'd ever lived on, was an amazing privilege. It's really nice to do it alone. There's nobody to mess it up. There's nobody to comment or contradict or tell you to hurry up. There's nobody complaining that they're hungry or they've gotta pee or your childhood home is a dump. You can take your time. It's bittersweet and sometimes brutal.

Our house on Washburn Avenue, next door to Charles Lee, had become a cliché: well, really, a parking lot. The next place we lived, our old house on Lafayette Street, was smaller than I'd remembered. Isn't that always the case? A white shingle house, worn-down grass, beat-up car in the gravel drive, it looked a lot like it did when we left it. The mimosa trees were bigger and smelled just as sweet as I'd remembered. Ah the mimosa trees, where the neighbor girls and I acted out *Moon Spinners*, taking turns being Hayley Mills trapped in the windmill, waiting for our dark, mysterious Greek sheepherder to rescue us.

I retraced my route to school: every porch, every doorway, every driveway and yard. A flood of familiarity wrapped around me and made me feel happy. There were the pink wrought-iron porch rails shaped like ivy, the painted brick bungalow with the black-lacquered shutters with the half-moon cutouts, the house with the weird screen door with the grey wooden slats from which you couldn't see in but the folks inside could see out. It always creeped me out to knock on that door when I was selling Camp Fire Girls candy, but they always bought two boxes: the mint patties and peanut clusters. There was the two-story house with the *"Beware of Dog"* sign which still hung from the gate, even though, Lord knows, that dog is long gone. There was the house where the lady gave out popcorn balls at Halloween and the house that always stunk like sauerkraut and the house where the ambulance came and rolled out the old man on a gurney, underneath a purple velvet drape.

The buckled sidewalk is what did me in though. On Clover Lane it's still there, the place where the tree roots created a hazard for the inattentive. On the first day of second grade, my mother had instructed my brother Don to show me the way to school. We'd carpooled with the Baker kids when I was in the first grade. I found them fascinating because they were Jewish. There weren't a lot of Jews in the working-class neighborhood in which we lived.

Don walked the route with me on the first day. "Go past Sutter, go past

Belle Place; when you get to Clover Lane, go left." I must have looked up with some uncertainty because he pivoted my shoulders left and said, "Just walk toward the barber shop," pointing to a landmark where I'd spent many a Saturday sitting in the wide windowsill next to the leggy jade plant, thumbing through dog-eared copies of *Science Digest, The Saturday Evening Post* and *Field & Stream,* waiting on my brothers to get their hair cut. Don was so patient with me; there was ten years' difference in our ages. I'm sure he was probably late for seminary school himself.

Day two, I was on my own. I loved that time alone as a citizen of the world, unencumbered on my one-mile trek (Google verified) to school and back each day. There's a lot a kid can think about during two miles of walking alone. Everything was fine until the day I stayed late for Spanish class on one of those overcast October days when it's dark by five. I left South High Mount about 4:30. I was walking fast. It was cold, spitting rain and the world felt menacing to me. Things looked different this late in day and there was a lot of traffic. Along about the dry cleaners, just beyond the spill of light from the drive-through, on the dark stretch of Clover Lane, I heard footsteps close behind me, hitting hard, like the sound of a man's dress shoes on the pavement. I picked up my pace. So did the person behind me. My seven-year-old mind conjured up all kinds of boogiemen, and this was long before child abductions were popular TV shows starring fathers of kids who'd been decapitated. In my little-girl mind, I envisioned some sinister goon in greasy Dickey work pants, a grimy zip-up jacket and skullcap pulled low on his brow. I was petrified with fear, walking so fast now that my skinny little legs, in crew socks and black-and-white saddle oxfords, where gliding like wheels, pumping the pavement, maximum torque. The heel strikes were gaining on me. I couldn't go any faster; I kept looking for Lafayette Street, Lafayette Street, that would be my right-hand turn. Right? Lafeyette Street, go right. Right, the hand I wrote with! Right? Where was it? I'd gone too far, I'd passed it, I kept telling myself, even while I kept moving forward, afraid to stop or break my pace to look over my shoulder. I was barely breathing, the brown canvas book bag criss-crossed over my chest was crushingly heavy. I was disoriented and cold and the person behind me was gaining. A car at the stop sign at the next corner turned left, coming toward me, splashing light briefly on the sidewalk in front of me. The buckled part, the ill-placed tree with its disruptive roots that had buckled the sidewalk, there it was! Halfway home, I was halfway home; I hadn't missed my turn. I knew my street was just twenty steps away. I was almost running.

"Jeannie Whatley? Jeannie? Is that you?" A girl's voice behind me spoke my name. I didn't stop, just turned to grab a quick glance over my shoulder. I did not know her, but she knew me. By the time I turned back around it was too late; I tripped over the uneven place in the sidewalk in a rolling stumble, the Jerry Lewis kind of exaggerated pratfall, where the person is falling, falling, falling in a slow-motion dive, face first, heading for the cold pavement. Then, *snatch!* She grabbed me by the book bag strap and pulled me back, just in time to break my fall.

"Jeannie, slow down! Why are you walking so fast?" She moved the umbrella over to cover both of us. "I've been trying to catch up with you!"

It was some junior-high girl who was friends with my brother Garrett. I, to this day, don't know her name. We made the right-hand turn onto Lafayette; she had only a few more houses to go.

"Be careful!" And then she left me. I made it home, soaking wet, my knees still wobbly.

The sight of that buckled sidewalk last summer brought me to tears. The tree was long gone. The jagged crack in the sidewalk, where the pooching slabs of concrete had once formed a stumbling block, had been filled in, patched over, season after season: more like a mound now. It's hard to explain the rush of recognition, almost affection, for some inanimate glob of familiarity. It was still there and so was I.

And then I thought, but not my brother Don.

"Fuck it. I need a new hat," I said out loud, completely at ease with talking to myself by now.

I got back in the car and navigated my way to the North Side. (We don't need no stinkin' GPS.) The North Side, that's where the stockyards are. Fort Worth is called "Cowtown" because it was a famous stop along the Chisholm Trail, back when there were real cowboys, not bronze ones, who drove real longhorn steers all the way from Mexico to Kansas City. Fort Worth was a hospitable stop, with stockyards to pen up the cattle and women to give the cowboys free range. Well, it wasn't exactly *free*. In a stroke of fortuitous timing, I actually got to see a few cowboys on a cattle drive. Oh, never mind that it was at the Disney-fied stockyards of today. Tourist trap or not, it's not every day you get to see Texas longhorns being led down the street, even if they do turn 'em around and lead them back the other way on the half-hour. Poor damn cows must be confused. I, on the other hand, was clearly directed to the Western-wear store.

Because that's what we do. My brothers and I inherited a slight affliction, begun by my maternal grandfather Booker Waddell, carried on by my mother, embraced with vigor by my older brothers, and indeed, appears to have been inherited by my own children. It comes from my mother's maxim, "Don't go 'round lookin' shabby" and if you're *feeling* that way, it's incumbent upon the shabby one to step up and step out to buy a new hat, or Tony Lama boots, or a Panhandle Slim shirt or, in my mother's case, often a new negligee. The object of our obsession has to be top shelf but not pimp-my-crib insanely expensive, you know: just quality. Often, quite often, it' a hat. One time for Don, it was a *kufi*. For the uneducated on the mode o' day for well-dressed West African men (and sometimes well-dressed southwestern American men), the *kufi* is the hat which tops off the *dashiki*. In hindsight, we really should have buried Don in his *kufi* and *dashiki*, but Lord knows he had already picked out the threads for his laying out. It was just two months before he died and he justified the somewhat indulgent capital outlay on a new sports coat, slacks, dress shirt and necktie thusly: "Two weddings and a funeral." Two out of three isn't bad. Don made it to my niece Madison's wedding just days after he picked up the ensemble from the tailor's shop where they took everything in, seeing as how Don was down to about 135 pounds by then. He did not, however, make it to my son Nathan's wedding just three months later, but, I'm telling you, he looked mighty fine at his wake. Oh, the lessons they teach us in life and in dying: how to find your way home and how to be carried home in style.

I had not had a new cowboy hat for close to thirty years—not since a pit boss at Caesar's Tahoe treated me to a custom-fitted brown Lady Stetson. He didn't get what he was hoping for out of that little deal. I lost that hat somewhere down the line and since we don't get much call for cowboy hats in St. Louis, I didn't miss it. But back home in Texas, when it's 90,000 degrees, a new straw cowboy hat is a pretty nice thing to have covering your melon. I went into the Fincher's White Front Store. It's been around since 1912, and my buddy Lalo fixed me right up with a nice custom-shaped Rodeo King. Best fit I've ever had. I stepped back out into the oppressive heat feeling halfway ridiculous (like I really should be riding a horse). It was a good thing Libby wasn't with me, because she would have barked or laughed at me, but mostly, I felt sublime. Do you know that feeling? When you've just done something so ridiculously hard to justify (especially after the monumental self-flagellation just hours before) that all you can do is shrug your shoulders and walk around with a stupid grin on your face? That was me. I felt serene. I felt satisfied.

I was carrying on our time-honored, over-extended family tradition. Plus, I had paid tribute to the Texas brand on my soul. Texas deserved it. My family played out a lot of history under her wide-open skies, in ways both good and tragic.

The house on Locke Street, the upgrade from the cracker box on Lafayette Avenue, was the backdrop for the worst of times. That's where I was headed next. My mother, newly divorced from Jim Whatley, her third husband, who allowed his name to appear on all our birth certificates, in her own inimitable way had managed to connive or charm a banker into giving her a mortgage on a rambling, two-story house which would plop us Whatley kids squarely into a slightly upgraded blue-collar neighborhood in a white-linen part of town. Vestiges of oil money run deep in the rolling hills of the west side of Fort Worth. The houses are big and so are the lawns in Westover Hills and Rivercrest Country Club. These are some of the wealthiest people in the Lone Star State. I went to elementary school with the daughter of the guy who owned the Coca-Cola bottling plant. She had a Coke machine and a white baby grand piano in the parlor outside her bedroom *on the second floor!* Just think of the help who had to hoist those two adolescent necessities up the stairs! The public schools, especially in this lily-white enclave of Fort Worth, were so good at that time, even the oil barons and the fine folks who bottle Coca-Cola sent their kids to them. That's how we Whatley kids got to brush up against the one-percenters, decades before the rest of us had been relegated to the other ninety-nine.

I was in awe of my friend Eva, who lived in a mansion with a spiral staircase. I swear to God it looked like the foyer to the Beverly Hillbillies' mansion, down to the black-and-white checkered marble floor. Every day in the cafeteria, while the rest of us ate peanut butter or bologna, Eva would open up her white or pale pink lunch sack (the rest of us had brown bags, or rusty, sour-smelling lunch boxes) and she'd take out a chicken salad or tuna salad sandwich, with the crusts cut off, and a tiny box of raisins or homemade brownie or cookie and the coveted single size serving of Fritos, all dutifully packed by her maid Ruby. I actually got to meet Ruby once at Eva's birthday party when we got picked up after school by the family chauffeur in the Mark V. She was so sweet, serving us all lemonade and cupcakes with sprinkles, but shooed us out of the kitchen when it got close to dinnertime. Ruby didn't suffer no spoiled white kids.

The hired help in Lincolns gave way to wheels of their own for the

Jean Ellen Whatley

Rivercrest Country Club set of kids, typically parked in the circular driveway on the morning of their sixteenth birthdays. The poor little rich kids would be presented with brand-new Camaros, Mustangs, VWs or GTOs which, tragically, by the time they were seventeen, often would be carting their obscenely spoiled asses over to the Stop Six part of town, where cousins or neighbors of the chauffeurs who formerly drove these little brats around town were more than happy to sell them heroin. Stop Six, not difficult to surmise, was the bad part of town, where one might expect to buy heroin. Nowadays, in Webster Groves where I live, the kids just text their heroin dealer, who delivers like the Jimmy John's guy: freakishly fast. Back in Fort Worth in 1968, there was as much risk in the fetching as there was in hitting it up. Heroin wasn't their first drug of choice. My brother Garrett and his Neiman-Marcus friends worked their way up from drinking to smoking dope, then speed, downers and LSD. You name it, they smoked it, swallowed it, drank it, snorted it and shot it—an endless array of recreational drugs, which, unfortunately for some, ceased being a thrill and ended being a trap. That's how it turned out for Garrett. The first time he went into rehab, I rode with my mother to take him to the lockup. It was a federally-funded drug treatment facility.

"Bye, Jeannie," he said and kissed me on the cheek, leaning through the open window, his wavy, black hair pulled back in a neat little ponytail. He always pronounced "Jeannie" with a soft "j," like "Jacques," as in Cousteau, and he put the emphasis on the last syllable, "jean-*nee*." I watched him walk away from me, up the grey concrete stairs, down the grey concrete sidewalk towards the redbrick institution. The gate rattled closed behind him; a chain-link fence with razor wire would hold him there long enough to try to beat the devil out of him, his budding addiction. He'd actually caught a break, getting court-ordered rehab instead of prison at seventeen. Garrett could charm a fucking snake and the judge had been lenient. I don't know that tougher measures would have changed the eventual outcome of him being bitten by such an addictive drug at such a young age. This marked the beginning of many trips in and out of rehab. My darling Garrett, my next-older brother, wrestled with this monkey on his back for years. In the end, it pinned him to the kitchen floor.

Garrett died alone in his San Francisco apartment on November 21, 2002 of an acute asthma attack. His wife was teaching school in Marin County. He had called her to say he wasn't feeling well. She called the doctor to get him in right away, the office was within walking distance of their house. She told him,

"Go to the doctor now and I'll be there as soon as I finish giving a test." For some inexplicable reason he decided to take a bath first. Garrett had become a bit dismissive about these asthma attacks. Decades of getting through them had worn down his wariness.

I remember them well. When we were growing up, in the stifling heat of summer, our tiny frame house on Lafayette Street would feel like an oven. It never cooled off at night. All we had was a miserable window air-conditioning unit in the living room. The cold air never made it down the hall to the bedrooms. Night after night, I woke up to the sound of Garrett wheezing. Sometimes I got up to check on him and found him sitting on the edge of the bed, his skinny arms propped on his knees, his skin stretched so tautly across his ribs it looked as though his bones would poke through his skin every time he tried to inhale. It must have been like sucking air through a pillow and Lord knows, he wasn't getting much. I'd get him some water or fetch his inhaler and then go back to bed, lying in the dark, listening to every tortured wheeze. Sometimes I cried. Usually I prayed.

Dear Lord, please let Gary breathe.
Please God, just let him breathe.
And be able to sleep.
Please, Lord. Amen.

It wasn't fair that he suffered like that, even though he could be as mean as cat shit to me during the day, and often was. He teased me, unmercifully, about being chubby. He called me Rotunda. Seriously. He made fun of me in front of his buddy Paul Ellis, whom I had a crush on, saying things like, "Jeannie, leave us alone. Go try on your new Spanky bra, although I don't know why you need one." I was mortified; what sixth-grade girl wouldn't be? When Garrett and I played pop-flies and grounders, he would magnanimously bat left-handed, ostensibly to give me a break on how far he could hit the slow pitches I'd lob over the pie tin. Even with that, he'd consistently knock them over the backyard fence and I'd have to chase the ball down the alley for half a block. After I'd trotted my chubby butt back up the stinky alley and it was my turn to bat, he'd quit, saying it was too hot to play.

The heat made his asthma worse, especially at night. In the dark, when everybody else in the house was asleep except Garrett and me, he was no longer my tormentor; he was simply my suffering, defenseless big brother and I just wanted him to breathe. Finally, the syrupy red asthma medicine or the inhaler would kick in and one long, thready breath at a time the rattling in his lungs would begin to subside. His breathing would come easier, sounding less like a vacuum attachment on upholstery and more like a skinny boy drawing a deep breath. Sometimes, it took hours. My mom, who was a teletype operator at the airport by now—a good, government job—would come home from her night shift and find him asleep, sitting up, his arms still propped on his knees. Other times, after his breathing was restored, I'd go in and tell him to lay down, tipping him over gently, tucking his legs under the sheet, and he'd let me cover him up, his uncharacteristic obedience disquieting.

There was nobody with him when he died. He'd drawn the bath but he hadn't caught his breath. The water in the tub was still warm when they found him, collapsed on the floor in the kitchen. It wasn't just the asthma that killed him though. Truth is, Garrett's health had been so compromised by his decades of drug abuse, on any given day any number of things could have killed him. He'd been off street drugs for decades but had traded in heroin for methadone. No matter where he moved around the country, he always had to make sure the methadone clinic was nearby. His teeth were decayed. His liver was shot. He was on a waiting list for a transplant. Lord knows the ethical questions that might have arisen if they'd found a match.

I just wanted to see him one more time. That's all. I wanted to tell him how much I loved him. I desperately wanted to have the conversation we'd never had; I wanted to ask him what it had been like for him, being an outsider like me. Garrett and I shared a unique bond. We were the outlaw kids among the five siblings. He and I were both illegitimate.

Illegitimate is such an archaic term, but factual nonetheless. I hesitate to sully my dear departed mother's reputation any more than I have already, because I loved her very much, but facts are facts. Parts are parts. During a prolonged estrangement from her legally wedded husband Mr. Whatley, the man who so graciously masqueraded as my father until I uncovered their little charade when I was eighteen, my mother gave birth to not only one but two children conceived with men other than the lawfully-wedded old man. I realize that "Who's your daddy?" and the blatant disregard for the silly institution of marriage as a prerequisite for having babies is quite in vogue these days, but in the mid-1950s, it was somewhat frowned upon.

As it turns out, Garrett was Nick Valdez the Mexican cab driver's son, followed by me, Tommy the Irish bartender's daughter. While I eventually came to terms with the circumstances surrounding my birth (as if we have any control over it), which included lots of purging to a shrink and driving across the country looking for my father's only other child, Garrett had complete *paternus interruptus*. He knew nothing about his father, and frankly, I don't think my mother knew a hell of a lot about him either. I believe this left a gap in Garrett's life, a hole so deep that no amount of dope in the world could fill it. Try as he might.

But if I might offer a brief observation here, it never works, my friends. You cannot fill up that void with drugs, or booze, or sex, or gambling, or work, or self-loathing, or jogging or fucking health food or missionary trips to Africa. You just have to learn to live with the gaps and enjoy the breeziness of it. It is the only thing that works.

There were long intervals, though, where Garrett's life did work. He was clean and sober for years at a stretch, during which time he got married (three times), went to college, coached soccer, taught pre-school, was a concert promoter, drug counselor for teens, a musician, a painter, a sculptor, a brother, a son, a husband—oh, and a father. This was the job he felt he failed at the worst.

Garrett had experienced life way beyond his years already when he became a father at nineteen. Bear in mind he turned eighteen in 1969, just to provide some context. The whole world was in upheaval; no wonder people wanted to go to the fucking moon! He hitchhiked all over America, landing in jail in Shreveport, Louisiana and a drug detox clinic in San Diego after he'd overdosed and been left in the street to die; all this before he married in true shotgun fashion just a few months before the baby was born. I'm not saying Garrett and his bride didn't love each other, I know they did. And they tried to make it work. He got a job at a landscaping company. He was clean. They rented a cute little house in Fort Worth and the baby's middle name "Ashland" was the name of the street on which they lived. For a while, he was happy and productive. He loved the baby very much and our family loved them all, doing the best we could to surround them with that love and support. Within two years they split up. The wife traipsed off to California taking the baby with her. They were hippies, okay? That's what hippies do. There were paternal visits—many at first—but time and money and distance takes a toll. After a while, he felt irrelevant, the older the son got, the further the father. My mother never lost touch though. She loved Garrett's son with a passion reserved for the son of the prodigal son. The rest of us Whatley sibs did our best to keep the nephew in the fold and we're blessed because he allows us to. Garrett's son is a very fine man—a family man, with a beautiful and smart wife (thank God she shares our politics), and two darling little girls. He's amazing. They're amazing.

That's what Garrett wanted to tell his son. Except the message has never been delivered. He had been writing him a letter. He told me he'd started and stopped it a dozen times. Garrett wanted to explain that he felt his son was better off without him and that's why he stayed away. This is largely supposition on my part because I have never seen said letter, but Garrett had told me for years that this was how he felt. When his health was declining and he knew he was dying, he wanted to explain all this to his son. Garrett died before he finished the letter. After he passed away, his widow promised she'd give the unfinished letter to his son. She should. It doesn't belong to her. But she's dropped out of sight. Despite our repeated attempts to find her, she remains incommunicado. Of all my reasons for making this journey, finding her and retrieving that letter was among the most important. I tried to find her in New York. I failed.

"Garrett, can you hear me?"

I had found our old house on Locke Avenue. I was parked across the street. There were two huge bedrooms upstairs, linoleum on the floor, ancient case windows, closets big as caves. Garret and I were the BMOCs, the upperclassmen. We were thick as thieves, Garrett and me. This is the house where, by the time I was thirteen, I'd fall asleep to Jimi Hendrix, the Doors, Janis Joplin, Tim Buckley, and Jefferson Airplane, before they were a Starship, spinning their peace, love and revolution on the Fisher turntable and giant Advent speakers from the room next door. We had these hollow bi-fold doors separating the two rooms which he'd blocked with a ratty couch bought at the thrift store. He had managed to steal a giant Frostie Root Beer soda cap sign made out of tin off the side of a quickie mart somewhere. Damn thing must have been five feet in diameter, just like a real bottle cap, only massive, with the little Frostie man in the red stocking cap. Garrett hung it on the wall over his bed like a crucifix. Good thing he drove the nail into a stud; it could have fallen off and killed him. He drew comic strips with Marks-A-Lots all over the wall-papered walls, with curvy, bare-breasted hippie chicks, anti-war slogans and peace signs and Alice B. Toklas-looking characters smoking joints as fat as Cuban cigars. My mother tossed it off with, "I've always hated that wallpaper anyway," a veiled admission of the damage done, and not limited to her home decor. His wall art went unhindered, as did his descent into drug abuse. It started with keg parties with his high-school frat boys. They called them "Charity Clubs," but they were really thinly-veiled gangs in button-down-collared Oxford shirts with white peg-leg Levis, and custom-made paddles with holes drilled into them to give them more torque on some terrified pledge's trembling white ass. The hazings these little hoods endured and then inflicted on the next batch of suckers make the Marines look like pussies. From the time of their freshman year to junior year, the country-club boys migrated to the counterculture revolution, abandoning their bourgeoisie influence and opting for dropping acid in dirty crash pads with records lining the walls, telephone cable spools made into coffee tables, and mattresses shoved up against the corners, with kids fucking each others' brains out behind tapestries hung from the ceiling while their friends sat like stumps across the room in a haze, if not purple. Peace and love, man.

"Gary D.?" This was his nickname, for Garrett Daniel. For some reason, my mom called him Toady.

"Can you hear me, honey? I need to tell you something."

I'd gotten out of the car where I'd been sitting for ten minutes, simply staring at our old house. Rivulets of condensation ran down the 7-11 iced tea I'd bought on Clover Lane, soaking the napkin I'd wrapped around the plastic cup. I'd be shit out of luck if I took to weeping again, with nothing to wipe off the snot. I leaned against the driver's door, warm against my back, legs crossed at the ankle, the brim of my hat pulled low. I whispered.

"I tried, baby, I tried. But I just couldn't find her. I couldn't find her. I didn't get the letter." I did have to bite my lip by now. "I'm so sorry, honey. I was going to deliver it in person. But I wasn't able to. I'm so sorry."

I paused. It was wickedly hot; the heat from the street was like a floor furnace.

"And there's one other thing. I've been needing to say this to you for a long time. I'm sorry I didn't get out of bed that night. I was just scared. I know you told me to stay in bed, but I should have told you no. I saw the blood, but I was lazy. And I was a coward. I should have gotten up, turned on the light, called bullshit on you, Garrett. I am so, so sorry."

I was thirteen when Garrett slit his wrists. The coolest cat in Arlington Heights High School had gotten in over his head. I heard later there'd been a fight. He'd mouthed off to the wrong person. He and his friends got jumped but Garrett ran off. He left. At least that's the half-assed explanation I got after the fact. He was drunk, maybe stoned on downers. His friends called him a chicken shit. He cut his wrists.

Of all the nights I lay awake on the other side of the bi-fold door, listening to his music, listening to him tinker at his desk, scribbling on the wall, making out with his girlfriend, all the nights I'd lain awake in the old house, praying for him to breathe, on the night he needed me the most, I rolled over. I fucking rolled over.

But he was drunk. I could smell liquor on his breath when he came into my room. It was dark. He was silhouetted in the sliver of light, just a hair, spilling through the folding door. He was holding his arms up against his rib cage. Was that blood? I thought I could see blood. Or was it mud smeared on his white tee-shirt? He seemed unsteady, stumbly. He leaned over and patted me on the arm.

"Jeannie, don't come in my room, okay?"

It seemed odd, him coming into my bedroom in the middle of the pitch-black night, waking me up to tell me *not* to come in his room. Why would I? I have played this scene over and over again in my head so many times, I cannot even count. Did he come in and wake me up to tell me *not* to come in because he was betting I would? Or was this the act of a loving big brother, incoherent as he may have been, trying to spare me the sight of him lying in a pool of blood? I will never, ever know. And I never had a conversation with another human being about what happened that night, not him, not anybody. And everyone in my family who knows what happened is dead.

To this day, I don't know how my stepdad found him. By this time, my mom had moved on to her fourth husband, Frank Garza (there had been two, brief marriages, but no kids, before she married Jim Whatley). I don't know if Frank came up to Garrett's room and found him bleeding in the bed. I don't know if Garrett stumbled down the stairs. All I know is that when I woke up the next day, he was in the hospital. They were keeping him for observation, after sewing up his wrists. Everybody was fighting. My mother was telling Don that his little brother's suicide attempt "had been a prank! Garrett never really intended to kill himself," the anger and resentment in her voice disguising what was undoubtedly fear, sadness and guilt over what must have felt like her failure. "He's just trying to get attention!" she closed. Amazing, the power of denial.

There was a French door with a crystal doorknob at the foot of our stairway. It separated the stairs and hallway from the front rooms of the house. I considered it fancy. It was delicate, elegant. I never minded cleaning the small glass panes; sometimes it seemed like the only truly nice thing in our house. The afternoon sun, from the west-facing windows in the dining room, shone through the glass, casting a windowpane shadow on the bland beige carpet, where I sat at the base of the stairs at times, watching the prisms of light bounce off the crystal doorknob. It was a kaleidoscope of light and pastel shades that happened every single day, observed or not. It was my secret show, performed only when the door was closed, only when I could shut out the others. They were yelling in the living room. I quietly closed the glass door and crept back up our well-worn staircase. I knew the silent spot on every wooden step, the lighter area, where the varnish had been rubbed away. I sat on the side of my bed looking at the bloodstains inside the cracks of the bi-fold door. She hadn't noticed those drops, my mother, when she'd come in early that morning to try to clean away her pain. She had no idea of the measure of mine. I felt as if I had almost killed him with my negligence, my fear, my laziness, my willingness to go along with something that I knew in my gut was amiss. I felt as guilty as if I had cut him myself. I never told anybody that he'd come into my room that night. I never told a soul. I never spoke to Garrett about it until this day in the blazing heat, some forty years later.

"So, I don't want to lay a big guilt trip on you. I know you don't want me to feel bad about it. I was just a kid, I know that now. I was a scared, half-asleep kid. I've just needed to tell you that I'm sorry."

I was directing my words towards the upstairs bathroom window, as if some ghost of Garrett remained. It was the bathroom he'd sneak out of, climbing down the wrought-iron railing of the front porch. It was the bathroom where I'd sneak cigarettes, blowing the smoke out the window. The bathroom where I'd run and close the door when I heard Frank's leather soles on the stairs. He didn't know the silent spots. I got the jump on him when he came creeping up the stairs, looking for something that didn't belong to him. I'd try to put him off by being on the phone, on the john, or in the bath. I'd slather Noxzema on my face in what he must have thought was some kind of obsessive-compulsive pre-teen ritual, I did it so often. It's because he hated the smell. I hated his transgressions.

He'd wait, of course, until my mom was at work, the little brothers out in the yard, Garrett out making trouble. My brother Don was married and gone by then. No one to protect me, nobody there, except himself and a little girl trapped in an unwinnable game of duck and cover. To go into detail about the sex abuse is pointless and would only hurt my children. But for three years this went on, until there came a week when he left me alone. A week led to a month. A month led to several, and then several months led to never again. I don't know why he stopped. It's not like I was going to ask him. Maybe it's because the situation with Garrett had gotten so intolerable. Maybe he lost interest, or maybe he simply couldn't get up the stairs. His diabetic ankles had gotten so swollen and purple by then, he was having trouble getting around. I'm just glad he was able to get to my brother that night. Maybe, just maybe, that's why I gave him a pass for all those years. In some kind of illogical atonement for undeserved guilt, I gave him a pass on a shitload of guilt he had earned because saved my brother Garrett's life.

For decades I buried my stuff. I pushed it so far down, it disappeared like the vanishing point of a Texas highway on a far horizon. This is modus operandi for children who are sexually molested. You dummy up. You dummy up, out of fear that if you do talk, the world as you know it will come to an end. You dummy up, because your mother just can't take another heartache and the stepdad just might take off and your mom won't have a husband. There won't be any money. You won't have a house. Everybody will hate you, because, secretly, you think it's really your fault. And the biggest fear of all, what if you did tell and nobody believed you? Decades go by, you dummy up.

At his deathbed, I felt pity for him. He suffered a massive heart attack in the intensive care unit at the VA hospital and no manner of crash carts, or paddles, nor hot and cold running doctors could save him. It was quite sad. My mother, in a rare moment, looked completely lost. She had devoted twenty five years of her life to him. Who was I to mar her memory? I had seen Frank seconds before the heart attack. They'd scooted us outside his death tent because he'd become violently ill. It happens that way, you know. One minute he was attempting to eat a few morsels of a nasty-looking piece of institutional chicken and the next minute he was gone. At the moment before his heart attack, when I saw his exhausted attempt to nourish himself, to live for maybe one more day, I saw him as just another human being, not someone I hated. I saw him as just another flawed human being like the rest of us, a fellow traveler with his own stuff to sort out and precious little time to sort it. I felt an urge to say, "Hey, Frank, it's okay, you know, about all that stuff. I'm over it." Of course, I couldn't whisper in his ear, since my mom and I had been whisked away from his bedside when he started having his heart attack and we were now standing outside the death tent, holding on to each other like two stranded birds in the middle of a hailstorm on a parking lot. Finally somebody came and escorted us into the "breaking-the-bad-news-to-the family" room, and sure enough they did, a very short time later. I didn't get to grant him absolution, as if it was mine to give, so, I just gave him a nice sendoff at his funeral instead. This would eventually become my inheritance, being the family eulogist. But I didn't do it for Frank, his sordid little secrets notwithstanding. I did it because my mother asked me to. Fuck it. Done and done.

Except it wasn't. "What you suppress you must express," said the shrink to a still-struggling woman named Jean many years later. So one day, when I just couldn't stomach my mother waxing nostalgic about some delusional Brady-Bunch-infused memory of Frank and how he'd saved our family, I blew. In the parking lot of a the Jade Garden Chinese Restaurant in the St. Louis suburbs, where I had just treated my mom to lunch, as we were leaving to go pick up my kids from elementary school, she started in one of her fond recollections of fabulous Frank.

"He loved you kids so much. The notes in his journal are so sweet, so funny!"

"Yeah, I bet the part about him fondling me was a laugh a minute!" The eruption was caustically overdue. I screeched on the brakes, put the car in park, and in the shadow of the Sports Authority I spilled my guts. I told her that dear old Frank had made my life a living hell. I told her that every time she'd back out the driveway for work, I stood at the bathroom window and cried, praying to God she would turn around and come back: *Please come back and catch him! Come back and save me! Come back and take me out of this wretched trap.*

She was crestfallen hearing the truth decades later from her forty-three-year-old daughter who was soon to feel the sting of her own delusions about the man she'd married. I will never forget, though, the guilt I felt in inflicting this pain on her. Her memories would be marred forever. I could have gone to my grave with this juicy tidbit of history, but I got to the point where I couldn't hold down the bile of secrecy and anger another day. She hadn't known. My mother truly did not know. But here's where the drama turns to comedy. No sooner were the words out of my mouth (well, maybe there was a ten-second pause after she said, "Oh my God, I had no idea..."), after she looked defeated momentarily, staring out into the strip center parking lot at the Babies R Us sign, after she contemplated my thirty years of silence for about eight seconds, here's what she said:

"Well, the very same thing happened to me when I was a girl and it just set me for life!"

Jean Ellen Whatley

Talk about a three-pointer at the buzzer, dude. She went on to describe how her grandfather had molested her as a young girl in Oklahoma. It took the Dust Bowl and her dad being run out of town for bootlegging to get her away from her molester; mine just grew disinterested. My long-held torment trumped by hers, this was one mother-daughter bond I would have preferred to do without. *Why didn't she save me? Why didn't she protect me?* Why didn't she think twice about leaving me in the care of a man who'd left his wife and daughter to move in with a gringa with five kids? This became the $64,000-worth-of-therapy question, screaming from my pores. *After what she had gone through as a young girl, why hadn't she been more careful with me?*

I eventually figured it out myself: it fucks you up. All of her recklessness, piousness, her insecurities, her pronouncements, denouncements, hubris, husbands, lovers and adoring masses, of which there were many, could not fill the gap where her self-respect was supposed to be. She might have made it look good on the outside, but deep down, she was going around feelin' shabby.

I was feeling hot and thirsty, all these years later, standing outside our old house on Locke Street, panning my eyes across it just one more time. The rock exterior is kind of like flagstone, but instead of flat, the rocks are round, a sort of boulder bubble wrap on the lower level, wooden siding on the top. The long narrow drive, still dirt, never paved, the deep flower box, on the east side of the porch, bare now. We'd fill it with pansies in the spring, geraniums in the summer. I loved planting flowers with my mother. The wrought-iron railing where I used to sit and hope for a mere glimpse of Vance, the stunning blond paperboy whom I worshipped and adored, remains an unchanged pale pink. I looked intently at my crying perch, the bathroom window. But not that day, nor ever again, would I cry for my lost innocence. Those tears had all been shed. I possessed the clear-eyed objectivity of somebody who'd taken those memories and put them in a box in the closet of their mind. They're still there. No need for further inventory. I remembered.

I remember a little girl who used to live here. She is me and I am still standing. The heat radiates from the street through the soles of my shoes and I could melt like a blob of grease into the pavement and into the heat-packed dirt beneath it, so connected am I at this moment to the earth which holds me firm. I could die right now and be happy because I have had it all. I've had everything I need, already. The very best and some of the worst. But, it's not my time. It's not my time because I've got a brand-new, mighty fine, mother-fuckin' cowboy hat.

I got in my car. I thought of Frank. Old Franky Boy, he taught me how to drive a VW stick when I was fourteen years old. Yep, fourteen, so I could take my mom to work in the morning and babysit my little brothers for the rest of the day. It wasn't a bad summer gig, going into ninth grade. I cleaned the house, grocery shopped, carted the kids to the pool by day and hauled my hippie friends with Spanada wine and bags of dope down to Trinity Park by night. You begin to see how the roof tile didn't fall too far from the garret.

I slammed the car door, took off my hat and placed it in the seat next to me. I took a long draw from the straw in my watered-down iced tea. I put the car in first gear and peeled the fuck out.

8
My Cousin Benny

The Texas cousins, I had disregarded them for the longest time. Not out of disrespect or lack of affection. It was that blood thing.

When I learned that Jim Whatley was not my biological father, something clicked off in my head like de-certifying an election. The whole thing felt like fraud. Oh yeah, that's right, it *was* fraud. My mother and I had been watching something on TV. It dealt with blended families and I casually remarked how grateful I was that all four of my brothers were "real" brothers.

"Well, Sissy," my mother started hesitantly, "we need to talk about this."

Now, you tell me, in your whole life, have you ever had a happy conversation that started with, "We need to talk?"

Mom took me by the hand and led me into her bedroom where Frank was in bed, reading. At this point, Frank had only one of his legs amputated just below the knee because of the diabetes. His prosthesis, wearing a neatly laced black dress shoe and a sock held up by a Velcro patch on the shin, was propped against the closet door. A few years later, he would lose the other leg. Mom and I sat on the corner of the bed, Frank's one and a half legs outlined by the white cotton chenille spread. It left us more space to sit.

She launched into a full-on confession that I wasn't *really* a Whatley kid, that my father's name was Tommy and he lived in California. She went on, since she was on a roll, to tell me that Garrett wasn't really a Whatley kid either. She wasn't sure where Garrett's father lived anymore, but his name was Nick. Nick Valdez. Garrett, who was by now twenty one with a kid of his own, had also not been informed of this patriarchal cover-up.

Here's how the whole thing started. Way back when, Jim and Beverly had made a deal that if she'd come back to him, leave California, and cut all ties to her misspent youth and former lovers and move to Texas, Jim would raise Garrett and me as his own. We'd never have to know. Jim just made my mom promise to keep it quiet, especially about Tommy. Apparently Jim knew him, hung out at the bar where Tommy was the bartender. They all ran in the same circles: Folsom, Placerville, Lake Tahoe. Jim didn't want to hear Tommy's name ever again. Maybe he felt threatened, I don't know, but it must have driven him to distraction every time he looked at me, the round-faced, brown-eyed baby girl who was the spittin' image of her round-faced daddy with the dark brown eyes.

I didn't really dwell on this whole who's-your-daddy deal at all. It seemed inconsequential. At eighteen I was already engaged to the cute boy around the corner. In six months, I'd be marrying into a normal family, a respectable family, a big Irish Catholic family who didn't have this spicy assortment of trysts to trot out at the most inopportune times. I was fixin' to be bona fide. I don't recall being particularly sidelined by pining for my father. My mother had made it abundantly clear that "It never would have worked with Tommy," waving her hand like brushing crumbs off a table. I gave her the benefit of the doubt and wrote it off as just one more example of her reckless behavior, which in this case, resulted in my life. I remain eternally in her debt for choosing to give birth to me and keeping me around. This earned her a pretty big chit in my book.

As for the Whatley poser, it made me less guilty about not liking him. Maybe it was because of all the times he'd said he was going out to work in the garage and I'd see the lanky son-of-a-bitch skulking down the alley, hands crammed down in his pockets, heading for the beer joint on Montgomery Boulevard. Maybe it was because he drowned our baby hamsters. The mama had been eaten by a cat or died in hamster birth or something. He dropped the babies by the tail into a quart-size canning jar full of scalding water. I remember him saying it was more humane than letting those hairless pink pet rodents slowly starve to death. How I desperately wanted to nurse them with an eye dropper. Watching baby hamsters being drowned by the tail can turn you into a hater. Or maybe I disliked him because he made me sit at the table until I'd eaten all my peas. In fairness, he had warned me that my eyes were bigger than my stomach. When he went back to reading his paper, blocking his view of me and the peas, I tossed them under the table, one at a time. How in the hell did I know each pea was tapping him on his crisply starched Fort

Worth Steel and Machinery uniform pant leg? At least he didn't whip me. He just made me get down under the table and pick up all the peas. I did not have to eat them; by this time, he was laughing in spite of himself.

All I know is, when I was nine and he and my mom split up, I was happy. I thought the Mexican bearing peppermint ice cream from the Carnation Ice Cream Shoppe, who actually took us on vacations and horseback riding and out for hamburgers was going to be a lot better than that lazy, lying, mean drunk who would rush home from the bar just before my mom got home from work. Oh, the silly ideas kids get in their heads.

And young women too. I didn't do it consciously. But somehow, knowing the truth about from whence I came, in my mind invalidated my entire Texas experience, which was a pretty significant chunk of development, the tender years of three to fifteen. How quickly I was willing to discard it, after I found out the whole thing had been predicated on a lie. It was like stepping out of a dirty pair of shorts. It's not that I held anything against my Texas kin. I felt like an outsider, like I didn't really belong anymore and somehow they were all complicit in the deceit. I thought I was, in fact, a tad bit fancy; *my* daddy was from California, I had no blood ties to that miserable, dry, scorpion-infested, Godforsaken patch of hardscrabble Texas land after all. I was a *Californian!* That sounded much more impressive. Years became decades as I moved all over the country; Texas and those memories grew more and more distant. I lost touch. I lost them. How fortunate, that they've welcomed me back.

Calling those long-lost cousins, however was even more nerve-wracking than calling the Carolina neighbors. I was reaching way, way back into the vault on this call. There was always a slight catch in my voice, a tightness in my stomach, when I'd tap the number, like ringing up a recalcitrant lover. You're always hoping for voicemail so you can leave a breezy message and hang up. Marker laid. But calling someone with whom I had not spoken in more than forty years, saying I'd be coming through town in a day or two and hey, "Could I spend the night?" required me to brave up. Rejection is a gut-twister. There was always the chance they'd say, "We have plans for the rest of our lives" or "Thanks anyway." Time and again, just the opposite occurred— Chicago, Philadelphia, New York City, Washington D.C, Culpeper, Winston-Salem, Atlanta, Fort Worth, and now it was Graford, Texas in the heart of Palo Pinto County, sixty miles west-northwest of Fort Worth, and it was my cousin Benny on the phone.

"I'm traveling with a big dog," I offered apologetically.

"Come on! We've got dogs!" Benny and his wife Sue, whom I'd never met, had me on speakerphone. Yes, even in tiny west Texas towns, technology rules. "Come on! One more dog isn't gonna bother us."

I drove due west out of Fort Worth feeling even more excited than I'd been about all my other visits thus far. For decades, I had longed to come home to this corner of Texas. In some ways, my rural Texas roots ran deeper than my Fort Worth memories. Even though I was amped up about getting to Albuquerque and seeing San Francisco again, I had yearned to lay my eyes on the horizon of my formative landscape. Why had I been so foolishly dismissive? This chunk of north central Texas is where I'd gardened with my Grandma, who always wore a bonnet, reminding me that no self-respecting white girl would ever allow herself to get a tan. To her, being tanned was degrading, made you look like a field hand. This is where we did laundry on the designated laundry day— Lord knows it took a full day, what with the wringer washer and hanging everything out on the line. How do you describe the scent of cotton sheets dried by the sun? This is where, on grocery day, we walked the half-mile to Morrow's General store, where the scent of decades-old, blood-soaked butcher-block counters, chewing tobacco and fresh bolts of fabric hit your nose before your eyes had adjusted from the raging sun to the cool darkness of wood-floor general store. They had everything at Morrow's. You could buy piece goods, dress patterns, fish bait, bullets and sides of beef. My little brothers and I lobbied for cap guns or coloring books from the toy aisle. The sun coated the backs of our legs on the way into town and beat our sweaty brows on the way back home, but we were contented commuters, lugging back the loot, because more often than not there was a Big Hunk candy bar or a strawberry Nehi tucked inside. This is where I'd sit out on my Grandma's porch at night, the constant chorus of insects in the trees interrupted every so often by the sound and headlights of an approaching car on the two-lane highway which passed in front of her house. I could see car lights from more than a mile away, closer, closer, closer, until they'd throw their beams across the yard, ripping through the darkened windows of the tiny frame house like searchlights, then gone, the thin red tail lights like devil eyes trailing farther and farther away until they vanished like a cursor on a black screen. I used to wonder about the people inside those passing cars on a country highway late at night. Who knew forty years later it would be me?

It was here, on my aunt's and uncle's little farm outside of town that I'd gotten my first taste of solitary fulfillment, swaying in the saddle on the back of a fly-flickin' Palomino pony, slowly plodding across a wide-open pasture on a blazing summer afternoon. I had saddled up the horse myself, something I normally depended on my scrappy, freckle-faced cousin Carol Jean or my Uncle Norman to do. My uncle delighted in putting us city kids up in the saddle and then whompin' the horse on the ass to make it take off with a jolt. On this particular day, I must have been ten or eleven, there was nobody else around, so I saddled him up myself. Blanket, then saddle, buckled it up, foot in the stirrup and up I went, only I hadn't cinched the saddle tightly enough and the whole damn saddle slid off sideways, dumping me on my ass, my foot stuck in the stirrup. I was halfway under the damn horse, one foot up in the air and I was praying to God he wouldn't step on me. This is a precarious situation for the equestrian novice. I'm lucky the horse didn't take off dragging me underneath him. I let go of the reins to extract my foot and I quickly crawled out from under the horse with the sideways saddle. I got back up, grabbed the reins, righted the saddle, tightened the strap and got back up the horse again. I could just hear him saying, sounding like Mr. Ed, "You idiot. I'm gonna throw you off so fast it's gonna make your head spin or split wide open once I bounce you off a rock." I smugly rode out of the corral, away from the barn, past shouting distance from the kitchen window, my Aunt Opal an ever-present sentinel.

"Jeannie, don't go too far," she hollered.

Horses are ornery. They're unpredictable. Likely to take off in a gallop at any given moment, run you under a tree limb, or stop short on the trail, hook a U-turn and head back to the barn. A horse will get the upper hand with you in a hurry. They absolutely sense fear, it's undeniable, especially when you are so nervous you're sucking air so hard it's lifting the saddle up off the horse's back. A person needs to learn to relax in the saddle, lean into the rhythm of the horse. The parallels to life in general are too self-evident.

I rode out far beyond the first cow tank, way beyond the second one, the deeper tank that we swam in, where the summer before I'd uncovered a nest of water moccasins, like snake spaghetti, all coiled up under some homemade water wings Aunt Opal had made out of giant Tang jars covered in denim scraps from old blue jeans. She'd sew a couple of the sealed jars together and the little kids would use them for floaties, except the snakes that day were using them for shelter. I have never run so fast in my entire life. I never looked back until I bolted up the back stairs, into the kitchen and the safety of my Aunt Opal's arms. She calmly remarked, "Gotta watch out for those snakes, Jeannie."

Opal had been living with pestilence of biblical proportions—grasshoppers, scorpions, snakes and coyotes—for so long that chopping the head off a water moccasin was like swatting a fly. Gotta love West Texas.

Actually, I do. At least my memories of it. That summer day from long ago, was the only solitary horseback ride I have ever taken in my life. I rode past earshot of the porch, past the place where the cattle clustered under the miserly shade of mesquite trees, beyond any semblance of a beaten path, where the terrain got more rocky, less flat, covered in brush as high as my knees. I couldn't detect any kind of trail in front of me, couldn't see the house behind me, no barn, no utility poles or well house and nary a drop of water out here. Jagged hills lay ahead of me, topped by black, skeletal remains of trees ravaged by wildfires, lined up on the ridge like a Mohawk haircut on a mountain. Leftover funeral pyres, they served as silent, stark witnesses to the deathly speed of a summer storm. The sun was going down. The whole damn situation was fraught with danger, as foolish as swimming in a lake at night by yourself. But I was strangely calm. It was so quiet. No noise, no airplanes, no hum from transformers, no TVs, no radio, no incessant jabber, just the comforting sound of steady hooves on the hard-packed red dirt, the swish and sometimes sting of a horses' tail that flicked me on the arm as he flicked flies off his back. They were bitin' bastards too, I'll tell you. Here I was a little girl, brown as a bun, with an endless sky, a radiant sun and a sturdy, if not reluctant mount whose equine brain was undoubtedly calculating his revenge. We rode a bit farther. I remember the sky, how vast, and me so small beneath it. It was the first time I ever contemplated my relative position in the universe, my insignificance, the transitory nature of our time here on earth. I was a mere speck, a lone traveler on a continuum of time, momentarily dependent upon the benevolence of another creature, but completely alone and I was fine. We stopped. I just sat there for a minute, my eyes scanning the landscape, the brush vibrating with the cyclical call and repeat of locusts, the late afternoon sun so powerful you'd swear you could hear the sunrays drilling like red-hot augers into the earth. I sat. Observation takes time. It takes time to watch clouds pull their shadows over an open field. It takes time to follow the flight of a hawk, as you contemplate which creature will become the hawk's supper that night, gone missing from their own den come sundown.

It was about to be me. My horse stomped to shake off a fly, bringing me back to the need to get us home. I pulled the rein to the left to turn him with that familiar clicking sound that somebody in India or China came up with in

4000 B.C. or thereabouts. He took that as a sign we were headed to the barn and that old plug horse took off like the fucking wind. Scared the piss out of me. All I could do was lean forward and ride that baby home. I've thought about this a lot since then. It was a larger lesson than I realized at the time.

It is unfortunate that, so often, our children are not afforded these experiences. As each generation gets farther away from the land, there are fewer opportunities for them to appreciate it, with all its torment and wonder. Even though all of us Fort Worth Whatleys thought we were somehow superior because we lived in the city, I believe each of us held our visits to the country quite dear. This was the place I'd wanted to bring my brother Don. I regret to this day that we didn't get to make that trip. As the oldest, Don had spent far more time out in the country than I had, fishing, riding horses, tending to the livestock, shooting guns and running away from grasshoppers. Benny remembered.

"There used to be a hog pen over in that corner," Benny said as he and I were out walking the property after I arrived. "But right here," he said, gesturing to scorched earth, "right here was this grassy area, probably the only place we didn't have cows, and Don and I used to play football out here." He waved his arm over the area he was referring to, as if to paint what he saw in his mind's eye on top of the brittle reality of never again. "I woke up thinking about that this morning." His voice trailed off to that empty place you go when words fail. Then Benny chuckled and looked at me with blue eyes just like his mama's. "Your poor brother was scared to death of grasshoppers. He would run like his pants were on fire when one of 'em landed on him. We kinda made that happen from time to time."

What is it with Texas boys and their proclivity for tossing grasshoppers on sissy California kids like me and my big bro? Through some unforgivable oversight, nobody in our family had notified the Graford cousins about Don's passing. I believe Benny was hurt to learn about Don's death almost a year after the fact. Sobering too, since Benny and Don were the same age: first cousins, blood.

I would learn in the best way possible that blood wouldn't have made my bond any tighter to this place or these people. After we'd been talking for hours and I brought it up, Benny said he'd heard talk when he was a kid that *Jeannie don't really belong to James,* but that minor biological detail must have dissipated as fast as spittin' rain, because to them it didn't matter. I was family. Benny's mother, my Aunt Opal, and his Granny (whom the Fort

Worth Whatleys called Grandma,) were two of the most influential women in my life, aside from my sweet mother. They sewed dresses for me, they taught me to cook, they braided my hair. We went to their country church where the entire congregation got their picture taken every spring on the front steps. We gardened, we canned, we watched wrestling. My grandmother loved her some wrastlin'.

We had a great visit. A gap of forty years can close pretty quickly with the simple sound of someone's voice or with an affirmative nod about a shared memory, or loved one, or time and place on the planet, coveted by a precious few. Benny's wife Sue was gracious, funny, cute, smart, hip—as much a family historian by marriage as Benny was by birth.

And I got to see 'em all, all my Texas cousins. I had stopped by Mineral Wells on my way out to Graford to visit with Benny's older brother, Harold, who let Libby stay in the cool air-conditioned comfort of his house while he took me out to lunch. Restaurant meals, inside, were a rare treat traveling with a dog. And it was as good a Texas-style lunch as I can ever recall—chicken-fried steak, cream gravy, fried okra, pinto beans and sweet tea. Yep, that's what I'm talkin' about. We drove by the old Baker Hotel in Mineral Wells, an amazing testament to grand old hotels of days gone by. It opened in 1929 and was the first skyscraper outside of Dallas or Fort Worth or Houston. Mineral Wells had a reputation for its nearby—you guessed it—mineral wells and the city got a reputation as a spa destination before spas were located in strip malls. Big stars stayed here like Glenn Miller, Clark Gable, Judy Garland. The locals will tell you with some certainty that Bonnie and Clyde engaged in a romp or two in one of the luxurious suites on the fourteenth floor.

However, Harold's prize steer only made it to the lobby. He checked in and then, uh, checked out. As we were driving by, after I'd asked cousin Harold to stop so I could take some pictures of the Baker Hotel, he shared with me that in 1951 he'd won a blue ribbon for the Grand Champion Steer. The owner of the Baker Hotel took a fancy to it. He bought Harold's steer for $1,500 and brought the calf up in the elevator and put him on display in the lobby for all the rich women and silly out-of-towners to fawn over, until it came such time to slaughter the calf and feature beef tenderloin on the menu. To this day, Harold has the eight-by-ten glossy of himself and his prize-winning steer hanging on the wall of his guest room. That would never work for me, as I'd be bawling every time I looked at it. But this is, after all, Texas.

I left Mineral Wells with that savory story under my belt and as full as a tick as I drove another fifteen miles to Graford. After Benny and Sue and I whipped through dozens of old stories and looked at pictures, we rode into town where my grandmother's house no longer stands but Morrow's grocery still does and believe it or not, it hasn't changed that much. It sits right next door to the world-famous Steak Shed. There's a sign that hangs out front: "Voted Best Steak House in Texas." I'd love to see the data on that.

Benny's sister Shirley came right over the minute she got off work as a Walmart greeter. Lest we be so hasty to criticize their labor practices, which I so often do, I have to temper what I say now because I have family who works at Walmart.

"Jeannie! I have thought of you so many times!" Shirley was so sweet I honestly wanted to cry. "I am so blessed to see you," she said with her immediately familiar, high-pitched voice, the dark brown hair that I remembered, now white. She threw her arms around me to hug my neck. That's what you say in Texas, "Come here and let me hug your neck."

Folks also say you can't go home again. Not true. Sitting there, in the log cabin home that Benny and Sue built by themselves, which reminded me of a western American lodge (think Fred Harvey) or a lodge in West Africa, so eclectic were the accoutrements, I felt like I had grabbed a handful of sacred dirt and rubbed it into my pores like Borax. This was part of me. They were part of me. We had shared the same grandmother. We'd eaten at the same table. We'd ridden the same horses and probably run from the same mean old snake. Their mother was the most beloved aunt of my entire life. We *were* blood.

At dawn, I lay on my belly and looked out the window from my upstairs room. I could see for miles. The magic was still there for me. Now, most people would look out this window and tell me I was certifiably crazy. It's pretty damn desolate. But for me, it was a healing view. I'd filled up a hole inside of me as big as Texas, patched up a longing to go back, to make it right with my kin.

"Let's go before it gets too hot!" Sue hollered up the stairs for me to get a move on for our scheduled tour of the blow hole.

Now, this had become local folklore, the blow hole, because several years prior there had been a natural gas explosion which blew the ever-living daylights out of a sizable chunk of land right there on Uncle Norman and Aunt Opal's farm. It was more like an earthquake: it split open the ground, upending massive rocks, setting them back down again like a haystack of mammoth slabs of rock. My Uncle Norman became somewhat of a local celebrity with all his news appearances.

Benny, Sue, four dogs and I walked past the cow tanks I'd remembered as a kid, dry as a bone now. It looked like that famous Georgia O'Keefe painting of the cracked, dry desert with the cow skull. Benny and Sue didn't find any cars or missing persons though, when their water dried up last summer, unlike a few other Texans who made some grisly discoveries about what those lakes had been hiding all those years. In one case there was a car with a suicide driver still strapped in her seatbelt. Texas was in the midst of the most severe drought in recorded history. More than three million acres were burnt up by 19,000 recorded fires inside of five months. From where we stood at the site of blow hole, Benny and Sue could point to places on a nearby ridge where fires had licked a little too close for comfort too many times, the fiendish wind deciding where to skip and what to singe. Fire was an ever-present threat last year, much more dangerous than snakes, scorpions, coyotes or mules. Mules, however, posed Libby's greatest threat.

"Come on, Libby! Get away from there!" Sue shooed Libby away when she went nuts barking and chasing a pair of donkeys we came across during our walk. "Don't let her get up behind them. They'll kick her in the head," Sue warned with a voice of wisdom that comes from having dogs in the country who go missing or turn up lame, chewed up by mountain lions or coyotes, or kicked senseless by some mule.

We walked through the ghost of my Aunt Opal and Uncle Norman's house, the house where Benny grew up. It's in bad shape, been empty for years. Gotta be sad, tearing it down, not to mention the cost of the asbestos removal. I suppose that's why you see so many abandoned houses and barns out in the country. It's not like there's some real estate developer licking his chops to get a hold of that particular parcel of land. And the cost to haul off the rubble? No wonder they just stand, and stand, and stand, until they just can't stand any longer. I took dozens of photos of ghost structures last summer.

And living, verdant, vibrant ones. I snapped a few pictures of Benny and Sue's incredible, hand-crafted home. Sue packed me a lunch. I patted their dogs and Libby, as always, jumped up enthusiastically into the back seat. Eight weeks, twenty one states, forty nine major metropolitan areas and my dog jumped right in every time I said, "Let's go." Amazing, isn't it?

I waved goodbye; they stood and watched as I drove down the gravel road toward the highway. It was better than I'd expected, honestly, the whole thing. I recorded some video of the old house, wiped my tears, said goodbye to my

Jean Ellen Whatley

Gram and my Aunt Opal, put on my cowboy hat and pulled out on to the two-lane, my soul expanded as far and as wide as the parched countryside. I was grateful. I felt peaceful. It was hotter than hell. I'd decided to take what I thought would be a shortcut to Amarillo, but would discover quite later that I'd taken a wrong turn on one of those lonely country highways and in fact was headed in the wrong direction. This was the only time in 8,600 miles that I took a wrong turn. Not bad, eh? But I'd been distracted. I had been distracted when I was supposed to turn onto another highway, preoccupied by all the thoughts and memories and images in my mind, the pictures Benny and I had pored over, the stories I'd never heard. It was 108-degrees, I was out on a deserted (well, there was an occasional cow) highway with no cell service and less than one gallon of water in my car, windows rolled down to save wear and tear on the engine and on my gas mileage, smiling like I didn't have good sense, when all of a sudden, I spotted this sign.

"Jean."

Swear to God, there's a green highway sign, "Jean" with an arrow to the right. "Jean," as in Jean, Texas. I even have photos to back this up. But wait; it gets better.

I slowed down a bit, thinking I ought to turn around and take a picture because it's just too damn funny, you know: "Jean" out in the middle of nowhere. But before I could make a decision to hook a U-turn, I came across another sign, "Kindley Park." Now, one might pronounce it with a short "i" like "*kend*-lee" Park, but I interpreted it as a direct command.

"Jean, kindly park."

Okey-doke. I hadn't come this far to ignore such obvious directives. I pulled over at Kindley Park, a nice, shaded roadside park with concrete picnic benches and blessed cottonwood trees, which always signals water close by. Lib and I got out. She sniffed around for food crumbs, I got us both some water and I hopped up on one of the tables.

And here's what I was thinking about. It was as plain as day. God, and probably my Grandmother Edna Whatley Ferguson and my aunt, Opal Whatley Brown, were all kind of on my back. They were urging me to rethink a few things. I had already come around to looking at my country cousins in a whole new light, to embrace again what I'd foolishly left behind, not out of malice, but simple misunderstanding—of myself. And then it occurred to me that perhaps I'd misunderstood Jim Whatley. I had never, for a single minute of my life, cut that poor man a break. When Jim and my mom divorced when

134

I was nine, I was simply relieved. Even though the next love of *her* life certainly regarded me in inappropriate manner, it did not make me look back on the Whatley dad with any nostalgia.

Being with my cousins, who spoke affectionately about their Uncle James, changed things. To them, he was the World War II veteran, Pearl Harbor survivor, the man who came back from the Marine Corps with a headstrong wife and a passel of kids to follow. Uncle James was the one who, after he divorced Beverly the tempest, traveled back and forth to Vietnam as a helicopter mechanic. He was an adventurer, accomplished. Sitting up late at night, looking at photos and letters he'd sent from overseas, hearing my cousins' fond recollections of Uncle James, took the hard edge off of *me*. *They* had loved him. Uncle James, to them, was a good man who died far too young. He wasn't even sixty when the cancer got him.

I had been indifferent to the whole Jim Whatley saga. Learning that I was, indeed, not his daughter was like inheriting a "Get Out of Jail Free" card from him. Truthfully, though, I'd been trapped, imprisoned in a very narrow cell of inconsideration. When kids are in the middle of a divorce, and especially girls, I think they tend to side with their mamas. My mother made a habit out of belittling Jim and he made a habit out of picking on Garrett. Perhaps it's because I was a girl, but I was rarely the target of Jim's pent-up anger. Plus, Garrett was a hellion, but he and I were thick as thieves and anybody who was mean to my brother was an enemy of mine. I hated Jim for being mean to Garrett, but, as I have learned over time, it's easy to demonize people, harder to discern certain truths. Truth is, my mother couldn't have said a kind word about Jim Whatley if her life depended on it. She did, however, have a rejoinder, which she carried around like a pistol on her hip, ready to shoot down any criticism of her hateful words or deeds, reckless or shameful behavior: "I did the best I could with the tools I had to work with."

I came to appreciate, over time, that she did indeed do pretty well, considering the circumstances, and to this day I give her undeserved credit, which some might label as Stockholm Syndrome. But this man, Jim, he had a few tall orders of his own. He took Garrett and me in, gave us his name and tried to make it work with the hellcat who was my mother. I had never given enough thought to what it must have been like for him to stick with her, with two kids who weren't even his. I can't imagine what my grandmother and Aunt Opal had to say about that!

He had his faults. Don't we all? He could be mean sometimes, he drank too much and he could be shiftless. "Ain't no 'count"—that's what my grandmother would say about the ne'er-do-wells who hung out and shot pool at the beer joints in Graford, with a notable exception if one of those ne'er-do-wells was her precious boy James. That said, I owed it to my Grandma to think it over.

"Jean, kindly park"

"Reconsider."

It was as if he himself were speaking to me in a quiet voice from a long time ago. Sometimes in life we are afforded opportunities to make amends, to evolve, to flip a nugget of hardness over in our minds, to transcend what we'd accepted as fact.

I remember a pair of maroon patent-leather shoes with black grosgrain ribbons in a tight, rippled bow on the toe. I wanted those shoes more than life itself when I saw them at Stripling's Department Store. When I tried them on and they actually fit and he paid sixty dollars for them, I thought I was royalty. Royalty! I had never had shoes so fancy.

Jim had taken me and my little brothers shopping when he was home on leave from Vietnam. I think I was twelve, he and my mother divorced for a few years already.

"What do the kids need?" he'd asked her when he came to pick us up, his voice could hardly disguise his lingering affection.

It wasn't mutual however. Her love for Jim had been irretrievably lost because of one drunken fight too many. It happened just minutes after she'd stepped off a plane at Love Field in Dallas, returning from her brother's funeral in California. The similarities in the patterns of events in her life and mine, in hindsight, are striking—one cataclysmic event on the heels of another. It wasn't until many years later, dealing with the loss of my two brothers, that I began to understand the magnitude of hers.

My mother's brother Dawes died in a fiery plane crash in the Nevada desert in November of 1963 when his A4 Skyhawk crashed into the mountains near Las Vegas. It was stormy. He was on a low-level navigational training flight as a Marine Corps reserve pilot. He was only eleven months younger than my mother, her only sibling. The Associated Press report about the plane crash, with the standard tag, "the name of the victim is being withheld pending notification of next of kin," crossed the teletype wire while my mom was at work at the flight service station. An hour later, my grandmother's trembling words, "We've lost our Dawes, Beverly. We've lost our Dawes," confirmed what my mother had felt in her gut from the beginning: that the downed pilot was her baby brother. My Uncle Dawes was a decorated World War II and Korean War veteran. He retired as a Marine Corps Major, came home, went to law school and became the Assistant District Attorney in El Dorado County, California. Dawes was the "good" kid, the show pony of the family, with a pretty wife, two cute kids and a picture perfect life in Lake Tahoe. My mother would tell me in later years that the last time she spoke to Dawes, he was down. He'd confided in his sister that he was disillusioned with his work and there was stress at home. "He sounded so tired," she said. A few days later his plane crashed into the side of a mountain.

When mom got back to Fort Worth after the funeral, Jim picked her up at the airport. He was drunk, spoiling for a fight. He accused her of sneaking around to see Tommy while she was in California. It's 1963, she has five kids, my youngest brother was just nine months old and she told Jim to get the hell out. That was it. They were finished.

Three years later, it's a visitation Saturday. Jim's Chrysler Imperial was idling in the driveway and he's come to take us kids shopping. Jim reached over and touched my mother's earring, a cluster of transparent blue glass beads with a matching necklace, a gift from her new man, Frank.

"Pretty," Jim said. "When did you pierce your ears?"

My mom stepped back. "The boys need pants; Jean needs shoes." She was sticking to the matter at hand, school clothes, but there was the faint strand of something that was beginning to sound like forgiveness.

"Jean, kindly park."

If that wasn't a message from the universe, well then, I hope to kiss a pig. That's another Texas saying. As I was sitting on top of that cement picnic table, Libby by now sniffed out, sacked out in the dirt, and time's a wastin' 'cause I need to figure out where in the hell I am and make it to Amarillo by dark. I dispatched my reply:

"I'm sorry I've been so hard on you. Thanks for not whippin' my butt for throwing those peas under the table. Thank you for three out of my four brothers and for giving Garrett and me your name. I know you did the best you could with the tools you had to work with. I hope you're in a good place. I really liked Texas after all; thanks for bringing me here."

"Oh, and thanks again for those shoes, Dad."

9

The Zen of Washing Your Panties in the Sink

Vending machines will never be the same for me. Not that I partook of their contents very often; in fact, I engaged in a somewhat smug avoidance of them throughout the road trip, preferring to refill my gallon water jug at grocery stores for a quarter and stopping at roadside stands for snacks. I had a continual craving for fresh peaches. As it was the height of summer, one would think there would be a lot of produce stands, right? I saw six—as in, *six* in 8,600 miles. No wonder we're all so damn fat.

The mere site of vending machines now immediately takes me back to last summer and my ritualistic trek to the well-appointed linoleum-floored breezeway next to the motel check-in desk, with the baritone drone of the condenser keeping the ice machine grinding and plopping in harmony with the annoying buzz of the fluorescent lights that kept the tantalizing midnight-snack smorgasbord of Chili Cheese Fritos and HoHos illuminated, eager as they were to leap to their certain death by consumption, from their corkscrew platforms for a mere 75-cents, fulfilling their destiny to wrap around your heart. Literally. For all the time I stood there waiting for a batch of ice to drop, I would have gladly bought something from one of the 9,000 vending machines I saw if some route driver had shown one grain of independent thinking and stocked even one of them with a Zagnut bar. I ask you, what the hell *is* a Zagnut bar?

As much as vending machines scratch the trip track in my memory, those green signs along the freeway with the gas stations, restaurants and hotel icons do even more. From St. Louis to New York all the way to San Francisco and back again, I wonder how many of those green signs Libby and I drove by?

I became quite adept at spotting and ruling out certain brands from a quarter-mile away, night or day. To whit, I did not consume a single morsel at any Burger King, Taco Bell, Long John *"Slivers"* or Pizza Hut. I did however partake of Starbucks, which incidentally, must have a bunch of highly caffeinated baristas giving blow jobs to state highway commissioners from Illinois to North Carolina. Starbucks has somehow secured its own self-standing highway signs, separate from all the other roadside restaurants that have been relegated to also-rans, their small, brand icons batched together on the signs that come right *after* Starbucks, which crop up, big and bold on their very own signs, whetting the caffeine-deprived appetites of fatigued Jersey turnpike drivers like me. And guess what? It worked. As much as I hate to pay for overpriced consumer gaga, monopoly coffee, it was really nice to get some decent coffee on the road.

Coffee is to drivers like gasoline is to engines, right? The other place I got fueled up was at McDonald's. Yeah, this trip paved the way for some serious bonding with my old buddy, Mickey D's. It was cheap. For three dollars I could get myself a cheeseburger, an iced coffee and a plain burger for Libby. It was quick, inexpensive and reliable. Libby liked those stops in particular. I am a self-described fast-food hater, McDonald's probably chief among them, but it did represent practicality, thrift, and on some level, solidarity.

It demonstrated solidarity with the Blackshoes of whom I am a part, not to be confused with the Blackfoot, which is an Indian tribe. The Blackshoes are a tribe in their own right, the ceremonial dress characterized by apron strings, blue shirts, skin-suffocating polyester, zip-up smocks and name tags pinned with flair. Their members far outnumber the entire Indian Nation and indeed count many Native Americans among their ranks, along with a disproportionately high number of African-Americans and Latinos, relative to the overall ethnic composition of our country.

In Oxford, Alabama which was checking in at a steamy 97-degrees, 84-percent humidity, but no rain on the day Libby and I breezed through town, I saw a lanky teenage boy sitting on the bumper of his car in the parking lot of a McDonalds where I had just driven through to get an iced coffee and a cheeseburger. He was changing his shoes. I'd pulled over to the waiting slot, the place where people idle-mindedly idle their cars while they wait for a fresh batch of fries, to blow on Libby's plain burger to cool it off. She was already a *hot* dog. It struck me how pleasantly resolute this young man was about taking off his street shoes to put on the black ones. A co-worker on shift change came out with a large soda and a purse strung over her shoulder; she was done for the day. "Hey Jason," she smiled and stopped by to invite him to a party later, while he was lacing up his shoes. It made me miss my Blackshoes back home, who trudge off, night after night, to wait tables for a living to get through college. There have been times when the mere site of Lauren's or Sean's pitiful-looking, curled-up, sauce-splattered non-skid black shoes, invariably left in the middle of the room, would make my eyes well with tears, not so much from sadness but more as an acknowledgement of what they have inherited. I know about the second shift; after you've gone to school all day, to come home, lace up those crappy shoes, put on your uniform and your happy face to wait on a whole 'nother shift full of gripy people whom you couldn't make happy if you gave them multiple orgasms in every bite. I know. I did it for years, except I wore a white peasant blouse and tiered, bright-red fiesta skirt with white shoes, waiting tables to get through school. It ruined my back. At eighteen I ruptured a disc and honestly, it's never been the same since. Every single day on the road, I crawled out of the cheap motel beds and got down on my knees for yoga and prayer. I prayed that I wouldn't pull up to some gas station, or restaurant, or motel, or picnic spot, and literally not be able to get out of the car. It is that bad. The day before I left St. Louis, my chiropractor/acupuncturist/healer dude actually came in on the Fourth of July to give me one more treatment before I hit the road, loading me up with joint medicine (joints would have probably worked fine, too) and Chinese poultices to slap on my back, just in case the pain was immobilizing.

I didn't see this future pain back when I was eighteen, hoisting giant silver trays onto my skinny shoulder, loaded with too many enchilada-taco combo plates in a tourist trap Mexican restaurant in Old Town Albuquerque. Tableful after tableful of rich, retiring (and I don't mean shy), mouthy New Yorkers were being imported by the dye-haired busloads by mega-developers hoping to sell them pre-fab homes in Rio Rancho, a sunbelt oasis if ever there was one, perched on the sandy, waterless mesas on the western outskirts of Albuquerque. Wiki "urban sprawl" and Rio Rancho's picture is there. Although now, Rio Rancho is affectionately called Little Queens. The restaurant where I was waiting on these east coast migrants, La Placita, was a destination in itself, a restored adobe hacienda dating back to 1764. Serving these cheapskates, "*chicken, fish or Mexican combination plate?*" and multitudes of other tightwads, is how I made my living, a good one, one 10-percent tip at a time. It was a volume proposition.

I thought about the working class every single day I was on the road; how could I not? They were the ones who dug the ditches, laid the track, blasted the tunnels, risked their lives and sometimes lost them to build the bridges and the dams, to cut switchback roads through perilous mountains for folks like me to glide along and take in the view. The working class: they were the cashiers at the gas station, the drive-through, the toll booth, the custodians at the rest areas, the flagmen on the highway crew, the front desk clerk. They are the aching backbone of our country and yet they are so often derided, or at the misdemeanor level of offense, simply disregarded.

I saw them, though. I *saw* them. I talked to them and they were my friends. There were days when the only human contact, the only other person I would speak to or interact with all day long, would be the waitress at the café, or the desk clerk at the motel, waiting for me like an angel in the white light of the lobby, a beacon leading to my bed. Sometimes there'd be other travelers standing in line at the counter like me, but not *like* me. Most of them were simply trying to get from point A to point B, whereas I was going from point A to Z. The distinction is not lost on me. I fully acknowledge that, more than likely, none of the other folks who were checking in at bargain motels at ten o'clock at night were writers on a quest for reclamation, crowd-funded as they rolled. Even though for the first leg of the trip, it was entirely possible that I could have ended up needing to jump behind the counter at some motel or café and work for a while, renting one of those rooms in the back of the motel with weekly rates just to get me home. God only knows what would have happened if my back had gone out. For the second half of the trip, I was already worried about how the hell I would make a living once I got back home. I related to huddling masses yearning just to pee, standing in the lobby there with me, holding their Styrofoam suppers, just waiting for the golden key, or plastic keycard to give them a place to lay their heads.

When I was traveling on the corporate dime and had the privilege of being put up in such austere hotels such as The W in Manhattan, Trump Tower in Chicago, the Fontainebleau in Miami or the Tivoli Lodge in Vail, the people seemed a lot less friendly. Have you ever noticed how those who appear to have the most appear to have the least to give? It's not like I was asking one of them to drop a diamond or fork over a Rolex. I'm just talking about a glance: you know, eye contact, an acknowledgment that there's another living, breathing human in the elevator with them, or meeting them on the flagstone path leading to the cabana. They're all just so *worried* all the time. Wealthy people just appear to be so burdened.

Jean Ellen Whatley

There was decency in the Motel 6 lobbies, almost an unspoken camaraderie, a "good morning" as you'd pass folks on the balcony or load up the car next to them in the parking lot. There was consideration: people held open the door if you were trying to juggle two cups of Styrofoam java. I relate to the Motel 6ers of the world. Although I know some might label this as condescending, I have lived from paycheck to hot check for so many years of my life I think I've got the street cred for this not being regarded as disingenuous empathy.

I come by it honestly. It's how I was raised. My mother had a way of relating to people worthy of study. She could size up a person in a matter of minutes, without acting superior or inferior and understand from whence *they* came.

"Poor people have poor ways," she'd say to me with a look of reproach if I said something hateful about a shabby person or place. It was an observation borne from experience. My mother was an adolescent when her family left Oklahoma for California. Dust bowl Okies, her dad was a cook, her mom a waitress, and she followed in the Blackshoe tradition, working in bars and cafés all up and down the California coast, from San Clemente to San Francisco. The restaurant ain't no life but it was her life and she could see where it would lead. Pregnant with me and soon to have three mouths to feed, she went to Western Union school in San Francisco to become a teletype operator which eventually got her a government job with the Federal Aviation Administration. This put food on our table for decades.

My mother did not do this by herself. She hired help. But this wasn't the fancy lady's kind of help, like the movie where the white women sat around and played bridge while the black women raised the kids and kept the house. This was where the white woman and the black woman were separated only by a narrow band of color, bound together in a social fabric of mutual need. "I've been blessed with good help," my mother would tell people when they'd inquire about how she kept our ship afloat. Working women were not the mainstream back then, "and whatever I make, I split with my help." It was a necessity. She was working to take care of her family; she hired women who were taking care of theirs. Simple as that.

Most people of a certain age remember where they were the day President Kennedy was killed. We were living in Fort Worth. My brother Don and his wife Beverly saw the president that very morning at the Texas Hotel before the motorcade left for Dallas. They called my mother at work to tell them how exciting it had been. When the shooting occurred, all of the school kids were sent home immediately. The principal at South High Mount Elementary, Nippie Scarborough, came over the loudspeaker. She spoke in a clipped voice.

"Attention pupils, this is Mrs. Scarborough. School is being dismissed early today. You are to go directly home."

Then the bell rang, like that. I remember walking down Clover Lane, a bright, crisp November day, must have been about noon, mystified as to why we'd suddenly been let out. Is it the product of my adult understanding of that day, which now makes me look back and recall a palpable sense of doom? Hard to say. But I definitely knew something was up when I saw my mom's car in the driveway after I'd crested the hill on Lafayette Avenue. It was an untethered anxiety as I ran the rest of the half-block home.

I walked in the door. I will never forget this sight for as long as I live. My mother and our maid Agnes were both standing in the middle of our modest little living room with the bent Venetian blinds and bargain-basement curtains, watching Walter Cronkite on TV, transfixed. Agnes had her hand over her mouth; Mother was standing beside but slightly behind her, shifting her attention from the television to Agnes and back again, with a preemptive empathetic perceptiveness, somewhat like a seizure-alert dog. She then turned to see me, standing just inside the door, but she reached for Agnes first, placing her hand on her shoulder. Agnes said nothing as the tears streamed down her face. I had never seen Agnes cry. I had never seen any black person cry. My mother looked at me again as Agnes turned around and buried her face on my mother's shoulder. White women hardly touched black women in those days, not that my mother had a racist bone in her body, but this generally was just not done. In public, it would have generated sneers, if not threats. In the privacy of her own living room though, my mother just stood there holding another woman, the woman who was watching over her babies, to allow her to work, so she could put food on *two* tables. The pain in my mother's face, I will never forget. This was just three weeks after she'd buried her only brother. Yet my mother knew, for all the compounded grief she felt at that moment, a light of hope had gone out for women like Agnes all over the world. The enormity of what they had lost was unfathomable. She could empathize but she truly could not know how it felt. With one arm around Agnes, my mother held out the other arm to me and I ran to her, wedged in between two women holding each other, weeping.

Such things leave lasting impressions. I thank her for cautioning me not to judge, not to hold myself up as superior simply because of another's station in life.

Pearl, Mississippi is a case in point. So pleasant were my plush accommodations, with the sparkling swimming pool, warm as bath water at ten o'clock at night, full of June bugs and pooty kids and the breathtaking view from my room overlooking the grease-stained parking lot and shredded strips of yellow crime-scene tape still drooping from the trees in the vacant lot just beyond the asphalt, so wonderful was this garden paradise, that I decided to stay over for a second night. Pearl was one of those "drive 'til you drop stops," adventurous but always a little bit unnerving when you don't really know where you'll stop for the night. Then all of a sudden it's nine o'clock and you've dawdled too long taking pictures of things like concrete lawn ornaments and concrete motor speedways in places like Talladega and you're exhausted and hungry, the dog's getting antsy in the back seat and you're just hoping there's a vacancy somewhere. There was.

For those planning a little cross-country jaunt of your own, know that Motel 6 in Pearl, Mississippi is thirty-nine dollars a night while the Motel 6 in San Luis Obispo, California is ninety-eight dollars a night, mostly because the parking lot isn't as greasy.

My reason for staying over in Pearl stemmed from fatigue that blossomed into curiosity. I had planned to drive all the way to Jackson, hotter than a pepper sprout, you know. But this little pepper was too pooped to pop when Jackson remained another forty miles away, so I took the exit to Pearl. Driving six to eight hours a day followed by writing until the wee hours to meet some mad, self-imposed blogging deadline tends to wear a girl out. When I stopped for the night and discovered come daylight that I was actually in a suburb quite close to Jackson, I wondered,

"What the hell do people *do* in Pearl, Mississippi?" More pointedly, "Why do they do it *here?*" There was a ton of fast food joints and hotels on motel row just like all the other homogeneous American outskirts of town I had traveled. They all look the same, except Pearl had every hotel chain and restaurant franchise you could ever imagine. In Waynesboro, Virginia, which had a similar fast-food-palooza, I figured you could justify that because of its proximity to the Blue Ridge Parkway. But what the hell did Pearl, Mississippi possess to warrant all this hospitality industry?

Baseball. Baseball has been very, very good to Pearl, Mississippi. When I ventured out the next morning for coffee, I was cheerfully greeted by a wholesome, red-headed, freckled-armed girl at the brand new Dunkin' Donuts (one tends to remember the outstretched arms of mercy in the mornings) which was right next door to a brand spankin' new Arby's. I sat semi-comatose in the drive-thru waiting for my caffeine to kick in and my turn to merge with a shitload of traffic. Rush hour in Pearl, Mississippi. I felt guilty for being a slacker. All the rest of these decent, God-fearing (I *was* in Mississippi) people were marching off to their work-a-day wars while I was in neutral at the drive-thru at their fancy Dunkin' Donuts, just another stop on my indulgent lolly-gaggin' across the country. I took another gulp of mighty fine coffee and decided that later, after the commuters had cleared the hell out, I'd explore ol' Pearl a bit and hang around an extra day.

"I'd like to stay over," I told the ponytailed brunette at the front desk back at the No Tell Motel 6. She was just leaving after pulling an overnighter and came around the counter to pet Libby after she'd remagnetized my card. "I love your dog. I used to have a pit mix, really cute dog. We had to give her up when we moved. I miss that dog," she said, rubbing Libby's head. Dogs are welcome, even in the lobby at Motel 6.

"So what's the big attraction here? Seems like there's a lot of motels for such a small town," I commented.

"Trustmark Park," she answered, like I should know this. The blank look on my face informed her she needed to continue. "It's where the Braves play. And we've got us a Bass Pro."

Well, all righty then, Double AA farm team for the Atlanta Braves and the fishin' and huntin' retail mecca of the world all in one small town? Doesn't get much better than that. Unless you have the Mississippi State Veterinary School and the State Hospital to boot. Now, we're talking *good* jobs. Throw in a state pen and you've got a trifecta. I spent the mid-morning meandering through steamy country back roads under green tunnels of live oaks draped in Spanish moss. I just happened to follow this one road that dead-ended at the Mississippi State Hospital—dead end being both a literal and figurative term. They don't cotton to folks clicking photos with their cellphones here either, reminiscent of the barn photo op back on the Blue Ridge Parkway. Only this time, the threat of being accosted was more than just some urban naiveté because a guy who had a gun, moseyed out of the guard shack and started coming my way when he spotted me taking photos of the entrance sign. I left before he had time to ask any questions.

Headed back towards town, I spotted a sign that made me laugh out loud. I had seen plenty of coin-op laundromats from coast-to-coast, but this was the

Jean Ellen Whatley

very first time I'd seen a washateria. When I was a kid my mother used to take Garrett and me to the washateria on Camp Bowie Boulevard in Fort Worth. We tied up mountains of laundry in sheets, knotted the corners together, and hauled the bundles of stinky clothes over our backs like hobos, trudging into the washateria to wash, dry and fold a week's worth of laundry while my mom did other stuff—like stock the larder. We'd load up as many as eight washers on some visits, but she'd always give us enough extra quarters to buy Dr. Peppers and peanuts. Some people actually poured the peanuts into the Dr. Pepper, but I thought that was gross. Once the washers were chugging, I'd curl up in one of those plastic orange chairs bolted onto a rail with a stack of *National Enquirers* or *True Confessions*, which were forbidden in our house, and Garrett looked for naked breasts in *National Geographic* or flipped through a *Field & Stream* or *Science Digest*. This made being stuck in the washateria bearable on a Saturday afternoon. Except Garrett always conned me on the folding. He'd find some way to sneak out and go across the street to the Green Front Store, an ancient dime store chock-full of the most worthless, made-in-China, job-lot crap you have ever seen. Or he'd have some urgent need to talk to some girl on the pay phone outside when it came time to get the red-hot towels and sheets out of the commercial dryers which were cutting the shelf life of the tumble-baked contents in half. If there was any consolation in being left alone to fold all those clothes, it was that my mother, once again, had passed along a valuable life lesson: be efficient. She taught me to fold the towels vertically first, then fold them down and down and stack them with the single edges all facing the same way.

"Be efficient" was the drumbeat by which we were raised, a throwback to her years as a Blackshoe, whether it was waiting tables, selling shoes, or working in a hotel laundry when she was fifteen. She taught me the secrets of the pros, the efficiency of folding towels the correct way. You see, most people fold towels like they're playing an accordion. Watch someone the next time you're in a washateria. They hold the towel horizontally, with their arms wide open like wings, then they bring the corners together, folding the towel in half, then folding it in half again, and then, folding it over. Then they stack the towels all willy-nilly, with multiple edges going every which way. With the vertical towel folding method, you save time; folding the towels longways first, then over and over, single edges together. This makes it easier to grab a single towel out of the closet, makes it easier for soapy-eyed motel guests to get just one towel instead of two and having one of them plop into the toilet. It makes it easier for the motel maid to grab a clean stack off the cart after she's picked up all the dirty ones. It's efficient. I thanked my mother for this years later, when at sixteen, I was a motel maid for a summer at the Western Skies in Albuquerque. Such lessons leave lasting impressions.

While I found only one washateria, there were churches a plenty in Pearl. They don't call this the Bible Belt for nothing. On the day I was in town they also had a bumper crop of political signs, batches and batches of them on every corner, which was also frequently occupied by a church, also known as a polling place. It was a municipal election day. Must have been a Tuesday; days of the week had no meaning for me by now. I spotted a man waving a sign and motioning for people to come on in, much like the Jamaican preacher in Brooklyn who was bringing in the sheaves. I pulled over, got my camera and figured I'd try to interview him. He was more than willing. He said he'd just returned from his second tour in Iraq, had to come home abruptly, because his wife had flipped out, wasn't taking care of their six-year-old boy. So he'd gotten a hardship discharge. Indeed, it was. He said he hadn't found a job yet, no longer had a wife because she'd "hooked up" with somebody else while he was in Iraq dodging IEDs. In a modern version of the "Dear John" letter, she dropped her own little bomb, informing him via email that she just couldn't handle the stress of him being over there and leaving her all alone, so when he got home he would be. So this veteran goes from dodging bullets to bill collectors and dealing with a soon-to-be ex-wife and probably a shell-shocked kid, plus all the bureaucratic hassles that veterans go through just to get the benefits they've earned. Hardship defined. Yet there he was. In stifling heat, there he was, standing by the side of the road, waving a sign, a citizen activist in our political process, flawed as it can often be. He's out there campaigning for his friend running for sheriff. I regarded him a hero.

"So what are the big law enforcement issues in Pearl?" I asked in a sightly condescending tone, assuming the cops ran around with only one bullet in their pocket, like Barney Fife.

"Drugs, cocaine, meth; it's bad. They're tearing stuff up, stealing stuff, shooting at people from cars, selling it at the high school," he said. The brim of his straw hat cast a basket-weave shadow across his beet-red forehead. "It's really bad here."

Welcome to rural America, friends. This guy wasn't going to take it lying down though, he had a plan. He was thinking if his buddy got elected Sheriff, there just might be a job in it for him. "I'd be out here doing this anyway, cause the sheriff we've got now, he's gotta go. He's just not doing anything!"

I bet soldiers make good cops. His politics, I could tell, were far different from mine; he volunteered that he's a Republican. But I'll tell you what, I admired the hell out of this guy. He was friendly, decent, civic-minded and somehow, at least from what I could tell, God bless him, he had kept his sense of humor. Even though he'd served two tours in an unpopular war only to come home and fight an even less winnable battle, he offered a quick smile and an "it will all work out" frame of mind.

I went back to my hotel room and wrote for a while. When it got close to the hour even the fast-foods would be closing shop, Libby and I went out for some gourmet dining at the Sonic, then a short moonlit stroll around the lush hotel grounds. I came back to the room, gave Libby the "no barking" command and went for a quick chlorine dip. It's kind of like a flea dip is for dogs. I left her because I'd learned early on that she freaked out when I went swimming. She'd stand by the side of the pool and bark like crazy when I went under water. Out of sight? Out of her mind!

Same thing applied if I left the room. After we got the hotel check-in routine down pat, ("Wait here, I'll get us a room" I'd say, much like a sailor to a barfly) it soon became apparent that we'd have to work on the "I'll be right back" part. I mean, I felt her pain. We'd be in the car all day long, then I'd put her in a hotel room and back out the door saying "I'll be right back." Why should she believe me? When I asked her in St. Louis if she wanted to go for a ride, I didn't disclose that we'd be gone for two months! I had zero credibility. Hell, I'd bark too if I saw my master getting ready to cut out! It's not that I left her for any length of time; I would run back out to the car just to fetch stuff I forgot. For eight weeks I lived out of the back of my car. It was like a really big rolling suitcase. There was no point in hauling in all my clothes every night. I'd just grab what I needed for the night. Invariably, I'd forget something. The first few motel stops, Libby barked the entire time I was gone; I could hear her from the parking lot or down the hall. I had to set her straight fast, especially in the places where I'd snuck her in! To train her, I would leave, she'd bark one time, and I'd bust back in the room with a "No barking!" command and scare the crap out of her. When she'd lay back down on the bed, I'd give her a hamburger. I'm kidding, I gave her a Milk Bone. Her reward, aside from dog treats, was that in the hotels with long hallways we'd play "drop the leash" and I'd let her race down the hall. This was by far her favorite game, besides riding in the elevator, where she'd stare at the floor. She could always sniff out our room by the second time we returned to it. I, of course, would not do this if there were other people in the hallway and I admit this is childish behavior, but, I mean, look at the whole trip.

Call me OCD, but I developed a lot of rituals on the road. I was alone, I had to. It was like a pre-flight check list before I pulled back out onto the highway.

1. Computer, cellphone, chargers, overnight bag, dog food, ice chest? Check.

2. Libby in the back seat? Check.

3. Rub the Our Lady of Guadalupe air freshener hanging from the mirror for good luck? Check.

4. Genuflect and say a prayer for the kids and Louie, each one, name by name? Check.

5. Get your underwear? Check.

No washaterias for this girl. I did a load of laundry when I stayed with people, but all points in between, I simply unwrapped the little bar of soap and washed my panties in the sink and hung them up to dry. A woman can travel across America with one black bra, one white bra and three pairs of panties. I was efficient.

I will be quite honest with you here: there is something very addictive about this kind of life. I fully admit it's escapism and part of it, frankly, was white-knuckled fear. But the one thing about traveling alone for eight weeks with scarce funds: it also teaches simplicity. It's good for you. There is something amazingly liberating about minimizing the excess in our lives. Less can indeed be plenty. How many households did I stay in with wall-sized flat-screen TVs and two or three cars in the driveway, where the beds were covered with designer pillows and chenille throws on top of comforters covered in duvets? Jesus Christ Almighty, it was summer! How many kitchen cabinets did I see stocked like grocery shelves? How many tubs and showers did I step into lined with enough products to fill a beauty shop and medicine chests filled with prescriptions for depression and anxiety? I wasn't snooping; they told me where to look for the Band-Aids! Please don't think I'm ungrateful or casting stones; I'm doing neither. I am deeply indebted to the people who put me up last summer, and I love them all, even though I am now virtually guaranteed never to be asked to return. I am also not saying I've never coveted things or had a drink or swallowed a pill to take the edge off. Hell, I drank a vodka tonic almost every night, sometimes wearing my brand-new cowboy hat! I'm just saying this: all that extra crap won't make us happy. I realize this is not a revolutionary concept, I just think it bears repeating. Admittedly, I didn't strap a happiness meter on every motel maid I encountered last summer, but I can tell you this: I heard a hell of a lot of laughing when those gals would cut out for lunch. When your only interaction for days on end is with people for whom the Motel 6 existence is not a temporary necessity, whose jobs are to rent you a room, hand you a sandwich or a cup of coffee, people who will be doing this same job next week, and the next week and the week after that, when you watch some folks get off work and walk to their room around in back of the motel, well, it has a way of calling bullshit on you for all the stuff you think you need and all the reasons why you're just not happy.

Want to know what made me happy last summer? A clean washcloth. At the end of the day, I was grateful for a clean washcloth and warm water to wash my face. I was extremely fortunate to experience a state of mind in which I could honestly say, *"At this moment, I have everything I need."* Simplicity is a great teacher. I was grateful for a fresh washcloth and the people who cleaned the room, restocked the towels with the single edge to the outside, who folded the top square of toilet paper into a perfect V and left me some soap. I was living large while they were living close to the bone. How many of us are just one disaster away from being there ourselves?

How many of us, myself included, have traveled through small-town America in our zipped-up, air-conditioned cocoons of self-importance, thinking about the fancy restaurants, theme parks, golf courses, ski slopes or spa treatments which await us at our destination, shuddering as we pass by ramshackle houses with a dog tied out on a chain and clothes on the line, shaking our heads, thinking "There but for the grace of God go I" when really, if we're honest, we're looking down our noses with affected sympathy at their hovels and hotels, which in a generous moment we might consider quaint, but we mostly regard as horrific? Who are we, motherfuckers, to say anything about how that other half lives? We have no control over the cosmic roll of the dice that lands us in Mumbai or Malibu. And there but for the grace of God? There *with* the grace of God, or Buddha, or Allah or nary a trace of divinity, these folks are simply living their lives.

We are all the same. We are all just trying to have a life. The people I met on the road at crappy EconoLodges with a foot of mud at the bottom of the pool in Youngstown to the woman at the Motel 6 in Salinas, Kansas who said, "Don't worry, honey, I'm saving your room," because Lord knows Salinas was the happening spot on the globe that Friday night and she held the last room in town for me, my last night on the road—these were some of the nicest people I have ever met in my life. And you know what? They didn't even have to be. They all could have been assholes and still kept their minimum wage jobs, but they were nice anyway. Close to the bone. Maybe it has a way of keeping you real. I'll bet you all the cheeseburgers from every McDonald's in America that if you asked them what they really want in life, they'd tell you they just want to be *free from worry*. They'd just like to know how it feels, *just once,* to not worry every goddamn day that something's going to happen to shatter their hand-to-mouth existence. I understand this. I have been living it for years.

They're card-carrying members of the Blackshoes. When I made it to Albuquerque, I was rummaging through a cardboard box of my mother's things at my sister-in-law Bev's house and I found a pocket-sized book of the by-laws from the Bartenders and Hotel Workers Union from El Dorado County, California to which my mother belonged in 1952. Inside that little booklet was her Communication Workers of America union card, dated 1956. This told a history. She had moved up from waiting tables to being a teletype operator. She'd moved up a notch among the Blackshoes with a better job, a fighting chance for a steady income, health care for her family, a paid vacation once a year, even a small pension. She could give the hired help a raise. "Whatever I make, I split with my help." Close to the bone. *She* understood this.

There is a rawness about it. You grow accustomed to being on high alert, the adrenalin drip of hoping to God that the kids don't get sick, the car won't crap out or the roof doesn't start to leak because you just can't make the money stretch any farther. How I would love to be in a spot where I didn't have to worry. Instead, I try to maximize the moments when I can remind myself, *"I have everything I need."*

The morning I left Pearl I rubbed my Blessed Virgin Mary air freshener and said my daily departure prayers. I had a lot of miles still to cover between Mississippi all the way to California and back to King Louie.

"Lord, please watch over me and Libby today. Please bless my babies' feet and backs, and oh, mine too, 'cause we're close to the bone."

Buckling my seat belt, I pulled out of the Motel 6 parking lot, spotting my ponytailed desk clerk buddy getting off work. I added a rejoinder "and God bless her too," with a wave goodbye. She waved back enthusiastically and hollered, "Good luck!"

It occurred to me how tightly we are knitted together, if we're open to the connective threads. Knit one, Pearl two. It had been worth the second day.

Just as I'm about to pull on to the highway, all ensconced in pure-hearted Blackshoe, family-of-man solidarity, she screams, "Wait!" pointing to the top of my car.

Where, I'd left the ice chest.

10

Land of Enchantment, Trail of Tears

Along about Adrian, I let Libby go.

August 4: We were approaching the halfway mark on what would end up being fifty seven days on the road and, as things turned out, we were just about at the halfway mark of the total number of miles we would travel as well. In complete coincidence (I wish I could say I planned it this way) our halfway point occurred in Adrian, Texas, which just happens to be the exact midway point on Route 66 from Chicago to Los Angeles. In a bit of providential timing, this is where I began to loosen up the chokehold I'd had on Libby.

It had taken 4,322 miles for me to relax. From the night I lay on top of the slippery floral bedspread at the Red Roof Inn in Springfield, scared to death, disbelieving that I had actually managed to leave town, my single biggest fear was that I'd somehow lose Libby.

"Don't run off, okay?" I whispered to her in the dark. She did not respond.

Logically speaking, how does one lose an 86-pound dog? It's irrational, I know, but my apprehension over this was at times nearly paralyzing. In Chicago when she'd bolted at a dog park next to Lake Michigan, I was afraid she'd run all the way to Canada. In Atlanta, she took off with my niece's dogs out into the woods and I was afraid she wouldn't find her way back again. In Graford, she'd taken off after a jackrabbit. From that moment on, unless I had visual confirmation of a chain-link or barbed wire, I wouldn't let her loose.

Until we got to Adrian. Well to be 100 percent cartographically correct, it was really Vega, Texas, which is only three miles away. One sprawling metropolis runs into the next one out in the teeming Texas Panhandle. I had stopped to take some photos of a football field adjacent to an outdoor rodeo arena, both empty in the summer. The ghost-town quality of two iconic Texas pastimes, smashed together in a single field, fascinated me. I let Libby jump out of the back seat free as a bird. It was a large field, far from the highway.

She looked at me quizzically, as if saying, "Didn't you forget something?"

"Stay with me," I said in my best dog-whisperer voice.

She did. She just hung out. She sniffed the few remaining traces of petrified cow patties, trotted along beside me when I pushed open the creaky cattle chutes and climbed up on the rusty gate to snap a few shots. "Come on, let's go over here," I said, trying to sound casual so as not to give her any indication that I was, honestly, still trapped in the irrational grip of fear that she would, for some inexplicable reason, decide to hook a U-turn and bolt for Route 66. She followed me over to the football field. This would become a turning point in our relationship.

"Good dog, Libby." I praised her more than I normally did.

We celebrated with a genuine Texas roadside diner meal a short piece down the road, a mighty-fine BLT and a piece of coconut cream pie to die for. She didn't dig on the coconut too much. As we sat on a bench in front of the restaurant eating, it was threatening rain, which is all it's done in Texas for about ten years now. People coming out of the diner with toothpicks clenched in their teeth, stopped to pat Libby on the head, saying how cute she was. I met some cool cats from Canada: four guys who were on a whirlwind tour of the American Southwest. We swapped photos and then I had to ease on down the road.

Albuquerque beckoned.

Not to use a cliché, but it's like getting one of your appendages returned; that's what going to Albuquerque feels like to me. Let's say it's your hand, which at fifty-six, you've witnessed with melancholy your once-lovely hands with slender long fingers turn into old-lady hands with gnarly veins and arthritic knuckles. There are nicks and scars from dull kitchen knives gone awry, the tiny freckles beginning to pool together like splats of mud and you find yourself shopping for Porcelana at the Walgreens, wondering, "Who broke in here in the middle of the night and stole my hands?" Albuquerque is like my hands: at once pristine, like the mountain sunrises which convince any sensing person who's up early enough to witness them that a day which starts with such intoxicating splendor holds unlimited possibility but is soon sobered by an unforgiving sun and relentless desert wind pitting and pounding in a masochistic pact, day after day, month after month, with nary a drop of rain, splitting open the desperate fissures in the desert floor into gaping, powder-dry arroyos. Ain't no lotion in the world which can smooth these cracks.

It's a hard town. It's written on the faces of the Indians on east Central. It's a hard place for me to be, for a multitude of reasons. Merely typing the word A-L-B-U-Q-U-E-R-Q-U-E evokes emotion, mostly because I had to type it 9,000 times in journalism school. A character in a play, she commands a leading role, Albuquerque. She is both hero and villain in my life. I had it all here once, but I lost so much more.

It started with Cully. Fresh off the boat—well, really it was a '70 Chevy BelAir which hauled my crying ass all the way from Fort Worth to Albuquerque when I was fifteen. It was one of those dragged-by-the-hair moves by the man du jour, my stepdad Frank, with my mother and two younger brothers. It was Godawful sitting in the back seat with my two pooty little brothers, feeling like I was going to throw up out of grief and car sickness for the entire 700 miles or so. I was probably having a nicotine fit as well, because I'd already been smoking cigarettes and a considerable amount of marijuana by then. I had begged and pleaded for my mom and stepdad to let me stay in Fort Worth with brother Don and his wife, Bev. Frank's FAA assignment in Albuquerque was scheduled to last just twelve months, only *one* year! Don and Bev would be living in our old house on Locke Avenue; it would be perfect! I had just finished the ninth grade, sort of. There had been that little issue of being suspended three times. The Dean of Women (they had such titles in high schools in Fort Worth back then) told my mother I was "incorrigible." That old spinster didn't know squat. I had the last laugh on her, eventually. Garrett and his wife were staying behind in Fort Worth too! They had a baby on the way! I could just stay in Texas, go to summer school, try to straighten out my act, while my mom and Frank went on their Land of Enchantment adventure with my little brothers. Sounded reasonable to me.

My mother eventually told me that she took me out of Fort Worth to save me. She had already, sorrowfully, seen the path of destruction Garrett had paved for himself and she warily watched me traipsing right along behind him. She was probably right. But there were plenty of ne'er-do-well hippies in Albuquerque I could get into trouble with and within one day I'd located a few. It was August when we arrived; by November, I was in love. I was in full-tilt teenage heat over Cully, the black-haired, blue-eyed Irish boy who, with time, would be allowed to sneak into my bedroom in the middle of the night at the height of a blizzard, leaving his tell-tale footprints in the snow the next morning and an indelible tattoo on my heart. I loved him more than he deserved, the Irish rascal.

Forty-one years later I cannot drive through Tijeras Canyon without thinking of him. On the eastern approach to Albuquerque, Interstate 40 cuts through the canyon, separating the Sandia Mountains to the north from the Manzanos to the south. At one time it was a narrow two-lane highway, part of the old Route 66, climbing to an altitude of some 7,000 feet where, after a person clears the curves and the last of the foothills, the entire city of Albuquerque sprawls in front of you, descending to the Valley and the precious swath of green that existed centuries before sod and automatic sprinklers created humidity and a water crisis. The canyon highway is quite beautiful. It's breathtaking, really, but treacherous. It is particularly dangerous at night, especially when you're a twenty-year-old kid driving back from a keg party. That's where I lost Cully, in Tijeras Canyon, in a head-on collision with a tractor-trailer rig. These things never turn out well. It didn't make it any easier on a heartbroken girl whose first true love was buried on her eighteenth birthday, that the news reports persistently included the grisly details about his decapitation. It made me hate the media. What an irony when I joined their vulture ranks a decade later. *Tijeras* means "scissors" in English. Brutally ironic.

Truth is, I had already lost Cully long before the car wreck. We'd broken up after just a few short months of what was a sophomore/senior love affair. But it had been a hot one, I'll tell you. I gave him everything. He gave me the heave-ho and went back to his straight-laced Italian Catholic girl next door, of whom his mama and hers approved. I mourned for months, wearing my loved-and-lost battle scars like a badge of courage. My girlfriends and I drank Spanada wine and we'd sing Carole King's "It's Too Late" at the top of our lungs. Truth is, it should have been Linda Ronstadt's "Love Has No Pride," because I would have taken him back in a minute. I pined for Cully with historic magnitude until the blonde long-haired guy from around the corner came totin' his guitar and rescued me from my disproportionate drama. I was dating him at the time Cully was killed. He helped me get through it, tenderly, and a year later we were married. There's a sadness that never completely leaves you, though, when the first boy you fall in love with doesn't get the chance to see how the rest of the story plays out.

And so it is with me and Tijeras Canyon—every time I clear the back side of the mountain and look at the city below, I think of all the scenes which have played out in this town. Albuquerque saturates my pores—a life-giving aquifer laced with DDT. This is where I finished high school, went to college, got married *twice!* I launched a successful journalism career here, launched three lives and lost half my family.

It's not the same. I love the peeps I still have here ferociously—my younger brothers, my sisters-in-law, nieces and nephews and the friends who always make time for me when I roll into town. I am so grateful. But somebody different lives in my mama's house now. My brother Don isn't on the front porch drinking a beer, watching the birds, waiting for me to pull up. My brother Garrett will never drop by in full animation, keeping us spellbound, killing ourselves laughing as he regales us with stories. The pickup isn't in the driveway anymore. The Harley has been sold. Our best storytellers have moved on, leaving us to the ghosts.

Or, conversely, feeling like one. There's a great New Mexico legend of *La Llorona* (okay, all you *gringos*, it's *yah-rona*), used by demented parents as a scare tactic to keep their kids away from the ditch. The "ditch" refers to the network of clear ditches (a misnomer, because they're muddy as hell) that parallel the Rio Grande. Even though Native Americans came up with a similar construct 600 years ago or more, a more formal network of ditches was created in the 1920s to better drain the Valley's waterlogged bottom and reclaim it for growing chiles and marijuana and stuff. The ditches are scenic, deep in the *bosque*, (which means woodlands) and cottonwoods trees provide great camo for skinny-dipping teenage girls. But the ditches are dangerous, especially after a summer rain, especially near the locks and drains. Parents would warn their kids to stay away from the ditch. They'd ask, "Can you hear that?" and of course the kids would shake their heads with sober stares. But the parents would proceed anyway, telling their children the story of La Llorona, the "crying woman" who roamed the ditch banks at night in search of her drowned children. They told them to stay away or she'd drown them too out of spite. Nice.

I'm like that dang old witch. I drive through my old hometown in search of some trace of lives lost. Many of them were mine. I was a wife, a sister, a daughter; hell, I was a semi-famous person! I was *somebody*, as the Reverend Jesse Jackson would say, the same Reverend Jackson who granted me an exclusive live interview when he was running for President back in 1988. Oh the power of the all-important local TV news. What a joke. It is patently absurd that broadcast journalists become celebrities—and yet they do. I guess I relished it when I was in the middle of it, a journalist in my own right, and married to an even more celebrated one. Rick was a household name. We had arrived. We thought we had it all. Twenty years later, I'm driving around the country trying to resuscitate a life and he's driving around making deliveries, just trying to stay alive.

I went to the bus station the day his Greyhound rolled into St. Louis with him straight from federal prison. I'm not sure why I felt so drawn to greet him. I suppose I just wanted to shake his hand and welcome him back to daylight. I found myself thinking about how overwhelmed he must have felt. A lot had happened on the outside over seven years. I missed his bus though, I've never been on time for anything in my life. I'd gotten tied up on a call at work, arrived at the station about ten minutes after his bus had come and he'd gone, by car, I think, the rest of the way to the halfway house where he'd be staying for a while. There was no way to contact him. For the first few days I kept imagining I was seeing him on the street, in stores, in the car next to me at the traffic light, *he* was the ghost now. It was an odd feeling, knowing he was out, not that I was scared or disturbed by this in any way. It was just knowing that he was back among the living and I could very well run into him on the produce aisle at the grocery store.

It was Panera Bread instead. He called me a couple of weeks after he got out to give me the number to the halfway house and to inquire about the kids. He asked me to let them know he was out, he was looking for a job, and he would not bother them or expect them to see him if they didn't want to. He just wanted them to know he was okay. I asked him to meet me for lunch. I wanted to look him in the eye, size him up, try to assess his frame of mind, to run interference for the kids, if I had to.

It was remarkably unemotional, seeing him for the first time in seven years. The last time I'd seen Rick was in the county jail. The way they show it in the movies, that's the way it really is. The guard brings the person in, sits them down on the other side of inch-thick glass and you pick up a phone to talk.

And then, after all that time, there he was, a free man, waiting in line with the rest of the lunch day crowd at Panera Bread. I saw him before he saw me. He was wearing blue jeans, a short sleeve plaid shirt, tucked in, with brand new white tennis shoes, the plain kind you buy at Walmart. He was a little heavier, more bald, and older. My God, he had aged. I was immediately sad. There was something about the way he stood there, tentative, like he didn't quite belong, a bit self-conscious, uncharacteristic for a man who used to walk in the room and own it. I definitely got the drop on him. Seeing how nervous he was made me feel bad for him.

The lunch meeting was a last minute arrangement, which was a good thing; it was good to break the ice, good that it left less time for my stomach to be in knots. Thinking about seeing him again after seven years and all the struggles, my God, Sean was thirteen when Rick left, now twenty years old, well, the anxiety over how I thought it was going to be was worse than how it actually was. Rick spotted me and grinned, his smile a bit apologetic now.

I walked up and hugged him. What else could I do?

"Sorry, it took me longer to get out of the office than I thought," I injected some filler words into a momentary silence. But an apology, was I nuts?

"Can I help the next person?" The guy at the bakery counter motioned for us to step over.

"What do you usually get?" Rick asked me.

"The Pick Two, soup and salad," I responded, grateful for the minutia to distract us while we both figured out the appropriate distance to stand apart and degree of familiarity to acknowledge.

"I'll have the same thing she's having," he said, which was weird because he had never done that in his life. He seemed so hesitant, like someone who's in a fancy restaurant for the first time, not sure how to pronounce the stuff on the menu. Or maybe it was simply that he'd forgotten what it was like to have a choice. I used to think about that when he was in prison, what he was eating. I figured he was probably remembering supper at our house, from time to time.

"I've got it," I pulled out my credit card to pay for our lunch. I reasoned a guy right out of prison probably had less money than I had.

Or any place to go on Christmas Eve. So, six months later, with the kids' permission, I asked Rick to come for Christmas Eve dinner. (This would be the year *before* King Louie and the pauper Christmas.) This gesture makes me neither simp nor saint. I reached out to Rick because I knew it would make things easier on my children. I didn't want them worrying about him being alone. Nor did I want them going out on Christmas Eve to meet their dad at some crappy Denny's. I did it because it felt like the right thing to do. I did it to open the door for some healing to come in. I did it because I think that's what my mother would have done.

My first night back in Albuquerque last summer, I stopped by to pay my respects to her. I used to think it morbid, going to the cemetery. Now I understand it. I go to talk to my mother, not that I don't frequently speak to her in the privacy of my own kitchen or my mobile crying chamber, also known as my car. Nobody prepares you for what it feels like to be an orphan. It sneaks up on you, the solemnity of no more buffer between you and being next in line. So when I am in town, I go see her. Her bronze headstone is the only one like it in the world. I wrote the inscription.

"One step forward, no steps back."

My mother had a vast repertoire of homespun sayings she could access like speed dial. "One step forward, two steps back" was number one on the list. It became the de facto anthem of her life and I figured she'd appreciate my slight revision, as a tacit nudge of affirmation to send her along to the next one.

It was almost sundown when I got to the cemetery. I always put it off until just before dark because it's just too damn hot otherwise. The sun affords no hiding in New Mexico, no way to cover your sorrow, your shame or your regrets. I wish I'd spent more time with my mother. I didn't realize until I read her journal last summer how lonely she was in the last year of her life. There was a job, always a job, which held me in its clutches. This particular job was a fluke though, the one I had when my mother took sick. It was a temporary leave of my sanity (well, aside from the road trip) that seduced me into thinking it was a good idea to join a medical start-up in 2005. I had done a little freelance marketing work for the founder of the company and he considered me clever after I'd come up with an ad campaign using the slogan *"It doesn't suck!"* I swear to God this is true. When the phone starting ringing off the hook after our first radio spots aired, he asked me to come on board and work full-time to run his advertising and marketing division. Never mind that the only advertising I'd ever bought in my life was for a garage sale. He believed in me! Entrepreneurs are notorious risk-takers.

"If you'll come to work for me and run like your hair's on fire for one year, I will make you rich," he said with a manic zeal in his eyes, I would later come to recognize as clinical.

Considering that at the time I had one kid in college, two more in high school, an ex-husband in the joint and had just been laid off from a high-paying PR job on my fiftieth birthday with nary a lead on selling the screenplay I was peddling in Hollywood, I figured signing a pact with the devil was a small price to pay for becoming a millionaire and having the freedom to write whatever the fuck I felt like after that. The lightning in a bottle which was going to make us all rich was a "revolutionary" compound injected into the body to dissolve fat cells instead of having them sucked out, hence the tag line, *"It doesn't suck!"* Eventually it did. The president of the company died of colon cancer; his uppity Australian partner ran the company into the ground, declared bankruptcy and made off to Fiji with what was left of the cash, rumored to be a cool twenty million. Instead of a quarter of a million shares of stock, which was supposed to bankroll my writing habit for the rest of my life, I was slapped with a lawsuit and two years gone from my life that I could never get back again. Nor my mother; she died while I was riding that goddamn, ridiculous tiger.

I can always find her grave easily. I had memorized the route from the day we rolled her shiny white casket, draped in a hand-stitched pastel quilt, out of the cool, stained-glass sanctuary and into the pounding July sun. We had chosen to roll her casket to her burial site not more than 200 yards from the chapel, out onto the sidewalk, around the circular drive, down the hill a bit, first a left, then a right, to the spot where two cedars were planted too close together and the Albuquerque Gravel billboard on the nearby freeway stands at ten o'clock. We could have put the casket in a hearse, but it seemed foolish to load her up, then unload her for a mere block and a half of lovely tree-lined perpetual care. Besides, the six grandsons who were pallbearers were honored to drive her home. That was some crowd walking down the street, a procession quite fitting for a little Okie girl whose kin on the paternal side came from New Orleans. My grandfather, Booker Waddell, was a charmer and somewhat a scoundrel in his younger days. When I told you how Booker set the standard for always being nattily attired, I failed to mention that he needed a lot of pomade for his nappy head. My mother always said, with a name like Booker, his New Orleans roots and kinky hair, my great-grandmother Nona was keeping a little secret. And for the record, casting no aspersions here, all of Booker's descendants have a hell of a sense of rhythm.

Libby waited in the car at the cemetery, her nose sticking out the back window, watching me walk over to Mom's grave, where I sat down cross-legged. I spoke out loud—told her about the trip, pulled some weeds, brushed the dirt from the headstone. I lay down on top of the grave and spoke into the grass.

"I miss you so much." I lay there for a second, curled on my side, my hands tucked under my face like a pillow. The constant, low hum of noise from Interstate 40 was not so much an urban soundtrack as it was an indifferent and ever-present crow cawing that life goes on, despite our sorrow. "I loved you the best, Mama. I loved you the best." I got up and brushed the grass from my pants.

As much as I enjoy talking to dead people, it's really about the survivors now, Albuquerque is. I stayed with my sister-in-law. I still can't wrap my head around her being referred to as a widow. Beverly had been married to my brother Don for more than four decades. My mother always mused that her eldest son had married a girl with the same name as his mama because he was looking for someone just like her. Couldn't have been further from the truth, because Don and Bev stuck it out. They were one of those couples who stuck it out through thick and thin, good and bad. Got married early, had their kids early, grandkids early, getting ready to retire. They could have been one of those couples who could celebrate a sixtieth or seventieth wedding anniversary, but they were robbed. Cancer's a thief.

Beverly is a survivor. It's tough being alone, but she's tougher. The days I spent with her were bittersweet. I had not been to their house since the funeral. Photos occupy the places where my brother used to be. The neighbors still stop by, raising the latch on the gate of their corner yard, coming to sit on the porch and visit with Bev and Baby Girl, the long-haired dachshund diva who tolerated me and the mongrel for five days. Jonathan the homeless man, to whom Don would assign odd jobs when Jonathan came looking for work, still stops by to see if Bev's got any chores for him. Sometimes she does, sometimes she doesn't. The day I was there he brought *her* food. Here's a guy who's sleeping in the church yard and yet he stops by to share his hand-me-down, left-over Chinese takeout. That's generosity, man.

Bev's neighbor Joe, still a practicing psychiatrist in his eighties, checks in while he is taking his daily constitutional. Dude's a rock star, rock solid, with his wisdom, compassion and pure life force. He counseled my brother, as a neighborly gesture, through many an hour, walking him through all manner of emotions in the face of death. I sat out on the porch and talked with Joe one afternoon. He told me that what I was doing was important, said Don would have liked it. That meant a lot coming from a therapist who's helped thousands of people. It made me feel less crazy. Guess that's what shrinks do.

J.R's a survivor. He's my next youngest Whatley brother. Out of the five, we're the closest in age. From the time I rolled out of St. Louis, J.R. had been monitoring my trip. He threw in fifty dollars on my Kickstarter campaign and said he'd be looking forward to showing me the dog park near his house once Libby and I reached Albuquerque. He can't drive anymore, since his stroke. Don died in August; J.R. had a stroke just eight months later. He was only fifty three. It was exacerbated by his drinking, which he'd be the first to tell you is the hardest thing he's ever tried to overcome, and this comes from somebody who's dealt with a lot. Most people who know J.R. would agree he's had more than his share of misfortune. He had an accident at a young age in which he was splitting logs, and a sliver of metal flew off the wedge, blinding him in one eye. I drove him to the hospital with my young sister-in-law Karen, not even twenty yet, holding the bloody towel over his eye. They lost their first baby, Beau, when he was just ten months old. J.R. battled cancer in his forties and survived it. He'd battled alcoholism and won, staying sober for twenty years or more. I marveled at his strength. Even though he never graduated from high school, he had built a solid career: from a being a plumber, taking classes at night to earn advanced technical skills, he eventually got a high-level job at a huge government facility overseeing all their computerized cooling systems. He went from flushing out sewers to writing code. Top security clearance, high-pressure, but good benefits and retirement in sight. The stroke took all of that away. He backslid. Decades of forward steps, then one giant step back into a treacherous hole of self-recrimination and regret. I do not tell you this to shame him. I asked J.R. if I could write about this and he said yes. "I screwed up. I made mistakes. I made some bad decisions," he said with a soberness that comes from knowing some are irrevocable. "But there have been a lot of successes. People seem to forget that."

He's raised two kids, he's been faithfully married to the same woman he met and fell in love with in high school. He is wickedly funny. He reminds me that lives are made up of many chapters. He is working on how to make the best of this one. He is still with us, and I am so grateful. His brain and his legendary sense of humor are amazingly, blessedly intact. He's holding on, one day at a time. He and the rest of his family, all of whom I love very much, are trying to figure it out. It's not what any of them signed up for. One day at a time, one step at a time, in the truest sense of the word.

I forget what I have in him until I see him. There's a sacred familiarity that comes with being raised under the same roof. Can I get a witness? He is one of mine. Childhood events we compare and contradict, just like an old married couple, but we were there. We were there when Garrett slit his wrists. We were there when my stepdad Frank's crazy ex-wife Carmen showed up at our house one night with a gun, stumbling drunk, stomping stiff-legged down the driveway on Locke Street, hollering like an enraged Jerry Springer guest, threatening to kill the *juera* who was sleeping with her man. We were there when the babysitter with no front teeth got drunk on the job and passed out while my mom was at work. This was the only white woman who ever took care of us, she lasted only one week. Her old man came to pick her up after my mother sped home to rescue us, Garrett armed with a baseball bat lest she gain consciousness and come after one of us. After my mother roused the drunken sot (we had found her empty bottles in the attic) and told her to get out and never come back, the poor old bag fell out of the passenger door of the pickup when her husband turned the corner hauling her sorry babysitter ass away. We laughed about that for years, much to the consternation of my mother, who was quick to remind us that we were none the worse for the wear. Ah, these are the memories we cherish. Like the summer of '68, when Mom bought us all brand-new Keds and we trekked all over the HemisFair in San Antonio, the freshly-poured black top burning through fresh rubber soles. But we were happy. The motel had a pool and life was good. We were there, J.R. and I, years before, when the bonus baby came home from the hospital, placed in the white-eyelet-draped bassinette, a figment of my adoration and J.R.'s bemusement. Baby made five; Paul would be the last of the line.

My last stop in Albuquerque was to locate him. It's alternately amusing and tragic that Paul doesn't have a pot to piss in, but he has a cellphone, or at least a steady loaner. The way in which this man survives defies belief. Somehow he does. Somehow he manages, God love him, to find a hovel, a meal, some cigarettes, musicians to jam with, a yard crew to work with and a cellphone to call his big sister once in a while. Usually, it's to ask, in a roundabout way, if I have a few dollars I can spare. I don't mind sending him a few when I do. Talk about close to the bone.

It would be impossible to know exactly what day, what year, or what inciting event nudged little brother Paul off the grid. He has been off longer than he was ever on. It started with drinking, then smoking pot and ended up with meth. The fact that my mother, may God grant her peace, was a textbook enabler, cajoling, threatening, pleading, caving, excusing, blaming, forgiving— that whole decades-long, co-dependent psychodrama, I am sure, contributed to his demise. Not as justification, but as context here, I would venture that we all know a family with at least one member who has failed to launch. Such was Paul's journey until my mother died and he was launched off her couch. Believe me when I tell you he got his share of the modest inheritance. It didn't last too long. In the six years since her passing, he has lived with a number of his *compadres* in Albuquerque's North Valley, within five miles of where the rest of us grew up. This is his universe. I have offered in years past to bring Paul to St. Louis, to try to help him find a job, to put him up until he can get back on his feet. But I knew it was lip service because I knew he wouldn't come. Heaven forbid if he'd taken me up on it. I truly don't know if I could have handled it; I've already done my share of raising kids. Plus I knew he'd never come because that ship has sailed. I can't fix him. I can't save him. I can't pay to replace his teeth. All I can do is round him up when I'm in town, buy him a meal, a pack of cigarettes, give him some pocket money and share a few laughs about what once was. He remembers.

Criminal and psychosis-inducing childhood memories notwithstanding, there was a lot of normal in the mix. It was a normal life—we had sack lunches, we went to church and Boy Scouts and Camp Fire Girls. We had a dog. We went on vacations to the Grand Canyon, even Disneyland! We had big family Christmases and Easter-egg hunts, trips to the zoo and a Slip 'n' Slide in the summertime. There was Little League baseball and piano lessons, summer camp and art classes at the museum. There was allowance and family meetings and leftovers in the fridge. How did Paul get left behind?

I miss my baby brother, the old Paul, the way he used to be. Yet, even in his syncopated, addlepated chatter, he reminds me with a certain look, an expression, or tilt of his head, of why I come home. I come home because he is still here. I come home because J.R. is here. No matter how far away I go, I always come back home. I come home to see my little brothers: they're the only homies I have left and I need them as much as they need me. We were five. Now we are three. I come home to hear *our* stories—the familiar pitch and tone, from blood to blood, the DNA of cadence, passed down from one generation to the next. I come home. I'm the matriarch, the oldest of the clan, a reluctant and somber guardian of the stories. The Indians had it right. They carved their stories as petroglyphs inside caves and on the huge lava rocks on the mesa. They knew, lest their voices fail them, lest their numbers dwindled to too few, they knew their stories would live on.

Night was descending on those ancient petroglyphs as I ascended Nine Mile Hill, old Route 66, heading west, leaving Albuquerque. She cut a divot out of my heart. But this time she also bestowed a gift: Albuquerque offered up a clue, a phone number. Sitting on the couch at Bev's house one night, we found a phone number for a man named Lester in El Dorado County, California. Forget Facebook or Ancestry.com or any other modern marvels; we found him the old-fashioned way, through tax records, which appeared to trace back to a man with the right name, the right time and the right place to have been my father. For the first time in my life, I had a tangible link to my California roots, a phone number for the brother I had never known. The number was scribbled on a scrap of paper tucked inside my coin purse. It would be days before I'd have the courage to call, lots of miles and lots to think about between New Mexico and northern California, but at least I had a number!

The lights of Albuquerque looked like sequins on a black velvet drape the farther I got outside the city. Already, the heat was subsiding. It is cool at night in the desert. Windows down, Libby in the back, lying on her side this time, long ol' legs dangling over the edge of the seat: as always, I was so blessed by her companionship. We'd try to make it to Gallup that night, but darkness was my enemy; it was the time I cried the most.

I was watching the road, but the twilight grey of the concrete before me was more like a projector screen for the grainy home movie playing in my mind: a birthday party from nearly thirty years ago. Nathan was just a toddler. I was divorced the first time, going to journalism school, working nights, poor as dirt. But I'd baked a cake. The boys brought beer. The whole damn family showed up. We were listening to "Minute By Minute" on a thirty-nine dollar boom box in my thinly furnished living room, the wood floors decades past the need for a new coat of varnish. Nathan was dancing around in his brand new Yoda Underoos, all hopped up on cake and ice cream.

"Hey, don't you worry..." Michael McDonald started it off. Garrett and J.R. rolled back the rug. *"I've been lied to..."*

The two of them started dancing, side-by-side, like the Temptations, except it was the Doobies.

"I've been here many times before..."

Brother Don got up. Brother Paul joined on the other end.

"Girl, don't you worry, I know where I stand...."

I jumped on the other end of the line.

"I don't need this love, I don't need your hand...."

We danced for the whole rest of the song, in some kind of ridiculous hippie white-people dance, cowboy boots and high-top Chucks, a few spins, a few kicks, mostly just side-stepping, arms laced around each others' waists. We were happy.

"I know I could turn, blink and you'd be gone...."

We were all just kids once, together, under one roof. We were just a pack of plain ol' kids, thrown together by a force of nature named Beverly, a remarkably smart and strong-willed woman with high ideals and occasional weak morals. God bless my mama. A passel of kids, all from one mother, but three different fathers. Five kids, me the only girl. In the bottomless, jagged-edged gaps where we longed for normal to reside, my brothers tried to fill the empty space with liquor or drugs. I'm the only one who dodged that bullet. I am not passing judgment. Like wads of paper ever mounting, in a metal trash can in a barren room save for a table, a chair and a typewriter, I stuff the holes of my life with words. Therein lies my addiction. I am a writer.

11

The Privilege of Breathing

If I had to choose a favorite landscape, I think I'd choose the desert. As much as I love the Carolina Coast with its dense, sweet, healing air, the desert frees me, much in the same way the flat land of Texas does. I am oddly comforted by the relative insignificance of my existence compared to such a majestic theater. Everything we are and have is a mere speck against the backdrop of the desert: a lizard scuttling across a sandstone boulder, a moment; then we're gone. The desert goes on.

The traffic, however, sometimes does not. Sometimes, it backs up for twenty miles or more, converting an interstate highway to a parking lot, or, as things turned out last summer, a stage.

August 15, I'm heading west on Interstate 10, about 200 miles east of L.A., when traffic comes to a dead halt. Need I mention it's hotter than hell? Probably not. But let me just insert a little factoid anyway: The average high temperature in mid-August for Blythe, California, where Libby and I had just stopped for a pee and water break, is 112-degrees. I later came to fully appreciate the providence of that pit stop. The traffic was going nowhere. I cut my engine right away; the last thing I wanted to do was overheat my car. Libby was fine. She stared out the window for a while, with a look of, "Are you crazy? Why are you stopping here?" then harrumphed and curled back up on the back seat. After about fifteen minutes, while I was making good use of my time by texting my kids in Los Angeles to tell them not to wait supper, catching up on comments on my blog and sending out pithy Tweets, I looked up and saw folks getting out of their cars to stretch their legs and/or play music.

I spotted this guy about four cars ahead of me, strapping on an acoustic guitar. I couldn't make out his face because the sun was behind him. We were heading west after all. I could tell, however, that he was sportin' dreads and sunglasses, a black muscle shirt and khaki cargo shorts, and also a guitar. Just as I was about to Tweet some smart-ass remark about a "hippie wanna-be" jammin' by the side of the highway, because Lord knows it's important for me to be witty 24/7, I see another guy lift a stand-up bass out of the trunk, the dark brown shape of it sharply outlined against his summery linen pants. He is soon joined by yet a third guy, who appears to be playing a harmonica. Hard to be sure on that one, because the harmonica didn't cast quite as distinctive a silhouette. The incongruity piqued my curiosity.

"Stay here, Lib," I told her, because she was infinitely better off in the car, now blessedly shaded by semi-trucks with a brisk breeze coming through the windows, as opposed to being out on the pavement which would have blistered her paws. I poured her a bowl of water. She lapped it up and took her post, watching me as I walked away, camera at the ready. Once a reporter, always a reporter. I walked up to these dudes with my iPhone poised and I hit "record." They never even hesitated, never even paused, nor missed a strum of the guitar or plunk of a bass string. For that matter, they didn't really pay much attention to me, barely acknowledged my presence. But what they sang and what I felt, I hope to remember forever. When it is time for me to draw my last breath, I hope to feel the same way I felt when I heard these lyrics:

"Hold on, hold on. There's something more than you've been wishing for."

The tractor-trailer rigs were idling, the truckers inside either asleep or Tweeting about how annoyed they were that this traffic snarl had turned into a camporee. Between the engine rumble and the battering wind, the audio quality on my camera was abysmal, but I was getting it. I had to. The sun was easing up, throwing down my favorite slant of shadows and diagonal sun flares through the lens of my camera, as their voices seared me to that spot. They were the Sirens in my Odyssey, but I was not a mariner and they would not shipwreck me. Oh no, quite the contrary.

"Sail on, sail on, there's something further than this compass can explore."

How could a twenty-something songwriter see into my heart? How could three boys, young enough to be my kids, in the middle of the California desert, stuck in a traffic jam on a blistering August afternoon, deliver a singing telegram personally addressed to Jean? There was nobody else in attendance at this concert. There were no other curious travelers who stretched their legs far enough to stroll up for a listen. Their loss, my infinite gain.

Jean Ellen Whatley

If nothing else, this entire road trip had been an exercise in perseverance. I struggled daily. Even with the encouragement from the people who were reading my posts and cheering me on, even with the "come on" from people who were waiting at the end of a day's drive with food and a futon, even with the loving support of my close friends, my family, and my children, I was often weak. I was full of self-doubt, fumbling with my own sense of direction. One minute I'd feel euphoric and empowered, truly in the driver's seat of my own life. The next minute some dark thought or an 800 number appearing on my phone, which always meant a bill collector, would pitch me back onto a giant heap of worry and despair. I got tired. Some days, just thinking about the heat, the driving, my aching back and the miles to go before I slept made me want to pull the scratchy sheets and microscopically-revolting bedspread over my head and hide out at the Motel 6 for days. I mean, 8,600 miles is a long way to drive.

Thank God I got out of my car and went to listen to those boys. *Thank God.* I doubt they'll ever fully know their gift to me. Yet isn't this why musicians write songs? Isn't this why sculptors sculpt, painters paint, writers write, chefs sauté? We create because we have to. There's something inside us that compels us to cut out our heart and lay it on a page, a screen, a canvas, a stage or a platter. We create because we have to, because if we don't, we might go crazy. We create so as to be understood. Isn't that all we really want, simply to be understood? We open our hearts, no matter whether it's song or sonnet, hoping desperately that someone might finally see us. *Really see us.* We're hoping that some goodness we possess, some beauty we express, might resonate in someone else's heart. I understood these guys. How could I not?

"Sail on, sail on, there's something further than this compass can explore."

We live with limited vision, we humans. We are much like moles. The most enlightened among us, I believe, concede that our vision is a small fraction of the light of the universe that does indeed guide our path. We make our plans. We dream our dreams. We trot along, so largely unaware of the immensity of the power that lies beyond our ability to yank on its leash. We drive our silly, mapped-out miles, oftentimes resisting the pull of our compass. I came to embrace the glory of surrendering to it.

I gradually panned my iPhone across the faces of these young musicians in their impromptu rehearsal among the tractor-trailer rigs, knowing that the spell could soon be broken. I knew we could be forced to bug out, race to our cars, throw them in gear and move on down the road before my song was through.

"Hold on, hold on, there's something more than you've been wishing for. "

I held the camera steady, shoulder height, but my eyes were raised above it, locked on the boys in the band. Andres Rodriquez, the lead singer and guitar player, has a very distinctive voice and style: crisply enunciated words, halfway spoken, halfway sung, with a soft edge, as nap is to fabric, the huskiness of his voice. When I tapped the video "record" button, it was more about the novelty of stumbling across a trio on the highway, but within the first couple of bars, however, I understood that this performance was meant to be. I distinctly recall a quiet, slow awakening which seemed to wrap around me, penetrating my scalp like the desert sun, a feeling that, of all the infinite points on the globe, the GPS of my life had resulted in my blue dot landing squarely on top of this red one. I had arrived at my destination. I was in precisely the right spot at precisely the right moment, doing precisely what I was supposed to be doing to experience precisely what I was experiencing. There are unlimited variables that could have prevented this from happening, yet they did not. Intersections such as this are rare and I was there. I was fully present. I felt incredibly lucky and glad to be alive.

There was a time though, a rock bottom time, when I felt like dying, a day back in January of 2004, when I was flat on my back on top of a picnic table in the parking lot behind a church in St. Louis and I was sobbing so loudly I'm surprised nobody called the cops. My shoulders were banging against the wood so hard it felt like my bones would bore a hole in the table. It was the loss. It was all the loss hemorrhaging out of me, creating a vortex so large it would be like pulling the plug on the Great Salt Lake. Except there was no sucking sound. There was just sobbing, choking, coughing with snot running out of my nose, a cussing-out-loud-at-God sound, soon after followed by a subtle wind chime. By the time I'd quieted myself down to hear that faint melody, the day had grown unseasonably mild, the sun actually bathing my face and arms in warmth. But it had started out bitter cold that morning with snow flurries driven by a wind too biting to allow the flakes to weave their blanket on the ground or line the edges of the red bricks of the courthouse where Rick awaited his sentencing. It was judgment day, fourteen months after his arrest. Rick waited inside the courthouse for the judge to rule while my friends in the press corps waited outside in the snow to report it.

The kids and I had chosen not to go to the sentencing hearing. It had been a tough fourteen months already. As I was figuring out how to deal with the emotional tsunami and the serious financial consequences of Rick being out of commission, there was almost constant chatter in the media regarding the circumstances of the case. Ultimately four men were implicated for having sexual encounters with the same teenage boy. It seemed like every time one of the defendants made a court appearance, the news media felt obligated to trot Rick's name out again. It was a never-ending perp walk. One of their own, one of their own, one of their own—they had to make sure they came clean, sufficiently distancing themselves from one of their own who'd turned bad, like a cop on the take. At the same time we were ducking continual media missiles, I was screening calls from collection agencies. Always and forever it seems, trying to keep my family afloat. Just because we were divorced didn't mean Rick wasn't contributing financially. He had just gotten current on the child support when his misdeeds closed the bank.

When we had first split up, Rick went into a tailspin, getting fired from his job just weeks after he'd moved out. He floundered around for a while: a baggage handler at the airport, a grocery-store clerk, a used-car salesman. The child support was spotty at best. I had to file for bankruptcy. What's a girl to do?

It was downright laughable the day I inventoried my assets. It didn't take long. I had very little money, maybe a couple thousand dollars. I withdrew it from the bank and sent it to Nathan, who was still in college in North Carolina. I was like a mogul off-loading cash to a foreign bank account. Then the little shit off-loaded a little bit of my off-loaded cash, not much, maybe a few hundred bucks, for some kind of emergency. Now that I think about it, I can't remember if he ever paid me back.

After I listed my cash on hand, and not my cash in Nate's hands, next came the household goods. Holy Mother of God. I had to inventory all my hand-me-down furniture, the lawnmower, the computer, the china, even our family jewels, which had already been pared down since I'd hocked my wedding ring to buy Sean his first set of drums. This whole asset-inventory exercise was ludicrous—just plain pitiful, really. I listed everything I owned except Pete our dog and Bob the guinea pig. The irony as to who had been the *real* guinea pig, all those years ago, way back in the beginning, when Rick first set his sights on me, did not go unnoticed.

To say that the kids and I had learned to roll with the punches in the ensuing years after breakup and before the lockup would be an understatement. On Rick's sentencing day, however, it was more a body blow. I had called my good friend Terry at the CBS station. He worked the assignment desk. I'd been out of the news business by now for a few years, had moved on to media relations consulting. There's a reason they call it *relations*.

"Terry, when you hear from Ray, will you let me know right away, please? Can you?"

"Sure, Jean," he said in the wonderfully familiar voice I'd come to know from hundreds of stories he'd dispatched me to cover. "I'll give you a call."

The Ray I was referring to was a reporter at Terry's station. I had worked in the same newsroom with him. Another colleague, Andy, was reporting for the FOX affiliate. These were my friends. Being in the news business is like being a cop or a fireman or politician; it's like family. You do battle, then you do shots. These were people who'd come to my house for birthday parties and baby showers, with whom we'd shared picnics, baseball games, and camping trips. I felt nauseous all morning, knowing the sentencing hearing was going on and knowing everybody would lead with it at noon. I could hear the stress in Terry's voice too, when he called me back, about 11:55 a.m.

"Jean?" He sounded serious, but sympathetic. "Eight years, Jean. He got eight years."

I don't remember gasping, don't remember dead air. I just remember Terry's urgency.

"Jean? Jean? Are you okay?" I could hear the police scanners and TVs turned up too loud in the background. Newsrooms are audio toxic.

"Yeah, Terry, thank you." My mind had already lurched ahead to, what does that feel like, to know you'd be locked in a cage for eight years?

"I gotta go. I'm sorry, Jean," he said. "Take care, all right?"

"Will do. Thank you so much for letting me know."

I moved from my office in the faux Florida room into the den. I clicked on the TV. I was home alone. At 11:57:30 they hit the pre-show tease. *"Coming up on Action News, a former newsman gets sentenced for sex crimes."* At 11:58 they hit the two-minute commercial break. I think it was for aluminum siding and a personal-injury attorney, then Lemon Pledge. At the top of the hour, they hit the show open. Those news jingles all sound the same, don't they? They all end with *dah-duh-dah-duh* and a swoosh with sound effects. The director cues the anchors and tells the reporter to stand by.

I had done this at least a thousand times, standing by to go live. Only this time this live report was about the next several years of my children's lives. I remember my friend Andy the most. I wondered if he thought about Sean just before he reported that his daddy would be in prison for eight years. Andy and Sean had history, man. We'd all been on a canoe trip on the Courtois River a few years back. Sean was nine. He'd gotten out of the canoe to swim and I'd spotted a snake in the water. I freaked out and screamed for Andy to swim to Sean to pull him away from the snake. Probably silly, I admit, but Andy did it anyway. Neither one of them got bitten. On this snowy, gray day, Sean was safely at school when Andy reported that his dad would be locked up for eight years.

I clicked off the TV, went outside and got on my bike. I guess by now you're detecting a pattern? I suppose it is my M.O., my modus operandi. When things get intense, I head outdoors: summer, winter, fall, or spring, running, walking, driving, around the country, up and down the sidewalk, around the corner. This time, I was on a bike. I got on my bike and pedaled up the drive, down our street, around the corner and into the main thoroughfare. I was crying. I guess most normal people would consider sitting still, like in a chair or standing by a window. I never could do just one thing at a time. Tears were flowing. I was having a hard time seeing. I reached for a tissue in my pocket but couldn't get to it. I lifted my left arm to wipe my eyes, the handlebars wobbled, the front wheel cut hard to the right. I pulled it back too hard and veered into the traffic coming up behind me. I was on the wrong side of the street to begin with. The driver of the car next to me swerved to miss me, honked and went around. I came so close to getting run over that day, I'm lucky to be alive. I rolled up into the next parking lot, shaken. It was a church, the same church I drive by every single day. It's right next to an elementary school. I cruised around to the back parking lot, out behind the church. There were basketball hoops, a baseball diamond, a barbecue grill and a picnic table near the grass. I parked the bike and sat on top of the picnic table.

"Eight years, eight years, eight years," kept repeating in my brain. I could not fathom what that felt like to Rick, could not imagine the depth of his pain and fear. Eight years of his life in a prison. Eight years! He would never see Sean play a single high-school football game, or attend one of Lauren's tennis matches. He would not see Nathan graduate from college and would miss all the rest of the kids' high-school graduations. He would never see his father again.

Yet, at that moment, I felt relieved. I know that sounds terrible, but in many ways, I honestly felt relieved to know we'd be free from his tormented presence in our lives. For fourteen months, from the time he was arrested to the time he was sentenced, we'd had this uncertainty hanging over us. Now, at least we knew: an eight-year sentence, which with good behavior and time served, he'd be out in seven. The kids and I could get on with our lives and I knew I had a block of time in which we could have some peace.

If only I could find it. I sat on that picnic table, watching kids playing soccer in the school yard next door. How many hundreds of Saturdays had Rick and I been the soccer parents, watching our kids, so innocent of what was ahead, with trusting hearts like mine. This wasn't what I signed up for. This isn't how things were supposed to turn out. I was completely overcome with loss: the loss of my children's innocence, the loss of the life I once thought I'd have and the loss of the one person I'd been clinging to, above all others, to comfort me during this time, to love me, to help ease the burden of what I was going through. It was the man I had fallen in love with at the very onset of all this turmoil.

Talk about bad timing. I had met Ian just a few days before Rick got arrested and it was at the most unlikely and completely inappropriate place to start a love affair. I met him at my brother Garrett's funeral. What a week. I traveled to New Mexico to be with my devastated mother and the rest of my family to attend to the arrangements. But, wonder of all wonders, there had also been this guy there, this Ian dude, who had called after we got news of Garrett's death.

"Your brother was a good friend of mine," Ian from Chicago said. "We were in a band together back in LaCrosse. I just felt a need to connect with somebody in the family to say how sorry I am for your loss."

His voice over the phone was sweet and comforting. "I'd like to come to his service," he said before hanging up.

He came, even spoke a few words. He told endearing stories about things the family never knew. He talked about their band days, one time when they drove nineteen hours straight to get from La Crosse, Wisconsin to Austin, Texas for a last-minute invitation to play at the South-by-Southwest Music Festival. Garrett would have been proud to hear Ian talk about their glory days.

He might have been ashamed of me though, when I hopped in the sack with Ian the next night. It was just one of those things. Seriously, it was just one of those crazy, crazy things. We were instantly attracted to each other the minute we met. It's like those ridiculously predictable scenes in a movie when two people make eye contact across a crowded room. Believe me, I understand how silly this sounds, but until you've experienced it, you don't know jack. I mean, this was happening in real life for the first time in my life and it was powerful. Our eyes would meet in that awkward way, when each person catches the other person looking at them, and usually one person has the decency to look away, scanning the room for something else to focus on. Ian did not. He locked on when I looked up and I caught him staring at me. He had the most inquisitive, luminescent blue eyes I had ever seen, and he apparently derived great satisfaction from putting them on me. Don't get me wrong: This was not a sleazy come-on. It was an "Oh my God, I might have just met the most important person in my life" look. It was thrilling.

After the service, I made a concerted effort to avoid him. I'd subtly move to the next circle of folks when Ian would join the circle containing me. It's like getting too close to the edge of a cliff, a heart-racing attraction like this. I felt ashamed. It seemed so inappropriate, my conflicting emotions of grief, exhaustion and serious attraction all jumbled together. A group of us mourners decided to meet for a mountain hike the next day. It would be everyone's last day in town, the weather forecast was favorable and it seemed an appropriate sendoff. Garrett loved the mountains. We all agreed to meet at noon, but nobody showed up except Ian and me. We went anyway. It was one of the sweetest days of my life. The thin air, the generous sun, the sixty-mile views from the foothills proved to be an intoxicating mix, especially for two world-weary forty-something grievers who were brought together by the passing of the lead guitar. I will never forget watching the sun go down at the end of our day together, my back to his chest, his arms draped around my shoulders. I wrote about it the next day.

Sometimes life grants us moments so perfect,
a person could die happy, having had just that one.
I had such a moment,
your face bathed, so golden,
the sky, your eyes, so breathtakingly blue,
and you held me.
Fiery orange and pinks gave way to twilight hues,
the eyelashes of the sun descending like a blanket,
good night.
And the world at that moment
was perfect.

After our day-long outdoor excursion, we dutifully attended the last supper:

a gathering of all the mourners who'd be heading out of town the next day. Afterward, I drove Ian to his hotel.

"I'm not ready to leave you," he said.

And so I went inside. The next morning, he flew off to Chicago, I flew home to St. Louis, where the very next day Rick was arrested. Saturday to Tuesday, that's the time span in which all of this drama occurred. *Saturday to Tuesday.* When Ian heard the news of what befell me when I returned home, he vowed to stand by me, to do anything he could to help. Poor dude, getting involved with a woman on the brink of catastrophe.

We lasted almost a year. On a clear November morning in Chicago, I left him. It's what he wanted; he just didn't have the backbone to do it himself. After a dozen or so back-and-forth trips, with him increasingly withdrawing and me increasingly clinging, I found my strength, or more like rescued my pride. I got up one morning after he'd said, "I just can't handle a long-distance relationship anymore," which was not followed by an offer to move to St. Louis. Instead he whined, "But I don't want to lose you," and promptly turned his back to me in bed. As soon as it was light, I got up and out. Up and out, packed and gone, in six minutes flat.

"I'm leaving before it gets ugly," I kissed him on the cheek at the door.

"I don't want you to go," he said.

But I had to. I knew we couldn't bridge the distance or different lifestyles. A writer and musician, with no children of his own, it wasn't in his DNA to take on a woman with four kids and a shitload of drama. He admitted as much. He echoed what I already knew in my head, but my heart was lagging behind.

The onslaught of tears commenced as I walked out of his building. A tree full of brilliant yellow gingko leaves had dumped on my car overnight, resembling hundreds of carping Pac Men: "I told you so, I told you so, I told you so," they seemed to mock me, as I brushed their annoying brightness off the windshield and away from my dark heart. I cried all the way from Lake Michigan to the miserable Mississippi. I parked a block from home where I had to suck it up, pull it together, slap on some concealer and get ready to explain to my disappointed kids why Mom was home early and why Ian would never be coming back. The timing sucked. The break-up was shortly before Rick's sentencing.

Boom. Boom.

I was lying on top of the picnic table by now. I'd been watching the children on the playground. Relief over the sentencing turned to grief over the loss turned to anger over my fate. I was so angry. I felt as though my kids were being punished for something they didn't do. It wasn't fair. It simply was not fair. And I felt like a chump, like I'd been the target of a series of cruel, perverted jokes— my husband, my brother, my lover—gone. They were all gone.

"What's the fucking point here, God?" I was on my back, yelling at the sky. "Why did you send him to me if you were just going to take him away? Fuck you, then. Just fuck you. I give up."

This is a scary thing to do, in hindsight, to pick a fight with God.

"What the fuck do you want from me?"

I was wailing. But seriously, a person can cry like that only for a while—it wears you out. The time between my sobs got longer, like a child who's been crying so hard she forgot to breathe, then stops to grab a few quick shallow breaths. I was getting my wind back when a breeze stirred a wind chime on someone's porch or patio. It's odd because I was quite far, really, from anybody's house, I never could pinpoint where the wind chimes were coming from. Plus, it was January. It had been snowing early in the day, but by now it was about 58-degrees and the winter sun was poking out in between the clouds, warming my face and stirring a slight breeze, barely a whisper, but enough to awaken the wind chimes, which always made me think of Garrett.

There is a brass bell on a pole on my back porch. It's a good size, maybe twelve inches in diameter across the bottom. I did not put it there. The man who owned my house before me did. He was handy that way, had been a rancher in Colorado for a while. He'd built a sturdy porch and deck off the fake Florida room in the back all by himself, then erected a bell on a pole. Reminded me of a ship. When I came to look at the house, I commented on it.

"Easy way to call the boys to supper," he smiled.

Or send a message to heaven. On the day Garrett died, some fourteen months prior to this day on which I wallowed in self-pity on top of some random picnic table, I had gone outside and rung that bell. I am not sure why. I guess I was trying to send a message. I think I was trying to help elevate Garrett's spirit to a higher plane.

Sail on, sail on.

Maybe I was just ringing that bell to signify that he had been alive. We do funny things in the midst of grief, such as handing over our hearts to blue-eyed musicians. I rang that bell every single morning for weeks, until tending to the backwash of Rick's shit storm robbed me of this spiritual offering.

On the picnic table, the soggy Kleenex now in shreds, I dabbed my swollen eyes under the cheap drug store sunglasses I'd slapped on before I got on the bike. I looked like crap. My hands dropped to my sides, limp. My knees were bent, leaning one against the other like a couple of drunks. I lay there on my back, motionless. The kids went in from recess and took with them their happy playground noise. The only sound I could hear was the occasional car on the road in front of the church and the wind chimes. Those tiny bells spoke to me, carrying the voice of my brother.

"Jeannie, get up. Don't waste this."

I have never gone that low again. If there is any redeeming grace—and they don't call it redeeming for nothing—to be gained from losing people you love long before their time, maybe it's survivor's guilt. I'm alive. It's a privilege, this breathing. It's a privilege to be present to the forces which cross our paths with unlikely, ill-timed lovers and unexpected, perfectly-timed musicians on a windblown California highway.

The boys in the band in the middle of the road in the middle of the desert finished their song in the way rehearsing musicians do, with a flurry of chords, a laugh or two, "So, how do we get out of this?" as if we'd ever want to. But our moment was through; I stopped recording. We shook hands and made introductions all around. The band, "The You and Me Thing," was on its way to California for a gig and to pick up a piano. I suspect they needed a truck instead of an SUV for the return trip to Phoenix. I ran back to my car to fetch a business card and Libby, to let her stretch her legs for a hot minute.

"They're opening it back up." A handsome man with salt-and-pepper hair, neatly dressed in crisply-pressed jeans and a Ralph Lauren polo shirt trotted alongside the cars letting the drivers know to start their engines. He got in the BMW two cars behind me. The boys loaded up their instruments, patted Libby on the head, gave me a CD, and we hugged and wished each other the best of luck. I trotted back to my car with Libby leaping into the back seat, happy to get off the blistering highway.

Slowly, the traffic began to creep forward. Cars sandwiched in between truck after truck, lurching forward, low gear, brakes whining, one at a time, crowded into the far right lane. Flares now nearly spent, we began to see the cause of the massive traffic jam. Up ahead, in the fast lane, near the median, four highway patrol cars, lights flashing, were like a fortress around the crash site. The windows of the crushed minivan were covered with blue tarps. There was no ambulance, no need. Their moment had passed.

12

I Know About You

Los Angeles: what a mess. No offense. I mean, I really like L.A., in the way you like your show-off cousin from the big city who blows into town, all trendy and cool and annoys you yet fascinates you at the same time. You're a little jealous cause she's skinnier, with naturally sun-bleached hair and has cuter clothes, but she's such a know-it-all and *so* high-maintenance! You are soon ready to be done with her. Such is my relationship with Los Angeles. Yet I admire Los Angeles for her ambition, as opposed to New York, which I admire for her tenacity.

My Los Angeles son, Nathan, is both ambitious and tenacious, a dreamer right off the old block. Nate's been in Los Angeles ever since he drove his Jeep all the way from film school in North Carolina to southern California in pursuit of his celluloid dreams. A boy after my own heart, he told me that by the time he got to Needles, California, it was so damn hot in his rattling Wrangler that he pulled off the highway, drove straight to a Motel 6 parking lot, and waited for some sophisticated hotel guest sipping a piña colada to open the passcard-protected gate, at which time Nate slipped in and jumped into the pool. That's my boy! He gets two "atta boys" for having the courage to dive right into his dream of being a screenwriter and marrying the lovely and lithe Melissa, a cartoon animator and southern girl, whom he found in Southern California. Some day they hope to actually purchase a home. They are wonderful people. They have a wonderfully long couch. It was long enough for me to stretch out my weary bones for a few days before I would head north to the motherland—more like fatherland.

So, L.A.'s a trip, man. I took time out to celebrate the fact that I had

Jean Ellen Whatley

actually made it! I couldn't believe I'd done it! By the time I got to Los Angeles, I had driven 6,075 miles—St. Louis to NYC, down the East Coast, through D.C., North Carolina, across the Deep South, then Texas followed by the desert Southwest. Hell, Texas took an entire month. I'm kidding; it only felt that way. Fact is, the whole damn trip could have ended in Amarillo with me being ax-murdered in a TraveLodge crawling with cockroaches by some fairly innocuous dude named Bob. It all worked out in the end, with me falling asleep across the street in a luxuriously cockroach-free Motel 6 with the new earth-friendly, bug-thwarting parquet floors instead of smelly, beige carpet, lulled to sleep by the soothing voice of Fran Drescher. It took a location swap to arrive at this nirvana.

You see, I had this coupon. I had been lured to the TraveLodge because I had a coupon. A nice desk clerk at the Quality Inn in Asheville, with a sweet accent, five states back, asked if I had "the coupon" when I checked in at her place. As it turns out, there are these nifty little coupon books at Quickie Marts from New York to California with which one can get a few bucks off their room for the night. The TraveLodge in Amarillo was ten dollars off! You can't beat a $39 room with a stick, if you're good with a shoe on cockroaches.

I didn't notice the bugs, however, until after I could not access the TraveLodge Wi-Fi. So I was already in a highly agitated state of being ready to get out of the state of Texas, mostly 'cause I was antsy about the family reunions, known and unknown, which lay ahead. Plus, I had just plopped down, worn out after a day's drive and the requisite load-in ritual, which also frequently included me going up and down a flight of stairs a few times, since I typically requested an upstairs room. I did this for my safety, as I had been warned by well-intentioned, paranoid girlfriends and elderly aunts not to get a first-floor room because bloodthirsty murderers would most certainly be crouching in the shrubs and observing me going into my room, where, later that night, they'd cut the window screen, come right in and ax me in my sleep.

Bob just knocked on the door.

"I heard you were having trouble with the Wi-Fi?"

I let him in. On the sheer sincerity of his voice, not even a peephole peep, I said, "Come on in." I had called the front desk to report that I could not get online, which is certain death to a writer with legions of adoring readers waiting with fevered anticipation for the next installment of my wild adventures from the road. The nice young man with the greasy hair and earring in his lip at the front desk said he'd send the maintenance man right away. I was dubious. I mean, this wasn't a leaky faucet or a burned-out light bulb or vibrating bed which won't quit shaking; this was a computer problem. Minutes later, there's a knock on the door. Libby did not even stir from her queen-sized bed. Great, this is great. Some watchdog.

"Hey, I'm Bob," he said when I opened my door. As if simply being Bob made it safe for me to let him into my room. There was no monogrammed TraveLodge polo shirt nor name tag to assure me that this guy was legit. This is a good indication of how the road was wearing me down. I'd become lax on my own security measures since the night in Toledo when I wouldn't even open the door for a guy with a badge, fake appearance notwithstanding. It did cross my mind, for a hot second, after I'd hollered, "Come on in," that I was letting a complete stranger into my room: a red-headed guy in denim shorts, a polo shirt, and grey New Balance tennis shoes, with a Texas accent and a ball cap that said, "You Are Here." Well, if he did attack me and I survived, at least I could provide a good description to the cops. I'm the person you want in the lobby during a bank robbery.

In the interest of full disclosure, Bob was carrying a laptop and not a hatchet, so that gave me some comfort. However, he could not give me Internet access. He was nice enough, said he just couldn't figure it out, gave me any number of codes, checked the firewall settings, managed to get online with his Dell laptop but not my Mac. "Sorry," he said. "Try the lobby, maybe?"

In desperation I called son Nathan in Los Angeles. He tried to troubleshoot from afar. As I was sitting there on the phone with Nate, with my computer on the blond dinged-up pressed-wood table, sitting far too low in the ergonomically incorrect, slouchy orange vinyl chair, with my legs sticking to it, I noticed the lumbering brown bug teetering atop the droopy shag-carpet threads.

"Nate, I gotta get out of here," I said. I hung up and bugged out. Earring-in-the-lip-guy at the front desk even gave my money back.

"We've had this problem with Macs," he said. I was grateful, despite thinking, "So, it's not like half the planet, or more, isn't using a Mac these days?" I didn't even mention the bugs. Whatever. Fortunately there was one vacancy across the street at the Motel 6. One room! It was forty-seven dollars, a full eight bucks more and worth every penny! Libby was confused. She looked completely baffled "Didn't we just do this?" as we repeated the load-in, this time, of course, upstairs, and only after we'd made a quick food run to the only place that was still open at ten o'clock, a drive-through Mexican joint.

I nodded and smiled as I passed folks on the balcony of our new home for the night. A skinny gal, oversized tee shirt down to her knees, with her hair in a scrunchied ponytail on top of her head, a cigarette clenched in her teeth, was running toward me, chasing a pit bull headed for the stairs.

"Hey," she said and I could hear the twang in her voice with only one word.

By the way, I saw more pit bulls than any other breed of dog last summer. Libby sniffed with an air of superiority, because Lord knows she'd never bolt like that now that she was so well-trained off the leash. I got to my room and the metal motel room door clanked behind me, a comfort by now. I made myself a vodka tonic and pulled the sheers together, but didn't close the black-out drapes even though there was a lot of foot traffic on the balcony that night, being Friday night and all. Those damn motel curtains make me feel claustrophobic. I figured, "Fuck 'em if they can't take a joke," as fellow lodgers would walk by and maybe catch a gauzy glimpse of a woman on the bed with her 86-pound yellow mutt, sharing takeout from the Taco Sal down the frontage road. Yeah, baby, get a load of this—Friday night in Amarillo, Texas, steppin' out! It was pretty bad—the food, that is. I gave Libby only a couple of tiny bites of the taco meat, not wanting to rouse her innards because I was too exhausted to take her out again. There was not a solitary blade of grass on that entire property. It was all blacktop. I had already walked a half mile or more with Libby after fleeing the insects across the street before we checked in at home sweet Motel 6. It took six blocks before she was inspired to pee. After half of an uninspired taco and picking at the beans and rice, I put the whole plastic mess back in the plastic sack and tied it up tight. This is another little trick you learn on the road. You don't want to wake up smelling last night's dinner. It's gross. As if staying in Motel 6s from Toledo to Amarillo wasn't gross enough already. This property, however, was one of the newer designs, more earth-friendly, Zen-like, with fake parquet floors and olive-green bars of soap, in which no animals had been used in the testing.

I told myself to catch up on my blog. I had a backlog of comedy and tragedy from Texas and I wanted to file those stories before I hit the New Mexico line, where there would be material o' plenty. But I was just too damn tired. Even though my muse is a slave driver, there is only so much she can whip out of me in a day. I clicked on the TV. Now here's a statistic for you—in eight weeks on the road, I turned on the TV in my motel like four times. I was completely disinterested in what was going on in the world during that time.

Selfish, I know: a bit creepy too. Truthfully, I was scared to death I'd click on the *Today* show and there would be some broad being interviewed about her bestselling book about a road trip with a dog. I would have run out in front of a truck. On this night, I was so brain-dead, I probably would have just said "fuck it" and ordered a copy off Amazon.com and turned around to go home the next day. The few times I did turn on the television, it was usually tuned to the Spanish channel with the novellas the housekeeping ladies catch up on while they clean the rooms. This night it was reruns of *The Nanny*. I was so lazy I did not even bother to change the channel. I fell asleep with my clothes on to the sounds of the nasal-toned nanny. In some inexplicable way it was comforting; all was right with the world.

By the time I rolled into Los Angeles, Amarillo seemed like a distant skid mark on the highway of my life. In the interim, I'd done the deep dive in Albuquerque, had spent two nights in Phoenix with my first husband and his wife, swam in their saltwater pool. Just need to insert an "OMG!" here because the pool was fabulous. It was not lost on me that my first ex-husband is living in a very nice home with a lovely remodeled kitchen complete with a wine rack and beer chiller and a lovely pool in the yard and I don't have two nickels to rub together, and yet, neither he nor his lovely wife rubbed my face in my apparent slightly-past-mid-life crisis. In fact, they were quite supportive, morally and financially. By Los Angeles, I had experienced a great deal of abundant benevolence from the road, including the amazing Interstate 10 cosmic smash-up at the car crash. So, by L.A., I'm thinking the journey has already been life-changing. I had no idea that the revelations had scarcely begun and Libby, sleeping contentedly on Nathan's floor, jubilant to be near a human who smelled familiar, had no idea that this stop would be the hallmark of her trip.

It's because of the beach. Nate and Melissa insisted we go to Huntington Beach, Surf City, USA and home to one of the longest, most popular dog beaches on the west coast. Dogs o' plenty. The day was absolutely perfect; what else would you expect for So Cal? Unlike Chicago, where I was in the grip of panic the whole time we were near Lake Michigan, at Huntington Beach I felt no fear of letting go. Even now, as I write this, it moves me to tears, remembering how she ran. After Nathan, Melissa and I got to the bottom of the long concrete ramp leading down to the sand, far below and far away from the highway, when I unsnapped the leash from her collar Libby just ran, and ran and ran. It's what dogs live for, right? I kept trying to be in her doggie brain, trying to imagine the sensation she was experiencing—encountering the ocean for the first time, free to run as hard and as fast as she could go with an unlimited supply of other dogs with whom to run.

I was amazed at how quickly Libby took to it: like a duck to water, except she's a dog. She didn't know which thrill to seek first; she'd scurry around and check out other dogs, then she'd follow them into the surf, chasing the receding waves back down to the ocean, like a sandpiper with four legs. Then she'd bolt up to some dog lover and grab a little lovin' on the side, then she'd spot the three of us, trailing behind, and she'd come bounding back, as if to make sure it was okay for her to be having so much fun. So many dogs, so many smells, so many people! And there wasn't a single solitary soul on that beach eating fried chicken. God, I love California! And so did my dog. She was free. Libby was running free. There was nobody yanking her chain or telling her no. There was no invisible fence, no wall of voltage between her and the object of her desire. There was just freedom and this freedom was my gift to her. For every extra minute too long that I made her wait in the car, for the times I scolded her in Chicago to hurry up and poop, and threatened to kill her in Toledo if she didn't stop barking at the rent-a-cop at the door, from the crinkly hot grass in Texas to the precious little shade outside the Dunkin' Donuts in Philadelphia, this was how I made recompense.

To give such joy is to experience it yourself. For the rest of my days, I am indebted to Libby for sharing hers with me. It is such an easy thing to do, to make our dogs happy: a ride in the car, a walk around the block, a bite of pizza crust, a place on the couch. Oh, that we could experience pure bliss.

I've often wondered if she dreams about the water. Chances are she dreams about the scraps of gyro meat the lady at the Greek diner gave her when we stopped at a great place on our way back to L.A., with milkshakes and gyros on the menu. What a combo. The lady who owns the place came out to our picnic table with a cup of meat shavings from the broiler. Libby thought she'd died and gone to heaven. I did too when I was actually able to take a nap in the back seat, with Libby's head in my lap, as Nate drove us home. For the first time in seven weeks and more than 6,400 miles, there was somebody else behind the wheel. Talk about bliss.

It dissipated into sadness, though, when I had to get back in the driver's seat the next day. Nathan is my firstborn. There's something about that, the person who introduces you to motherhood. It is a unique pact, a kind of mutual understanding, a different level of regard.

"Hey, I've never done this before," says the young mother as she looks down at this warm, soft creature with the heavenly fresh-from-the-womb scent, which is even better than the aroma of freshly-baked bread.

"No worries; I'm new too," the infant replies as he leans his fresh-milled cheek toward tender breast, instinctively rooting for survival.

Nathan probably saved me. He doesn't know that. I'd be the first to admit there are millions of examples that repudiate this assertion, but at least for this mother, the instant I knew I had another life to account for, any predisposition for self-destruction quickly vanished. I was unwilling to allow any of my babies to ever become collateral damage.

Now, I was about to learn the extent of my own. I waved goodbye to Nate and Melissa on their front stoop, smiling behind my sunglasses, making it all the way to the stop sign at the corner of Wilshire and Burnside before the tears reached my chin. By the time I was heading north on the 101, melancholy had been usurped by nerves. Despite the beauty of the central California coast and me telling myself, *"Be in the moment Jean, be in the moment!"* it's hard to be lulled into relaxing when your inner voice is browbeating you to take care of business. I hadn't felt precisely like this before. Granted, one would think that a gal with a dog, who's not too adept at changing tires or reading GPS, facing a daunting journey of more than 8,000 miles would be a little jumpy from time to time. Well, sure, when the sun went down and I still had 162 miles to go until my next stop and my eyes were so tired I was cross-eyed and there's no rest area or gas station, nothing but two lanes and cactus as far as the eye can see, that's one brand of being on edge. But this was something entirely different. I'd deliberately avoided thinking about that Lester brother until the other stops along this journey were contentedly tucked away. Every time I popped the hatch and rearranged the yoga quilt, my cowboy hat, the Milk Bones, my pitiful dusty, seam-split loafers, I had one more city, one more chapter, one more round of goodbye hugs under my belt. But thanks to the Windex and paper towels that my thoughtful friend Charles told me to bring along to clean the bugs off the windshield, I now had an unimpeded view of what might lie ahead. "Might" being the operative word.

Of course the view along CA 101 was breathtaking, impossible for it not to be, even with my paternal preoccupation. I got as far as San Luis Obispo and decided to stop early for the day. Good thing I did. Another road lesson: as alluring as the carefree adventure of rolling into town not knowing where you'll stay for the night might be, don't try it on a Saturday night in California tourist towns. I'm just saying. I went to three places before I found a vacancy at, of course, the Motel 6, which was masquerading as a Motel 99—as in ninety-nine dollars. At least that's how much they wanted to charge me. I wasn't in the mood to drive inland and farther north, seeing how I'd be staying with friends in San Francisco the next night, and I needed to contemplate what lay ahead in the Bay area. Or not.

I needed a night to not speak to anyone, and, as always, I had traveled farther than my blog had kept up. I had some things I needed to get out, some words I needed to wrest free to relieve the creative constipation that had built up from four days in L.A. catching up with my son and socializing. This had been my routine: a few days with kinfolk, a couple of days to tattle on them. I had to clear the logjam so I could wipe my mind clean and be ready to fill it up again with the northern expedition. I checked in at Motel $99. Then Libby and I went hunting for food.

Be careful what you ask for, this solitude. Saturday night in San Luis Obispo, the main drag was lively. Stores still open, cool currents of refrigerated air, light and noise and the smell of fresh hundred-dollar denim jeans spilled onto the sidewalk. Teenagers in cars were draggin' the strip while yuppies with baby strollers and drippy ice-cream cones crowded the sidewalk; friendly folks copped a feel of my dog as they passed us by; couples leaned forward over half-filled, full-priced glasses of California red at their tables next to the window; the vivid kaleidoscope conspired to splash the chapters of my life in my face like a puddle of rainwater pitched up from the street by an innocent driver who came too close to the curb. Or close to home. It was hitting close to home. On this buzzing Saturday night in the heart of the California Central Coast, here we were, my golden girl and I, on a hot date on a warm evening, a woman alone with a dog, in stark contrast to every other pairing on the street. Nobody seemed to notice but me. I tied Libby to the pole outside the pizza joint with the red-and-white checkered tablecloths and neon beer signs. I could get a slice to go and keep an eye on her while I waited in line. That was our modus operandi, the *"MVC."* That stands for "maintain visual contact" with the dog. I could be Libby's fucking Secret Service agent by now.

Lord knows I'd already achieved world-class procrastinator status by this time. I was midway up the coast of California, seven weeks on the road, and I had not reached out to the mystery bro. I think I had put it off because I was scared. As much as I'd been brave in calling up old friends and cousins whom I had not seen in decades, the phone call I needed to make was the one

I most dreaded making. I would be reaching out to someone so far back on my timeline I wasn't even sure he existed. Talk about hostile—he could turn out to be even less friendly than those lovely young girls who pounded on my door and called me a bitch in Toledo. Now it would be the long-lost girl who belonged to his father. From the measly scraps of information I'd gotten from my mother, this half-brother, the only other child from my father, had not laid eyes on me in fifty three years.

What if I'd waited too long? What if he wasn't there? What if he was gone too? I realize that in the modern, healthy world in which we live, with the average life expectancy of Americans (McDonalds cheeseburgers notwithstanding) now standing at seventy eight years of age, chances are this dude would still be standing at sixty five. I had been told he was the same age as my brother Don, and we see what happened there. Garrett was only fifty one when we lost him, so it's not like I didn't have just cause for my urgency. Finding Lester had been one of the most important drivers of the entire journey and there was a part of me that was so afraid that once I finally got the courage to make the call I'd hear, "Sorry, you're a week too late."

That's what had happened with my father. I had twelve weeks of opportunity in 1983 to visit my father when I was working in Lake Tahoe. I'd gone up there for a summer, lived with friends, waited tables at Caesar's, made a ton of cash before I finished journalism school.

"You know, you could see Tommy while you're up at the lake," my mother had said to me in a rare moment of magnanimity regarding my father. "I'm sure he still lives near Placerville; it's only about thirty miles." I was twenty eight years old and it was the first time I would ever be without Nathan for an extended period while he visited his dad and new stepmom in Phoenix. They did not have the saltwater pool back then. I was adrift without my boy. I took my friend Sue up on her offer to come up to "the lake" (that's what the trendy set in California calls Lake Tahoe) and I could live with her and work. Mom was dead set against it. In one final and failed attempt to control me, she said, "You'll only go up there and get in trouble." She knew from whence she spoke and apparently knew me fairly well, but I did manage to escape California fairly unscathed. Before I left for my defiant summer as a single girl, she rose to her bigger self and told me she would help me track down Tommy while I was up there, if so inclined.

I wasn't. I thought about it. I thought about it quite a bit, as a matter of fact, sandwiched in between Carl the ginger, a mustached pit boss at the craps tables who sat in my station every night so he could flirt with me, and Joe, the Jersey Italian transplant who captivated me with the crescent moon scar across his chin, with his dark eyes and white teeth, who despite being six years my junior thought I hung the moon. Sure, I thought about reaching out to that sad sack father of mine who hadn't bothered to look me up all those years. Honestly, I wanted to. I really did. Especially after my mother and Frank brought Nate up to the lake from Phoenix to spend the last four weeks of the summer there with me. I could have taken Nathan to see Tommy. I could have shown him his grandson. But I chickened out. I didn't know what I'd say. I didn't know what I'd find or how I would feel. I didn't go.

Instead, I went back to Albuquerque, wiping off the barroom-scented remains of the only single summer in my life (married at nineteen, a mother at twenty three) got on with my senior year of college, got a job at a TV station by October, started dating the anchor man by November, was married and pregnant again by the following June. Why waste time, right?

It was in the newsroom, a couple of years later on a Saturday night. I was on deadline, about 8:30, when my mother called my direct line. She had just returned from a visit to California. She'd been to San Francisco, then up to Placerville, her old hometown. She'd heard some news.

"Jean, Tommy's dead, honey."

I don't know why she felt compelled to share that little wad of information at that precise moment. My news shooter Eddie was waiting by the door to leave. Bob, my editor, was standing by to edit and I still had voice tracks to cut. My husband Rick was sitting across the newsroom, his back to me, typing away at his beige IBM Selectric and soon would be on my beige ass if I didn't get my story filed and into editing and get out the door to report on the latest ditch drowning. (I never said the *drownings* were folklore, just the witch.)

I think I said, "Okay, Mom," and hung up. The power of concentration is an amazing thing. I recorded my voice tracks, I jumped in the truck, we barreled down the road to a concrete reservoir where the diversion channels dump their contents, sometimes bodies. The front of my brain was broadcasting words on live TV while the back of my brain was thinking, *Fuck all of you people out there! I don't need no stinking father!* I climbed back into the truck, another live report done. I am nothing if not a performer. "Money in the bank," that's what Eddie always called me. I'm glad he wasn't in the mood to talk. We rode along in the live truck back to the TV station, my face turned toward the window so Eddie wouldn't see my eyes brimming with tears as the Police sang, "Every

Breath You Take" but my father would not be watching every move I'd make. That vault had been slammed shut.

That's what had me so freaked out about making the cold call from the road twenty four years later. I didn't think I could stand it if another door might have been closed, but I sure as hell could not stand to watch that damn horse's tail twitch another second. Traffic was crawling on the 101; I was in the right middle lane with a fancy white horse trailer in front of me with a brown horse twitching his tail, side to side. I had just passed the exit to Gilroy and was pondering what folks *do* at a garlic festival when I just couldn't put it off a moment longer. Hell, I'd had the phone number from the time I'd left Albuquerque. I kept thinking there would be a perfect moment. I'd pull over, maybe a rest stop, maybe some nice quiet park, maybe a bridge, next to a river or a lake, or a pasture full of horses, some place quiet, with nobody else around so I could focus on what to say.

What exactly *do* you say to somebody you don't know but with whom you share the same father?

"Hi, I'm your long-lost sister, the one your daddy got in big trouble over."

At the very least, I wanted to be parked to have this conversation. In a way, I was. Traffic was going nowhere. It was getting late. I wanted to give him a couple days' notice and I didn't know exactly where he lived, didn't know if the address and phone number I had in El Dorado County was the right guy. But like standing at the edge of a swimming pool looking at the water, it wasn't getting any warmer. Staring at the back of a white horse trailer with a chocolate-brown tail twitching back and forth, back and forth, in bumper-to-bumper traffic on Highway 101, eighty miles outside San Francisco, I dove head first. This was a phone call I had thought about for decades.

"Hi, Angela?" I took a wild guess, since this was one of the names in the county tax records.

"Yes," she said.

Bingo.

"My name is Jean and I'm looking for a Michael Lester who's father's name was Tommy. Do I have the right house?"

There was a slight pause and then, "Yes."

In one call, *one phone call*, I had found him.

"My mother was an old family friend. I believe my older brother Don may have known Mike. I was hoping to talk to him."

"Mike's my dad. I believe he's sleeping right now. He's got kind of a cold

Jean Ellen Whatley

or something."

I told her no problem, I could call back. I was afraid if I got off the line, though, I might not get her back again. I didn't want to sound desperate.

"No problem, just tell your dad that Jean called. And I believe he might have known my older brother Don in San Francisco and maybe my mom. They've both passed away, but I'm trying to back track with some old... acquaintances."

Another pause. "Let me see if he's awake."

She left and came back, long enough for traffic to creep along another forty-five feet. With each inch of forward motion, the suspense mounted and I was petrified that some semi-truck would come between me and my cellphone signal, disconnecting my first connection to half of my genetic makeup.

"Yeah, he's asleep," was followed by a long pause. Just as I was about to give her my number and hang up, she asked, in the same tone you'd ask someone to pass the salt, "Was my grandpa your father?"

Just like that. Way to cut to the chase, homegirl.

"Yep."

It was all I could muster, staring at the horse's tail and a sea of taillights in front of me. For someone who's been throwing words out like grass seed from a broadcast spreader all my life, that's all I had: just "yep."

"I know about you."

In those four words a lifetime of wondering if anybody else had ever wondered was resolved. To hear that in someone else's house, at some point in time, whether sitting around a kitchen table, on the front porch, in the living room, in a beer joint or on a deathbed, that some words had been spoken about a little brown-eyed girl, a baby, really, who'd gone away on the train with her mama, the fact that somebody, anybody, had talked about me, had remembered or wondered, moved me beyond words.

I know about you. How I had wanted them to know about me. I had wanted him, my father, to know about me. I wanted him to know what a wonderful, loving, beautiful soul had been born from his indiscretion. We had missed our chance, Tommy and I. He never came around to see me and I had been too spineless to track him down while I had the chance. But now, in one phone call, the first try, on the second ring, I had found a trace of him, my brother.

"Are you okay?" Angela asked, as by now there had been a gap long enough to drive a horse trailer through. Of course, I was completely choked up, center lane, traffic moving at the breakneck speed of 12.5 MPH and my eyes were welling with tears as I tried not to bump into the horse's butt which now had Libby's rapt attention. She'd sat up miles ago.

"I'm sorry," I replied. Why do I always apologize? "This just means a lot to me. Thank you, Angela, so much, for taking this call. I am so glad you picked up." As if she'd had ESP that the long-lost sister/aunt was the person on the other end of the line.

"Don't cry! Be careful!" She had a laugh in her voice. "It will be okay. Just don't have a car wreck, okay? It will all be okay." How's that for a woman whom I've never met, my new niece, having the immediate generosity of spirit, sense of humor and common sense to snap me out of my CA 101 meltdown? Fast on our feet apparently runs in the family.

"I will have him call you, I promise."

An hour later, he did. Thank God it wasn't as I was navigating the mixmaster where you can either head west toward San Fran or head north to San Rafael. Out of all the freeway knots I untangled last summer, the I-80, 880 and 580 interchange was by far the most challenging, exacerbated by the fact that I lost my glasses at Huntington Beach and I had been using drugstore readers all the way up the coast, off and on, off and on, staring over the tops of them to see road signs, peering through them to see the map on my phone. It rang while I was doing doughnuts in a parking lot in suburban Novato, about thirty miles north of San Francisco, following the pulsing blue ball, trying to find the street to my friend Dan's house where I was spending the night. I was already late for supper when Mike's number came up in my iPhone. Such a weird feeling, to see "Mike Lester" in my cellphone, the mystery brother, suddenly real. I had to pick up.

"Jean, I guess this is your brother Mike." I pulled over at the Shell station as he continued. "I always knew this day would come."

We talked for about half an hour. Libby did not understand why I was neither getting gas nor going to the bathroom. She whined a couple of times, sighed loudly to register her disgust, then lay back down. She is so accommodating when I need her to be. "I'm so glad you called," my new older brother said. "I didn't know how to find you. All I knew was I had a little sister named Jeannie, someplace."

This was Sunday, August 20. Libby and I had been on the road for nearly seven weeks. Mike and I agreed to meet on Tuesday. I'd drive up to El Dorado Hills, which is northeast of Sacramento, after I tooled around San Francisco for a day. I got to Dan's house late. He was a news shooter I'd worked with in Albuquerque whom I had not seen for twenty six years. This was no small reunion in itself, once again to be welcomed with open arms by someone I hadn't seen in a very long time. I'll be damned if this sweetheart of a man, and Tracey, his darling wife, whom I had never met, didn't have a steak dinner and a nice California pinot noir ready to put on the table. They totally understood why I'd been delayed, talking to my never-seen brother for the first time. We took their two dogs and mine out for a moonlit walk with their teenage daughters, who are beautiful, leggy, California girls through and through. That night I slept in a seventeen-year-old girl's room with posters of hot soccer boys on the wall. I felt so blessed to be sleeping in the home of yet another kind family. I felt so blessed to have my own brood. They were so excited when I'd told them the news.

The next day, I would pay homage to my mother. I got up and out early, since I had only one day in San Francisco. I was running out of money and time. I had to do San Francisco, head northeast to El Dorado Hills to meet my brother, and then I had one more, free overnight stop in Lake Tahoe with the same girlfriend who'd invited me there years before. Then I would need to get the hell home.

I felt my mother's spirit with me when I was overlooking the Golden Gate Bridge. Standing there next to the bay with that world-famous view, for the first time in my life I thought about how hard it must have been to leave San Francisco to live in Texas. *Texas?* But she was going there for a man. She was leaving northern California, the Golden State to which she'd been delivered from the choking dust of Oklahoma when she was just fourteen, leaving all this beauty behind to reunite with the man she thought she needed. I could relate. How full-circle the lives of mothers and daughters can be. Her California was my Carolina: a sad farewell, one more move, a last-ditch effort to make it work. God bless our naïve hearts.

I stood there for the longest time staring at the bay, channeling my mother. She was both reckless and responsible and this was the land that had branded her. She learned to drive on mountain roads, she married at sixteen, took a bus to Reno to dump her first husband at the ripe old age of seventeen. She worked in seaside cafés and fancy mountain resorts until she met the tall Mr. Whatley with whom she thought she could have a life. They had a tortured relationship, as evidenced by long separations with babies on the side. Pregnant with me but not showing yet, she moved from Placerville to San Francisco to go to Western

Union school. She wanted a better life. She rented a tiny flat in the Mission District with my two big brothers, Don and Garrett, and she finished teletype school before I was born.

She was all alone when she went into labor. Took a cab to the hospital, calling Kybie, the German lady who kept Garrett during the day, to come watch him and Don while she went to have another baby.

"She looks like Archie Moore," was Booker's assessment of his infant granddaughter after he and my grandmother Marie got there from Placerville. If you Google "Archie Moore," you'll see my baby picture there, I swear to God. Never mind that Archie Moore was a black man, whom God only knows how many uppercuts he took to the face. He was possibly the greatest light-heavyweight of all time. He was called the "Old Mongoose" and the "Ageless Warrior." He scored 140 knockouts in a career that spanned from 1936 to 1963. The dude never lost his crown in the ring and in 228 recorded bouts, Archie was stopped only seven times. Okay, even if perhaps my mother wasn't too thrilled being told that her newborn daughter looked like an aging prizefighter, maybe she willed his stamina on me. Ageless Warrior? I'll take it any fucking day of the week.

I don't know how Tommy reacted when he saw me the first time, but his son just smiled. Mike was out in the yard when I pulled up in front of the modest, single-story, brown bungalow at the end of a long, gravel road nestled in rolling hills, which when there's not a drought are probably green, instead of golden brown. The "No Trespassing" sign nailed to a wooden pole at the beginning of the lane is perhaps a deterrent to those who might be looking to steal auto parts, but simply noted by me. Mike has built an automotive shop out at Tommy's old place, made a lot of improvements, I'm told. On the drive out there I kept wondering, *will he be short or tall, blue eyes or brown? Fat or thin, bald or full head of hair? Will Mike look like me?*

Of course he did. I mean, just think about everything else that happened on this journey. Would it be any other way? The half-brother I had never seen is handsome, sweet and funny. We look like family.

"So, I guess you must be the sister," he said as I walked into the yard. He shook my hand and then pulled me in for a brotherly hug. He had a sweet Chevelle, electric blue, which he'd just finished restoring, parked beneath a protective tent in the front yard. Later, when we took pictures in front of the car, he told me, "Move your arm, you're covering my new wheels."

The man's got a sense of humor; I like that. Angela, or Angie as she goes by, is the one who took the pictures. I was so grateful to meet the wonderful voice on the phone from two nights before. This was my niece. My smart, sweet, reassuring niece, who had been so comforting to a strung-out stranger searching for a scrap of family.

"Well, let's check it out," Angie said as Mike and I squinted in the noonday sun to study each other's faces. Can you imagine how it feels to look at a grown man for the first time, realizing that half of his genetic fiber came from the same source as your own and for both of your lives you've coexisted on the planet not knowing each other? It was so much easier than I'd expected: the sweetest sparkle in his dark brown eyes, dark as mine.

"Yeah," we kind of nodded knowingly, it was like looking into the mirror, only a different gender with nine years' difference. When we got into the house, out of the glaring sun, it was uncanny—to me, anyway—how much we'd inherited from our father. Mike was the only son of his mother and Tommy. I was the only daughter of my mother and Tommy. Each of us had other siblings from our respective mothers, with enough marriages and divorces among our extended families to keep the El Dorado County Clerk in business for a month, both of us with a couple under our own belts.

We sat at the kitchen table. Mike's pit bull Sweet Pea actually hopped up and sat, like a human, in an empty chair across the table from me, quizzically observing. It was quite funny, really. Seems misbehaving dogs run in the family. After Libby and Sweet Pea had performed their requisite posturing and Sweet Pea was satisfied that neither I nor Libby posed a threat, both dogs flopped on the floor and fell asleep. Angie apologized for the house, said she'd recently moved back in with her dad so she could go back to school. I'd done that a time or two in my life. There were clothes and boxes everywhere and she'd soon have to leave to go pick up her daughter from school. They had taken the time to round up some old photos of Tommy, the album and loose pictures spread out on the table. I had only seen one tiny picture of my father to this point.

I learned that he was as much English as he was Irish. He was a logger in his young days, in Washington State. I saw fantastic photos of my paternal grandparents and my father as a strapping young man, standing behind a flatbed carrying a log some twenty feet in diameter. I was astounded by how much the young Tommy Lester looked like my son Nathan. Mom had told me from the minute he was born, "Nathan favors Tommy." She was right.

There were a few snapshots from the bar, the infamous Louie's Place in Folsom. That's where he undoubtedly met my mom and they grew cozy. I don't know whose respective spouse was around at the time, but I am forever grateful that nature took its course. Sometime after I was born, when I must have been a toddler, Tommy and his little boy Mike took a short side trip on their way home from an outing.

"We were coming home from salmon fishing," said Mike. "I must have been ten or eleven. We went to your house and I remember there were some kids in the room, I don't remember their names. But my dad says to me, "This is your baby sister, Mike," and I remember thinking how cute you were. You were in a little playpen in the living room and you were standing up, holding the rail, and you just had the cutest little eyes. They left us kids in there, just sitting in the living room, and went off in the bedroom for awhile."

I don't think he meant to offend me, as squirmy as it feels knowing that my mom was still putting out for this guy who may or may not have been worthy. And as much as it slightly hurts me to know that he was making a booty call, rather than a welfare check on his baby girl, how can I be offended by an additional romp when I was conceived from an earlier one?

"Anyway, he came back out and I knew we were in trouble with my mom, 'cause we were late getting back home and he was drunk. I had to drive us home, like thirty miles, and I was just a little kid. I got home and told my mom we'd seen my baby sister and all hell broke loose."

That very well might have been the crowning blow. I don't know for sure; all I do know is that Mike's mom gave Tommy his walking papers. Made things rough on him. Mike lived for a while in the projects in Sacramento, his mother, like mine, working hard to provide for her kids. Tommy wasn't around sometimes when he should have been. He'd tell Mike he was coming to take him fishing and then wouldn't show, leaving his little boy waiting out on the street. But when I asked him for one of the photos that he and Angela had rounded up to show me, Mike took a long time considering which one. I sat patiently.

"Okay, this one," he said, handing me a particular snapshot I was coveting, a color photo of my father at Louie's place at Christmas. Mike thought long and hard about parting with it. Such remnants are rare. I appreciate the value of limited artifacts. Hell, I drove all over the country searching for mine.

I could see the affection in Mike's face as he was studying the photos. Tommy died at only sixty-seven. He'd been running a bar and a card room for decades. It takes a toll. He drank too much, developed diabetes; things went from bad to worse. Mike had seen him just a day or two before he passed. They seemed to have patched things up by then. Life, if we're lucky, teaches us, I think, that over time hurt might not go away completely, but the heart can expand to move stuff in next to it. Stuff like forgiveness, love of the here and now, understanding and grace. If we're lucky, this is what we load up front, relegating bitterness, disappointment and regret to the trunk.

"Dude, we are staring into the face of our future."

"Isn't that the truth," Mike laughed at my reaction to a photo of my father, grey hair and glasses.

I had never seen any pictures of him as an older man. I had only one: a small black-and-white photo of him from back in the early '60s, serving my grandfather a beer. Looking at the older Tommy, the round-faced, brown-eyed grandpa to Angie, I found myself wanting to know what it felt like to hug him: really, to be hugged *by* him, my daddy. I wanted him to know me, but I do not blame him for not coming around. My mother had made her deal; Tommy was to stay away.

Just before I got up to leave, I pulled out a wallet-sized photo of Nathan and me. I wanted to show Mike and Angie the family resemblance. When Angie saw it, her voice went up. "Oh my God! I just came across that picture two weeks ago when I was cleaning out some of Grandpa's stuff! I threw it away. I'm sorry, I just didn't make the connection."

The photo was taken the same year I was working in Tahoe. The only other person who had a copy of that photo was my mother. She had assured me, long ago, when she first confessed about her duplicitous deed, that she kept Tommy up to date on how I was growing up. She sent my grandfather an extra school picture every year for him to give to Tommy. I had assumed the photos stopped when my grandfather passed away, long before Tommy did. Yet, here it was, proof that my mother had kept sending those photos to my father, right up until the time he died.

He *knew* about me.

13

Duty to the Dead

The parting shot from the Lester bro was, "Mission accomplished."

"You drove all the way out here to find me," he said with a look of affection not developed over a lifetime but, instead, an hour. "Well, you found me. You can go home now."

Oh, if only it were so. I was ready to go home. The novelty of the road was wearing thin. I'd grown weary of the industrial-disinfectant smell of rest-stop bathrooms, scratchy white towels rolled up into tubes crammed into cheap chrome towel racks, the baritone hum of the condenser on the air conditioner responding to my demand for "low cool," knowing that I'd be freezing within an hour of pushing the button. There is no middle ground between suffocation and arctic chill. And those Motel 6 bedspreads with the planes, trains and automobiles, oh please! If I could have transported my golden mutt and me back to St. Louis in an instant, I would have done so.

Mission accomplished; Mike was right. I felt satisfied. I felt, wow, I felt happy. I felt so grateful for every good person and good fortune that had come our way. I had driven completely across the country, I'd seen almost every human on the planet that I wanted to see (okay, I wasn't able to connect with my nephew Gabe in Dallas, and I didn't track down my Italian sister-in-law in New York to claim Garrett's letter) and I found my brother Mike. Meeting him didn't mean we'd start planning vacations together or family reunions. It isn't really necessary. I had achieved what I set out to do. This is rare, at least in my experience, thus far.

So often road trips are paved with good intentions, especially vacations. On the way to your destination, you're thinking about all the fun you're going to have, how much you've been looking forward to it, how much you deserve it, how exhausted you are with the grind. You justify the excess, the money, the calories, the alcohol, the trinkets, by reminding yourself just how hard you've slaved all year to earn the decadence. The drive back home you atone for your sins. *When I get back home, I'm going to finally lose this twenty pounds, tackle the basement, work out every day, find a new job, quit bitching about the job I do have, not drink so much, paint the bathroom and oh yeah, lose that twenty pounds.* Is it just me or is this a fairly common phenomenon? Maybe I'm just driven (no pun intended), but for me the open road has a way of making me take stock, a truth serum providing some measure of how far I've come and how far I have to go to make good on my intentions.

But for the first and only time in my life, for eight weeks last summer, I was acting upon my absolute highest intention. I was doing the very thing I had always intended to do. There wasn't any dream, or goal or vision that I would have to "get back to" after I got home because I was actually getting on *with* it. This was my shot. This was my chance. This was my highest purpose and there was nothing I was putting off or feeling guilty about neglecting. After I made it to San Francisco and continued northeast to El Dorado Hills and Placerville where my mother grew up and grew fond of Tommy, after I had set my eyes on the never-seen brother, it was case closed. Mission accomplished! I would have high-fived myself if I could have figured out how to do it! Time to get back home and start writing my bestseller: end of story.

Until I saw a single playing card floating face up in a narrow stream, from which a whole new chapter would flow. I will not be offended if you slam this book shut or click off your e-reader at this very moment because you think I'm lying, but I swear to God, you cannot make this shit up.

That was a favorite rejoinder of my brother Don. As the oldest of the five of us, he had seen it all. God love him, he *really* had seen it all. He saw my mother's belly grow large, time after time, with one more sibling after another, one from the cabbie, one from the barkeep, and two more Whatley boys who favor their big brother Don quite a bit. He had suffered the indignity of wearing my mother's penny loafers on the first day of school in the sixth grade because back-to-school time arrived before her paycheck did. He had suffered, with dignity, the pain and isolation of polio at a very young age, forced to stay alone at a hospital in San Francisco more than 100 miles from home for more than three months with my mother and grandparents taking turns riding the bus from Placerville to visit him on weekends. Even now my sister-in-law repeats the story that Don told her about his extended stay in the polio suite. My mother had called the hospital to tell my brother Don she'd be there on the weekend, "and I have a surprise for you!" Don was excited, seeing how he was a six-year-old at the polio sanitarium all alone all week. When my mother arrived, she gushed, "Guess what the surprise is? I flew on an airplane!" Suffice it to say he was expecting, at the very least, a fucking candy bar.

Don was wise, analytical, rarely flustered, took stuff in stride. In fact, he refused to allow his stride to get in the way. His left leg was noticeably smaller than his right leg, a lasting gift of the polio. Instead of allowing it be a handicap, he pushed himself: he played tennis, softball, and golf. He went on bike marathons and week-long, solo backpacking trips in the mountains of New Mexico. Oh, never mind that he ran out of gorp just two days into the man-versus-mountain expedition and was getting pounded by rain and had nothing but a crappy tarp and Beverly and J.R. had to stop everything and drive up to the Pecos Wilderness to fetch an embarrassed and slightly emasculated mountain man who had to hike back out of the wilderness to find a phone booth. Don made them stop at the first Lota' Burger in sight. To this day my little brother J.R. feels a tad guilty for giving Don grief about his failed survival trek. But Don had pluck. I hadn't thought enough about that until the three of spades made me stop and give him his due.

I was staying with my friend Sue in Truckee, on the north shore of Lake Tahoe. I was resting up, writing up, and gearing up for the long drive back to Missouri, the prospect of Utah and Kansas not very enticing. I took Libby for a walk. I was a little preoccupied by the bear warning signs, thinking about how Libby would react to a bear compared to the donkey in Texas when there it was, the three of spades, face up, slowly gliding along in the current alongside a residential road. I plucked it from the water, got back to Sue's condo and Googled like a fiend. By this time, these clues were beginning to feel a bit like a reality show. What I read wasn't funny though. It was frightening.

"The Three of Swords, also called The Lord of Sorrow, signifies extreme pain and sorrow, separation, disruption, upheaval, discord, conflict, strife, sadness, loneliness, heartbreak, betrayal, inevitability, loss and grief, but with a positive view in the end, released tension."

How's that for a list of adjectives you'd just as soon never have associated with this life or the next one? It went on:

"Such events feel so painful because they are unexpected. However, the Three of Swords often serves as a warning sign to show when one or more of these are

possible. By preparing for this difficult event, the emotional blow can be minimized or even prevented entirely."

Oh, gee thanks. If I'm on the lookout, I just might be able to minimize the extreme pain and sorrow, separation, disruption, upheaval, discord, conflict, strife, sadness, loneliness, heartbreak, betrayal, inevitability, loss and grief. Okay, dude, I'm all over that. I was like Radar on high alert, waiting for the sound of "incoming." I mean, are you kidding me? The Lord of Sorrow floating right towards me in a babbling mountain stream? Really? The three of spades, which is the Three of Swords in Tarot-card decks, is illustrated as a heart with three bloody swords pierced through it. I suddenly regretted picking up that card. Damn signs.

It was unnerving. My mind raced through scenarios: "What if something goes wrong at home, or if Libby or I get in a wreck?" We both know that if I'd thought like that from the beginning I never would have backed out my driveway. But believe me, over the course of 8,600 miles, I did consider what a disaster it would be if Libby and I had gotten in an accident, or if I'd gotten sick or one of the kids needed me in an emergency.

I shuddered. And then I prayed. I mean, wouldn't you? Fully realizing that cross-pollinating Tarot and the Trinity might make for a dangerous spiritual cocktail, I prayed that the Tarot was wrong. I was more than a thousand miles from home on the tail end of an odyssey in which I had already cheated the devil on a number of turns, literally and figuratively; I wasn't willing to take any chances. I availed myself to any higher power which came a-calling or to whom I could place a long-distance call.

"Please, God, please. You've brought us this far. Please, Lord, just get us home safely."

I stewed, I studied and I left myself open to try to be open. Gotta play the cards you're dealt, right?

It was Don. According to Hoyle, it was all about my brother Don. It seemed fitting that this reminder would float through the air, or fall from someone's hand, or out of a trash bag, or blow out of the car window and land in a stream in the mountains of northern California, so near to where Don was born. Don, like my mother, was a Californian, first and foremost, in his heart. And it was here, in the pine forests of the Sierra Nevada mountains where his spirit came around, reminding me, in the gentle but uncompromising way in which he would counsel a student, pointing his finger in a teaching, not punishing way, that I had rushed through my homework. I hadn't intended to give my grief for Don the short shrift. I just hadn't gotten around to absorbing the thud of his absence.

Of course I cried when it happened. I'd allowed myself time to curse the unfairness of it all. And in much the same way your leg pops up involuntarily when the doctor tests your reflexes, when my heart was pounded with a mallet, I wrote.

He Is Leaving
The August breeze carries them,
descending
twirling
floating
like so many gold foil flecks shimmering inside diagonal rays of late summer
sun.
"Why?" I ask indignantly. "Why are you falling?"
Even as the fullness of summer still gives off her scent—life, life, everywhere!
Crickets calling, bugs crawling, the birds so busy, as the garden snake lounges
in the shady, chocolate clay of the flower bed, flush with color—pinks, yellow,
purple
with buds yet to bloom.
"It's too early. Why must you do this now?" hands on my hips, accusing eyes to
the sky.
"Because," say the leaves. "It's our time."

But I had not enough time. No time to consider the days ahead without my big brother, the real big brother, the one who showed me the way to school, the one who took me to Forest Park pool in Fort Worth on his Lambretta scooter, the one who picked me up first in the church bus on Sunday mornings before he went to pick up the kids in the projects, *this*, my friends, is bringing in the sheaves. Preacher turned teacher, Don went through his hippie years just like every other self-respecting liberal in the late '60s and '70s. Little sister went along for that ride too. The Texas International Pop Festival, just outside of Dallas in Lewisville, was the next major outdoor festival following Woodstock, just two weeks after. Ten Years After, along with Janis Joplin, Santana, Led Zeppelin, B.B. King, Canned Heat, Sly and the Family Stone, Chicago, and Herbie Mann were among the headliners. A lot of the Woodstock hippies had not had a bath since they left New York, so they were skinny-dipping in Lewisville Lake while the rest of the 150,000 of us watched the *other* show. I was a mere fourteen under the sometimes attentive eye of Don and Beverly who would later report to my mother that they were worried when it took me more than an hour to get to the Porta-Johns and back. It would have taken anybody that long to walk across acres of bodies on blankets. I never smelled so much pot and patchouli oil or saw so many bare breasts in my life. Even then, the summer of '69, I had a tendency to be a lone voyeur.

Christmas of '72, we took a road trip to northern California. Don and Bev were still living in Fort Worth, where I had so desperately wanted to remain. They stopped in Albuquerque to pick up an eager seventeen-year-old champing at the bit to get out from under the 'rents and drive up the Pacific Coast highway with her cool big brother and family, my niece and nephew just little kids then. I will never forget Don, singing along with the radio to "You're So Vain." It was just about the time we reached Monterey Bay. It was late afternoon; Don was leaning forward, the way tall men and bus drivers drape their forearms over the wheel. His handsome profile, with his long hair and dapper tweed cap, which I'm sure was a Pendleton, was backlit by the ocean and sun. Bev was asleep with the kids in the back. Don got sleepy, so we pulled over and swapped drivers real quick, a thrill for me, since I'd been eager to test my road skills and he figured it'd be less distraction for me with everybody else asleep. After I thought he was safely asleep, his seat reclined and his wool cap pulled down over his eyes, I lit a cig, blowing the smoke out the window. Don didn't even raise the brim of his cap.

"That shit will kill you."

I had wanted to do this trip with him. I had wanted to take him back to Texas, go see our cousins and then retrace that trip from 1972: the Grand Canyon, Monterey Bay, San Francisco, Placerville and the Lake. I wanted to repay a kindness, to be his driver for all the times he had been mine. This was to be my gift to him.

Grief was his stand-in. It rode with me from Philadelphia to Pearl, from Atlanta to Albuquerque, with me obligingly dripping tears from the dense green forests of the Appalachians to the grey-shrouded San Francisco Bay, parceling them out like water from a rain barrel, but I had yet to pull out the stopper for Don.

I had not given him his due. Sure, I had done him proud before a sellout crowd at his funeral. I believe he would have been pleased. But as anyone who has ever made a speech or delivered a eulogy will attest, at times like this you are in performance mode. That was my job. Make 'em cry. I am a fucking master. When was there time for my tears?

Three days' bereavement and I was back on the job, back to the grind, distracted by deadlines, no time for sadness 'cause we had clients waiting and videos to make!

Americans, for the most part, don't know how to deal with grief. It's like a disease. People at work did not know what to say, so they just didn't say anything, at least most of them. My cubbie, the guy whose office was adjacent to mine, simply hugged me, no words needed. My production assistant left flowers on my desk, our finance guy dropped off a card. My boss popped his head in the door and asked, "How ya doin'?"

I remain grateful for those kindnesses. Anyone who is going through this process remembers these kindnesses, yet people are afraid to say anything for fear you'll cry. I understand this, but it is infinitely easier and far more comforting if people will just come out with it and say the words that need to be spoken, the way Ethan did.

A thirteen-year-old kid named Ethan taught me a lot about what to say when you're not sure what to say. Ethan was very close friends with my son Sean at the time Rick was arrested. Sean and Ethan were in the seventh grade. Ethan spent many a weekend at my home, shuffling up the basement stairs at the crack of noon on Saturdays to eat pancakes in my kitchen. Boysenberry syrup was his favorite. In the days immediately following Rick's arrest, some of the parents of my kids' friends, naturally, were forced to have a conversation with their children that I'm sure they would have preferred not to have. Even though Rick and I were already divorced at the time and he had minimal interaction with the friends of our children, he did take a turn at carpool or football practice or baseball games now and again.

"Did that man ever touch you?"

My friends told me they had to ask the obligatory question. I told them I understood. But just one day after the story was blasted all over the news, Ethan's mom called and said:

"Ethan wants to come over to your house after school and hang out. He said he thinks Sean needs his friends close by. Is that okay?"

I was so grateful. At 3:15 Sean and Ethan were standing out in front of middle school as I inched forward in the carpool line. They were cutting up as seventh-graders do. The boys climbed in the back seat of my Subaru when it was my turn at the front of the line.

"I'm really sorry about what's happened to your family," said this shaggy-haired, brown-eyed, darling boy named Ethan, before the door was even closed. I caught Sean's eyes in the mirror. He was looking pained. I would *not* cry.

"Thank you, Ethan. That is the absolute nicest thing you could say."

People just need to be more like Ethan. Just say you're sorry. You're sorry for someone's loss. That's all you have to say. And if it makes the bereaved cry, so be it. Most people will not wail and fall down on their knees. Unless you are Paco.

Paco was my mother's immigrant boyfriend for many years after my stepdad Frank died. Given her history with men, she did not wait very long to make a love connection after Frank suffered his massive heart attack and we carried his two artificial legs out of the VA hospital, upside-down in a brown paper grocery sack, both of his black dress shoes still attached to the fake feet, laces neatly tied. By the time Frank passed, he had lost the second leg just below the knee because of diabetes. We figured there was no point in burying him in them. I'm sure my mother must have donated his prostheses to some good cause. They didn't have Craigslist back then.

Paco appeared on the scene, more specifically on her couch, within about four months following Frank's funeral.

"Why am I not surprised, when I stopped by to visit my widowed sixty-three-year-old mother this week, to find a wetback asleep on her couch?" Don had asked this rhetorical question at a gathering of the sibs shortly after Paco was introduced to our lives. "I am probably the only grown man on the planet who would simply say, "Well, of course!'"

The details surrounding Paco and my mother's initial introduction and ensuing courtship remain sketchy. It had something to do with Paco being an acquaintance of Frank's from the G.I. Forum, where all the Mexicans in Albuquerque's North Valley would go to dance on Sunday afternoons. Being a friend of Frank's meant he was a friend to my mother, the *"juera"* which loosely translated means "blonde" or *gringa*. From there, it blossomed to help around the house, and, well, out of respect for my wonderful mother, the rest is nobody's goddamn business.

Bottom line was, Paco was utterly and absolutely devoted to my mother and attended to her for the remaining nineteen years of her life, even after her stroke. The nurses told us that Paco came every day, often early in the morning and late at night to see his darling Beverly. He was seventeen years her junior, I might add, so to say that my mother still had it going on is an understatement. She looked twenty years younger than her age. They made quite a scene, the flamboyant and always well-dressed *gringa*, champion of the downtrodden illegals, and her one-eyed Mexican escort (Paco had sustained an accident and was blind in one eye) in boots and a straw cowboy hat.

The hat came off the minute we stepped inside the cool, demurely-lit and air-fragranced funeral home on the July day we took him for my mother's visitation. We had met at my brother Don's and caravanned to the funeral home in yuppie cars and Paco's pickup, which my mother had gone to the ends of the earth to help him obtain.

"Patricio, *venga con migo.*" Paco asked my son Patrick to ride with him.

It's not easy seeing your mama in a coffin. It's just not. She would have been happy, though, I believe, in what we'd chosen as her parting wardrobe: her favorite denim skirt, a lacy blouse she'd chosen to wear in a recent portrait photo, which she'd proudly framed and sent 8 x 10 glossies to all of her kids and grandkids exclaiming, "I made the front cover of the Senior Expo Program!" which was a source of great pride, given her decades of being on the Mayor's Senior Advisory Board. And she wore two pretty pieces of turquoise we'd all agreed upon. I did make the funeral director change the color of her nail polish, though. My niece had innocently selected a coral shade, but Mom wouldn't have been caught dead in that color. She liked pink.

As the rest of us, sons, daughter, grandchildren and great-grandchildren somberly stood by her casket, muted tears absorbed by thoughtfully-placed tissues on every table, Paco took his time walking up to her white sateen quilted bed. Eventually, it was down to him. Hat in hand, he approached the side of the casket and then split the room apart with the sound of his grief.

"Bever-leeeeee!" he wailed out loud.

He laid his head on her chest and sobbed. The sound of that man weeping could pierce the coldest heart; it was that painful to witness. Then, slowly, he raised his head up and patted her hands, touched her hair, made the sign of the cross on her forehead, pulled his handkerchief from his pocket, wiped his eyes and said, "Okay."

Oh that we Americans could be so expressive. And as my shrink always said, "What you suppress you must express." The devil is in knowing what you are hiding.

I go to church sometimes just to watch the old ladies. It's one of the few places in our modern society where we can actually mix with older folks, for those of us who live apart from our elders or our elders have passed away. I steal sidelong glances at the little old ladies, with their grey-haired bobs, hands in laps, the way they tuck one tissue inside their sleeves, the slow gait to take communion. My mother did not stand on religion. She was saved at a summer tent revival in Sayre, Oklahoma by a Church of Christ preacher, whom she sought out and thanked some sixty years later when he was preaching at a church in Albuquerque. She went to Catholic Church for years, seeing how she'd married a Mexican and Frank was Catholic. She never converted, although I think my mother was far more spiritually inclined than most of those who went to Mass every day. The last words I ever heard my mother speak from her stroke-ridden bed were, "This is my darling daughter," as she graciously introduced me to her nurses, who adored her and whom she kept entertained as long as she was able. Then, in one of her final days of being lucid, she opened up her eyes and sang, "Jesus loves me. This I know."

They teach us even as they're dying. And precisely in the same way that a wise thirteen-year-old kid had the courage to say the words that needed to be spoken, so too, did my brother. I had gone to New Mexico shortly after he was diagnosed with cancer. It was early on; he had not even started chemo. He would live for only nine more months.

I went to kiss him goodnight and crawled up in the bed next to him instead. I laid my head on his shoulder, thin from the cancer. We talked about God and baseball, two things he held in high esteem.

I told him I was angry and he told me it was okay.

I told him I was sad and he said he was too.

I told him I loved him and he said,

"I love you too. I'm proud of you and the way you've raised your kids."

I told him I didn't want him to die.

"I don't really want to die either," he responded, matter-of-factly. "But I'm not afraid to die because I have a deep faith."

I asked if he was looking forward to getting started on his chemo and he said yes. He had been on hold for weeks while the doctors figured out which protocol they would pursue.

"It's weird to think I'm actually excited about having my body bombarded with toxic drugs, but I am."

He was already behind on the count because his pancreatic cancer had spread to his liver. Lying there in his bed with him, the circumstances trumping even the slightest awkwardness, my brother gave me a gift. In a moment of blessed clarity, his thinking often muddled by the morphine, he crafted an analogy. He compared his cancer to standing in the batter's box.

"There's an infinite number of things that can determine how that ball comes across the plate," he said in that quiet little voice that cancer had given him. "Standing there is both thrilling and frightening, because you might get a piece of it and smack a line drive or a home run or you might get hit with the ball. So I have two choices. I can drop my bat and walk away or I can stand there and take the pitch. I'm gonna stay in the box, because either way, it's gonna be okay."

14

I Will Never Leave You

The man walking on U.S. 50, out in the middle of nowhere, waves back at me. The sun is slightly to the west of noon. I can see from twenty yards that his skin is far more leathery than my own. He doesn't appear alarmed or armed as he continues pushing the zipped-up baby jogger my way. No baby inside.

"Hey!" he hollers back. I am still a little uneasy.

Is he going to hit me up for money? Maybe he's walking for some disease, you know, like a Walk-A-Thon. Or, maybe he's just crazy. I'm sure he's harmless, like the people who sit around and talk to themselves in the park. Wonder if he'll take off on some rant about the international monetary fund or global warming or MIAs in Vietnam still being held as prisoners?

He's not that old. As I get closer, I am able to verify that yes, indeed, he is a kid.

"Hello," I say. "I just *had* to stop!" I offer in my friendliest voice.

"Sure! I'm glad you did!" He sounds normal, as much as I can tell with the desert wind buffeting my ears like sponges tapping a live microphone.

He's smiling. That's a good sign. He must be used to this.

I get within two feet and he pulls off his Ray-Bans to reveal sweet, youthful, inquisitive, green eyes.

We shake hands.

"My name is Jean. I'm traveling across the country with my dog," I say looking back over my right shoulder, where Libby remains in the back seat, her nose fully extended out the window.

"That's awesome," he says. "I'm Nate Damm. I'm walking across America, um, without a dog."

"Like all the way across the country?" I ask with some incredulity. "Man, I thought I had it rough, and I'm driving!"

Nate Damm proceeds to tell me that this very day—August 26, 2011— marks six months since he began his solitary walk across America. He is from Maine, but actually started his trek in Delaware in February. Hell, no wonder he headed toward the desert! His ultimate goal: San Francisco.

"Do you want to sit down?" My maternal instinct kicks in immediately. "Do you need any food? I've got granola bars and some fruit and water!"

He smiles. His teeth are like an ad for Crest White Strips, especially with his tanned face and blond hair. "You wouldn't believe the food I've got in there," he gestures over his shoulder to *his* vehicle. "I'm good. Really."

Nate tells me his story, how he went to community college but it just wasn't his thing. He tells me about his longing to see the whole country, this crazy idea to walk across America, how it just took hold of him and wouldn't let go. He smiles, stopping short, "Like I'm telling you, right?"

He explains his routine, how he rests when he needs to, moving away from the highway for a nap or when it's time to call it a day, seeks coverage away from the noise and potential road bandits. He tells me in vivid detail about a close call with a bear in the Sangre de Cristo Mountains in Colorado. He'd stumbled upon the bear's kill and was in between the bear and its supper. The bear charged toward him and then simply stopped, lumbering off into the forest. Lucky change of heart. The biggest threat of all? Lightning.

"The people I've met have been wonderful," Nate says, in the warm, approachable voice of a highly enlightened, brave and benevolent young man. "It's crazy. People stop and give me food, or they'll give me their phone numbers and tell me to call them when I roll into town and they put me up for the night, sometimes for days. I've kept in touch with everybody I've met."

I tell him, "Me, too," and the positive energy around us at this point, two complete and total strangers face-to-face, on the side of a sparsely-traveled highway, waxing poetic about the family of man, could have deflected a Scud missile.

"I call it abundant benevolence," I laugh. "That's my name for all the amazing, sweet and kind people I've met. I'm writing a book about it. I'm a writer. That's my deal, you know, to take this trip with my dog and write about it. Oh! Let me go get my dog!"

I gesture toward my vehicle and run to fetch Libby.

"I wish I had a dog," Nate says as Libby makes an absolute slut of herself, rolling on her back in the warm gravel. Nate squats down to rub her belly as I worry about the extra wear and tear on his knees. Once a mom, always a mom, I guess. "It would be so much better if I had a dog. I almost picked up a dog or two along the way, but I think it would be too hard on 'em. You know? How is she doing in the car?"

"She jumps in with glee every time I jingle the keys."

I tell Nate how Libby inspired my trip, made me leave my job, get away, clear my head and write my stories. I tell him about my brothers past, present and the one who was absent.

"So did you find him?" he asks enthusiastically as an AirStream rattles past, shaking our pant legs.

"Yeah, man! One phone call!"

The hair on his legs and arms is albino white from six months' walking in the sun. Six months *walking*. His stars-and-stripes cotton bandana is also faded from the sun from six months' walking, six months alone.

"Do you get lonely?" We are simpatico at this point. We can afford to be honest.

"At first, the first few months. Not as much now. There's so much to look at, I don't get bored. My mind is very active. You can really think when you're just out here like this," he says, his eyes panning the wide-open sky behind me.

"What are you going to do when you get to San Francisco?"

"I don't know," he says wistfully in a confession I can relate to.

We talk about his girlfriend who might or might not be there when he gets back.

"This kind of thing is hard on relationships," he says. I smile.

I inquire about his family. His mother's fears are allayed by iPhone and iChat and all things Mac (hell, Apple should have sponsored the both of us!). We laugh about how hard it is to *truly* get away. We've come to appreciate the silence in the cellphone service gaps. He's been lucky: hasn't been sick, no serious injuries, no malice, just mile after mile after mile of solitary walking.

"Are you sure you don't want to sit down?" I ask, but I know it's time to go. I record a quick video interview. We take turns taking photos. He's missing Libby already, I can tell; it's hard to let her go. We vow to stay in touch.

"Okay, gotta go," I say. It's emotional for me, of course. I open my arms for a hug, a natural reflex, and he is right there. He hugs me back, tight. His arms and shoulders are strong. There's no hurry to let go. There was nobody on the planet right then but us. We might not touch another human for days.

This was the real deal. Pure.

What if I had taken the Interstate? What if I had won at the casino at the Nevada line and played a little longer? What if I'd stayed an extra day in Tahoe? What if Libby had been a cat?

But that wouldn't have happened. We know better. To assume that this was simply a random event which caused two people who were on life-defining journeys via different means and modes of travel to cross paths on U.S. Highway 50, twenty miles west of Delta, Utah assigns to the holder of such assumptions the inheritance of fools. We know better.

As I continue eastbound, I am yammering to Libby, "Can you believe what just happened?" I am completely cocooned in the providential afterglow of our encounter. In my mind's eye, I can see him as clearly as when he was still standing right in front of me. But really, it is the trace of him. Ten miles farther east, a few miles closer to the people I have now informed I will not be seeing until lunchtime tomorrow, ten miles down the road is when I realize it. I raise the crew-neck collar of my white tee-shirt over my nose and take a deep breath.

I smell like him.

Nate's scent is still with me; the lingering scent of his sun-baked shirt has rubbed off on mine, a comforting, reassuring reminder of the human touch, the mingling of two different fabrics, two different detergents and two different bodies underneath the garments, a lingering trace of two people embracing. I don't want the scent to fade.

It reminds me of my mama's black trenchcoat. "How do you like my new coat?" She turned the collar up, spy style, and spun a little turn at the St. Louis airport, just after she'd walked off the plane for what would be her last visit.

"Cute, huh?" She was proud of the bargain she'd gotten at Macy's on her new London Fog, staying true to her credo of never going around looking shabby. "Looks like a million bucks," she answered her own question before I had a chance to.

I found that coat in a suitcase a few years later when I went to the storage shed in Albuquerque to claim what artifacts I had left of her. My brothers had stowed all of her belongings after the house sold and I was there to load up a U-Haul truck and tote all traces of my mama a thousand miles to Missouri. When I hung up the coat at home I found a clean tissue neatly folded inside the right pocket; I pulled it out and smelled it. It smelled like her perfume. I have worn her coat every fall for the past six years. For the first three, I left the Kleenex there, lovingly tapping it in my pocket, as if to say hello to her, to tell her where we were going, to let her know I appreciated her being with me. It finally disintegrated into shreds after I blew my nose on it in a moment of desperation. One more trace of her, gone. How can someone be sad about throwing away a ridiculously tattered, reminder of their mother?

Or feel sad about the fading scent of another human? I cover my nose with my shirt and breathe even more deeply this time, but it's the memories I am inhaling now, a flood of memories of the loving arms of every man I have loved and lost. *That darn Nate, he's reminded me.* He has forced my artful-dodger brain to go to places I have detoured around all summer, memories I would just as soon extract like an abscessed tooth. But I simply cannot drive around them anymore. The trailing goosebumps which surface involuntarily, even years after the fact, accompany the memories of the men I have loved with a pure heart: a sunny window seat, his fingers sliding over frets, a gait, a look, a gesture, the silver chain just under his collar, his laugh, his touch, those shining blue eyes. I've loved those blue-eyed boys the most. And where are they now? What happened?

Will I always be alone?

I'm looking out at the dusk draped highway and I'm laying my heart out on the pavement.

Come on, Jean, let's just be honest here. Whose fault is this?

I have tried so hard not to think about it, this one little longing, which remains. I've comforted myself with the magic of the present, the duty to my grief, this amazing opportunity, the adventure, my freedom, my family, the friends I've made or rediscovered, my backers, my blog followers and my Libby, I've got my darling Libby.

Yeah, but she doesn't keep you warm at night. Well, yes she does, but that's kind of pathetic.

I had meant to get around to it, you know, finding somebody to love. It's not like I haven't tried. But it always comes down to too much of this, not enough of that, bad timing, bad manners, bad haircut, you name it. So easy to toss 'em, you know, because time was on my side. I'd get around to it. Just like I'd get around to patching the dining room ceiling or taking piano lessons or cleaning out the basement. I just needed to *schedule* it. Everything is programmable these days, right? On demand, we live in a world where we can get anything we want, on demand, 24/7, operators standing by. Besides, I've been busy raising up those kids, taking care of the dogs, taking care of clients, taking out the trash, combining all those half-empty boxes of corn flakes in the pantry.

Okay, so maybe I'm ready now.

The crosswind whips the last lingering scent of Nate off my shirt, like shaking out a rug. I run my hands through my tangled mop of hair: a busted bale of hay, my bangs annoying me now. I grab my hat and plunk it over my head, squashing the annoying glistening fringe around my eyes. The highway commands my full attention now. Flat surface, wide open has turned to steep grade, sharp curves. I pass the third fatal car wreck I've seen in eight weeks. Traffic is so sparse out here, I hardly need to downshift to third to catch a quick glimpse of an upside-down, silver sedan in a deep ravine, a white sheet this time. The state trooper nods and waves. I shudder. Libby sits up. Heebie-jeebies, man, she always knows. She rests her nose on my left shoulder, just under my seatbelt strap, with a slight groan. It's uncanny; I don't know if it's the switchbacks or my tight grip on the wheel, but she sits up the second I tense up.

Besides, the desert is calling. I've been straining to catch the sunset through the back window and it's a dangerous distraction. I have to stop and pay my respects. My desert vistas are dwindling down to a precious two. Finally I find a scenic overlook that is truly off the highway. Fantastic. Libby and I pull over.

The view at Castle Valley is breathtaking. The colors are magnificent: the sound of the wind, easing up at twilight, is amazing, like a sound track to a western. The road has fallen still. Gazing out over this desert, *this desert,* which I had expected to hate, it sings to me. It sings a holy psalm of peace. Libby and I are next to each other. We're on giant, flat rock and the sun is going down. It's dry where we are, but there's a thunderstorm far off in the distance, must be fifty miles or more. It falls to the desert floor in a vertical grey shaft, in Spanish, it's called *"virga."* The column of rain tumbles from giant pink and purple clouds piled high like cotton candy skyscrapers as far as the eye can see. I am humbled. The desert is simply so grand, so powerful, so vast and mighty, there is nothing, no pain or disappointment or fear or failure, loneliness or regret, which cannot be pulverized into particulates, dispersed on the back of a change-up gust.

In a once in a lifetime gift of discernment borne on this desert wind, I am inspired to let it go. I simply let it *all* go. I come to understand that the egregious assaults that have been thrown my way as a little girl, a trusting wife, over time, have ceased to matter. They simply do not matter anymore. Like transient dark stabs into a porous surface, they're sustained, absorbed, infused and used. *Used* in my life to create a new one, a better one, because I know there is far more surface than there is rain. I've acknowledged the losses. I took the time to grieve. I allowed myself to feel the pain of missing people whom I will never see, never hear the sound of their voices or touch them again. I have driven through these grey daggers and in so doing, the remaining Tarot tutelage is revealed.

"Pain, sorrow and grief are often a necessity in the journey of life. Without pain, there would be no challenge and no lessons learned. Pain can be a great motivator because it encourages you to surmount obstacles and ultimately learn from your mistakes. Each challenge you encounter creates that initial pain, which is inevitably turned into an opportunity to grow stronger and to change the direction of your life as a result of the lessons learned. While the pain may cloud your vision for a certain period, it will eventually allow you to see clearly and to put the past behind you. Though life seems meaningless at the time, recovery can and will occur. It takes faith, self-love, forgiveness and time. Count your blessings."

"Come on, Lib."

I have treacherous miles from here to Green River, our stop for the night. Libby and I are the only ones at the overlook. Darkness is coming fast.

"Let's go."

Libby jumps down off the rock and trots alongside me. No leash. She hops back in her beloved back seat, always in the moment, no hesitation. I rub Our Lady hanging from the mirror and perform the Act of Acceleration, merging with the dusky road. She is my seductress. The sky behind me is painted with horizontal bands of orange and purple lying on the horizon like a blanket. There, in the backseat, I see my girl Libby, her dark eyes looking back at me, contented, no fear.

Freedom from fear: what a gift, when we give that to another creature. Just the day before, in much the same way as she'd performed her little stunt in the front yard which launched this expedition, once again, Libby became my teacher, delivering one of the most profound lessons of my life. We were still in Lake Tahoe. I was packing up to get on the road.

"Stay," I told her, as I hauled the first load of gear to the car outside my friend's condo. Libby was standing inside the foyer, behind a glass door. I tossed the suitcase in the back and was rearranging the backpack, the ice chest, the yoga mat, the cowboy hat. I looked up to see her through the door, the reflection of my white car, rear hatch open, reflected in the door glass and behind it, the face of my dog, full of fear. The look of panic in her eyes broke my heart.

From New York to California, she must have gone through this anxiety every time I packed up! I just didn't realize it because I could never see her from the motel parking lot. Every single time, Libby could hear me loading up the car, but this time, in Lake Tahoe, *I could see her!* There she stood, anxiously waiting on the other side of the door, worried, heart racing, riveted gaze, watching my every move, afraid I would *leave her!*

Leave her?

As if I ever could. Libby was my rock! She was my bed buddy, my muse, my witness, my confessor, my accomplice and my friend. Leave her? Never! But how in the world could I show my love? How could I possibly prove my devotion, convince this golden, darling mutt, that I could not, would not ever abandon her because she *belonged to me.* I was her faithful guardian, then and forever more.

I came back inside, got down on the parquet floor and whispered in her ear.

"I will never leave you."

"I will never leave you."

"I will *never* leave you."

I was telling her as much as I was telling myself.

Eight weeks, 8,600 miles, a lifetime—and I am still with me. I belong to me. I am the faithful guardian of this one life. *My* life. There is no one better qualified to watch over me than me. Lucky is the little girl who is now in the loving hands of the woman I've become.

I am still with me.

Through abandonment, betrayal, loss and pain, I am still with me. The same little girl who rode out far from the house, still I ride unworried, alone. We come in alone, we go out alone. We have these blessed companions: husbands, wives, sons and daughters, brothers, sisters, friends and lovers, and we have our dogs, our blessed dogs. We are bound together in ways we scarcely understand. Whether through blood, choice or chance, for a lifetime or a minute, we're like traffic on the highway, pulsing blue spheres on the GPS of time. We merge with other people with an invitation to share their lane or share their life, until such time as our paths diverge and we're traveling solo, seeking our own true north.

How fortunate are those who find and follow.

Jean Ellen Whatley

Led by love: self-love, brotherly love, maternal, passionate, and puppy. Love is all that matters. Love knows no boundaries. It transcends all race, gender, geography, station in life and species. Love is what we're sent here for, or, more importantly, the courage to love, the willingness to face our fears, to turn the key and start the engine.

Epilogue

I'm sitting on my front porch in early August, record heat, having just moved the sprinkler to the next patch of forlorn grass. I'm trying to revive it. This time last year, I was reviving my life. This summer, I'm just trying to survive, ready to hand off a manuscript and hope for the best.

So much has changed. Lauren finished college and moved out-of-state to Teach for America. Rick got to see her graduate, then came to her graduation party here at the house. It gets easier with time.

Patrick has moved to a different house in Brooklyn, Nate has moved to a different house in the Hills, Beverly has moved out of the house that she and Don lived in for more than thirty years. This makes me sad. J.R. has a new grandson, Paul still has a cell phone. Sean's still working his way through college. I'm so proud of how he handled things last summer while I was gone. I know it made him anxious. Makes me shudder now to even think about it, I mean, we were *out* there.

So many images from the road shuttle through my mind as I sit here eating a bowl of Grape Nuts (which are neither grapes nor nuts) trying to decide if I should wait until it rains to pull the weeds out of the driveway. Libby and Louie, golden, warm, sun-baked furriness, lap-high with nuzzling puppy dog snouts, lean against my legs, one on either side, Louie still mischievous, Libby ever soulful, both clinging to the desperate hope I'll leave them one crunchy morsel or at least the chance to lick the bowl.

I look into Libby's Cleopatra eyes, unfathomably deep, dark brown. How many times have I peered into her loyal, expectant glassy spheres, kissing her nose, rubbing her mutt forehead, asking, pleading, *Libby, do you remember?*

Do you remember, Lib? How proud I was when we crossed the Verrazano Bridge? How I cried for my mama at the Golden Gate? Oh my darling dog, do you remember all the hundreds of stops we made? Rest areas, grassy fields next to barns and gas stations, the cafés, the QuikTrips, motels and casinos? The wild mustangs—oh Libby, I tried to get a picture. What a fool! They were just for you and me to see. And my madness, you never questioned my madness, when I detoured and went to the Grand Canyon, just to show you! I went just to show you, Libby. How crazy is that? Remember how wonderful those pine trees smelled? Oh, and the ocean? I took you to the ocean! Do you remember the dog beach ? That's where I lost my glasses, remember? And the fried shrimp at Fisherman's Wharf. You chased the seagulls and the pigeons, the donkeys and cows and cats and we stopped for sunsets, especially the sunsets. Do you remember the sunsets, Lib?

How you desperately want someone else to remember. How you long to talk it over with that person, just one more time. *Do you remember?* If only you could go back, just long enough to smell the smells, to feel the breeze, to hear the songs, to touch, oh, to touch that person, that wonderful person, just one more time, for just one more second.

'Tis the writer's privilege then, I suppose, to wrestle the calf to the ground, or the words to the page, creating a reasonable facsimile of the real thing. Fools though, who fail to realize it's the writer who is being led like a calf on a rope by the ever-present cursor, pulling us along to our revisitation, be it glorified or tainted in the retelling. Beat, beat, beat, goes the cursor, until it, and we, beat no more.

But how I do wish Libby could respond. How I wish she could soothe me with some reassurance that yes, indeed, she does recall and yes, indeed, it was as marvelous as I have spun it in my memory. But we know, intellectually, that this is not possible. As much as I'd love some movie scene in which she looks at me in a matter-of-fact way and speaks in a matter-of-fact voice that I would imagine to sound like Maggie Gyllenhall's, *Yes, Jean, I remember; it was great. My favorite thing was the hamburgers,* as much as I would dearly love to know that some other heartbeat on this planet could verify these intimacies with me, I know better. Such is the tyranny of a solitary journey.

Which makes me weep. Like an advance team for a political event, a locations crew for a movie shoot, or a writer who knows well the craft of foreshadowing, I weep at this moment for the day when the sole witness to my journey passes from this earth. My Lib, my darling, the dog whom I love above all others. Why? Why do I torment myself now with the thought of how

I will go on without her? Because I know. Because I know the heart's boundless capacity for love. *We know these things.* It's like the first sip of whiskey, the first drag off a cigarette; we know how fast we'll fall. We know the price we'll pay for love, and yet, silly humans, we do it time and time again. We gather the ecstasy of thousands of perfect moments, like the precise boiling point in candy-making when the syrup spins a thread, we string and bind, bundle and patch these brittle strands together like a steel rod up our back to brace us for the bad moments, which, like ecstasy, have no regard for limits. Boundless joy, endless grief, we opt in like innocent babies at the baptismal font, willing parents doing the soul-lending. We opt in because we've already done it. We did it when we drew our first breath.

Enter trust. We are totally dependent, aren't we? On the benevolent forces of nature and timing, lust or love, design or accident which squeezes us into our situation, our plop on the planet where we begin the lifelong barter of this for that: win some, lose some, pros and cons. We rationalize, calculate, scheme and plan and hedge our silly bets, all the while complicit recruits with an unspoken allegiance to trust. We must trust, mustn't we? That snakes won't bite on desert strolls at sunset, that tires won't blow and rest areas won't harbor murderers; trust that there was a reason the seven of spades was thrown in my path, that Andres sang his song to me, that Nate shared his glistening warmth and that my newfound niece picked up the phone and that my dog, on that tear-sodden morning as I sat in this very same spot, spoke to me more clearly than if she was a human megaphone. Trust. Dogs do it. They don't appear to need us to bark at them to understand what they cannot repeat nor verify with human words. We can take a lesson from our dogs to throw ourselves into forces greater, stronger, and longer-lasting than our ability to comprehend or manage them. It's like jogging with my eyes closed on the straightaway at the track—I imagine the air currents weaving through my fingers, cooler, hotter, different shades of blue. There are so many swirling, layered, circling, binding, fleeting, attainable ribbons of connectedness that we cannot see but can feel, just as certain as a rock in our shoe, if we'll just slow down enough to *notice* the discomfort. Enter trust. Leave it on your dashboard, your mantel, paint it on your sunglasses, add it to the contacts on your fucking cellphone, put it in your shower head, your morning coffee. Drink that sucker up, dude. Rely on it. Believe in the bonds you feel, whether it's devotion to some four-legged, mud-slung hound or a lover who sweeps you up then lands you safely back again, swaddled in panting afterglow, or the steadfast gaze from your children

Jean Ellen Whatley

in the front row at your mama's funeral: trust.

Some call it faith. It's not a dirty word, really, faith. Too bad it's so maligned. I learned from the masters: Garrett, reaching down, ringing those wind chimes on a windless day to tell me to get off my ass: "Any day you wake up and you're not in a ditch is a good day." My mother's pitch-perfect, "Jesus, loves me," to assure us she would be okay, and my blessed brother Don, preacher, teacher, who by his witness, "I have a deep faith," reaffirms mine.

Libby and I were not alone.

I lift my face toward the sun and offer myself up for further instruction. "Next?"

Acknowledgments

I am grateful to so many.

Kickstarter funders, this never would have happened without you. Libby and I are eternally in your debt.

Kristina Blank Makansi at Blank Slate Press, thanks for not holding back the tears, even as you were rolling up your sleeves. I am grateful for the partnership.

Greg and Mark, you never blinked when it came time to help, I am blown away by your love and support.

To David Allen, who still picks up the phone when most men would not, I am amazed by your generosity and faith in me.

Bev, you teach me every day about courage. Thank you for doing what you think Don would have wanted. Love and thanks to J.R. and Karen, little brother Paul and all my extended family in Virginia, Georgia, Texas, New Mexico, Arizona and California.

Special thanks are due to some long-time true believers. Bobbie Lautenschlager, you are the role model of role models, never say die. I remain your devoted pupil. To Gerry Mandel, you continually inspire me, make me laugh and make me look good with your effusive prose. Linda O'Connell, your words of encouragement saved my hide on days when I wondered if I could make it. You are a wonderful woman and writer, I owe Gerry double for you.

Craig Barnes, I love you like a brother. Thank you for always reminding me to "take it back to one." You were there from the beginning and I will never forget.

Drew McClellan, why do I deserve you? Oh yeah, cause you get it. Snap. I appreciate your insight, both commercial and human.

Will Zweigart, I could never repay you for the camaraderie and consulting, mostly because I could never afford your fees. All the cool cats know you're brilliant.

Cyndi Papia, you got me at hello. Thanks for going above and beyond on the website.

Catherine Rankovic, thanks for the edit and advice.

Thanks to my ground crew, those who threw parties, did video, photos, business cards, publicity, booked hotel rooms, designed my website, book covers, pitched me, placated me and talked me off some ledges.

Kelly Barnes
Brant Hadfield
Sean Sandefur
Michelle Fielden
Patrick Sandefur
Lauren Sandefur
Whitney Gelnett
Christina Geisen
Matt Neatock
Julia Bishop-Cross
Tracy Collins
Ariel Poster
JoAnne Westcott
Nathan Shepherd

Thanks to Megan Reeg for the IAMS connection. Sarah Castano and Bev VanZant, at IAMs, thanks for Libby's kibble and free publicity. Greg Holsclaw at DogGoes, you were wonderful last summer. Thanks to the Open Salon community of writers, who made me believe I had something worth sharing and to Sarah Hepola for sharing on Salon.

Sincere thanks to The You and Me Thing for allowing me a few lyrics from your song, "Sail On" and for the blessed serendipity.

Thanks also to the Hal Leonard Corporation:

Libby and I are indebted to everyone who fed us, housed us, bathed us and let us use their salt water pool last summer.

Melissa, thank you joining our small legion of mutineers. We are truly soldiers of good fortune.

Special thanks to Steve Edwards, my lawyer, friend, confidant, pitchman, editor, arbiter, trench mate and occasional Santa, who wisely waits for the dictator to become enlightened.

Finally, with love and gratitude for Vincent, who needs no explanation.

About the Author

Jean Ellen Whatley is an Emmy Award-winning journalist cum author who's been published on Salon.com, More.com, SheWrites.com and, at the low ebb of her writing career, as the Bedding Columnist for *Furniture Retailer Magazine*.

Jean has been a guest columnist for the *St. Louis Post-Dispatch*, the *Winston-Salem Journal*, and the *Albuquerque Tribune* and has been featured as guest host on "The Evening Special" on KMOX (CBS) radio in St. Louis. Jean's broadcast career spans nearly twenty years and several diverse regions of the country. She has been a news reporter and anchor in Albuquerque, New Mexico (KOAT) Winston-Salem/Greensboro, North Carolina (WXLV) and St. Louis, MO (KDNL). Her reporting has been featured on CNN and ABC. Bridging the gap between reporting news and wrangling reporters, Jean has also served as Press Secretary to a New Mexico Attorney General, a Governor of Missouri, and a member of the U.S. House of Representatives. Excerpts from her popular blog, *A Woman With a Past: The Post-Apocalyptic Approach to Men*, earned "Editor's Picks" on Open Salon. Jean is the proud parent of four, remarkably well-adjusted, mostly-grown kids and two high-maintenance mutts. In her spare time, she deletes names of former boyfriends from her cell phone. She lives in St. Louis.

CPSIA information can be obtained at www.ICGtesting.com
Printed in the USA
LVOW13s1510090814

398337LV00001B/2/P